P9-CLY-704

Level 1

¡Avancemos!

Cuaderno práctica por niveles

HOLT McDOUGAL
a division of Houghton Mifflin Harcourt

ISBN-13: 978-0-618-76593-5
ISBN-10: 0-618-76593-X
Internet: www.holtmcdougal.com

38 39   1026 16 15
4500569529

TABLE OF CONTENTS

UNIDAD 1
Lección 1

Vocabulario A, B, C 1
Gramática A, B, C 4
Gramática A, B, C 7
Integración 10
Escuchar A, B, C 12
Leer A, B, C 15
Escribir A, B, C 18
Cultura A, B, C 21

Lección 2

Vocabulario A, B, C 24
Gramática A, B, C 27
Gramática A, B, C 30
Integración 33
Escuchar A, B, C 35
Leer A, B, C 38
Escribir A, B, C 41
Cultura A, B, C 44

Comparación cultural 47

UNIDAD 2
Lección 1

Vocabulario A, B, C 50
Gramática A, B, C 53
Gramática A, B, C 56
Integración 59
Escuchar A, B, C 61
Leer A, B, C 64
Escribir A, B, C 67
Cultura A, B, C 70

Lección 2

Vocabulario A, B, C 73
Gramática A, B, C 76
Gramática A, B, C 79
Integración 82
Escuchar A, B, C 84
Leer A, B, C 87
Escribir A, B, C 90
Cultura A, B, C 93

Comparación cultural 96

UNIDAD 3
Lección 1

Vocabulario A, B, C 99
Gramática A, B, C 102
Gramática A, B, C 105
Integración 108
Escuchar A, B, C 110
Leer A, B, C 113
Escribir A, B, C 116
Cultura A, B, C 119

Lección 2

Vocabulario A, B, C 122
Gramática A, B, C 125
Gramática A, B, C 128
Integración 131
Escuchar A, B, C 133
Leer A, B, C 136
Escribir A, B, C 139
Cultura A, B, C 142

Comparación cultural 145

UNIDAD 4
Lección 1

Vocabulario A, B, C 148
Gramática A, B, C 151
Gramática A, B, C 154
Integración 157
Escuchar A, B, C 159
Leer A, B, C 162
Escribir A, B, C 165
Cultura A, B, C 168

Lección 2

Vocabulario A, B, C 171
Gramática A, B, C 174
Gramática A, B, C 177
Integración 180
Escuchar A, B, C 182
Leer A, B, C 185
Escribir A, B, C 188
Cultura A, B, C 191

Comparación cultural 194

UNIDAD 5
Lección 1
Vocabulario A, B, C 197

Gramática A, B, C 200

Gramática A, B, C 203

Integración 206

Escuchar A, B, C 208

Leer A, B, C 211

Escribir A, B, C 214

Cultura A, B, C 217

Lección 2
Vocabulario A, B, C 220

Gramática A, B, C 223

Gramática A, B, C 226

Integración 229

Escuchar A, B, C 231

Leer A, B, C 234

Escribir A, B, C 237

Cultura A, B, C 240

Comparación cultural 243

UNIDAD 6
Lección 1
Vocabulario A, B, C 246

Gramática A, B, C 249

Gramática A, B, C 252

Integración 255

Escuchar A, B, C 257

Leer A, B, C 260

Escribir A, B, C 263

Cultura A, B, C 266

Lección 2
Vocabulario A, B, C 269

Gramática A, B, C 272

Gramática A, B, C 275

Integración 278

Escuchar A, B, C 280

Leer A, B, C 283

Escribir A, B, C 286

Cultura A, B, C 289

Comparación cultural 292

UNIDAD 7
Lección 1
Vocabulario A, B, C 295

Gramática A, B, C 298

Gramática A, B, C 301

Integración 304

Escuchar A, B, C 306

Leer A, B, C 309

Escribir A, B, C 312

Cultura A, B, C 315

Lección 2
Vocabulario A, B, C 318

Gramática A, B, C 321

Gramática A, B, C 324

Integración 327

Escuchar A, B, C 329

Leer A, B, C 332

Escribir A, B, C 335

Cultura A, B, C 338

Comparación cultural 341

UNIDAD 8
Lección 1
Vocabulario A, B, C 344

Gramática A, B, C 347

Gramática A, B, C 350

Integración 353

Escuchar A, B, C 355

Leer A, B, C 358

Escribir A, B, C 361

Cultura A, B, C 364

Lección 2
Vocabulario A, B, C 367

Gramática A, B, C 370

Gramática A, B, C 373

Integración 376

Escuchar A, B, C 378

Leer A, B, C 381

Escribir A, B, C 384

Cultura A, B, C 387

Comparación cultural 390

Vocabulary & Grammar
Review Bookmarks 393

TO THE STUDENT:

Cuaderno práctica por niveles provides activities for practice at different levels of difficulty. Leveled vocabulary and grammar activities cover the entire content of each lesson of your student book. Other activity pages practice the content of the lesson while targeting a specific skill, such as listening. Within most categories of practice there are three pages, each at a different level of difficulty (A, B, and C). The A level is the easiest and C is the most challenging. The different levels of difficulty (A, B, C) are distinguished by the amount of support you're given. A level activities usually give you choices, B level activities often call for short answers to be written, and C level activities require longer answers.

The following sections are included in the **Cuaderno** for each lesson:

- **Vocabulario**

  Each page in this section has three activities that practice the lesson vocabulary.

- **Gramática**

  This section follows the same pattern as the **Vocabulario** section and reinforces the grammar points taught in each lesson.

- **Gramática**

  Follows the same pattern as the Vocabulario section and reinforce the grammar points taught in each lesson.

- **Integración**

  Each of these pages requires you to gather information from two different sources and respond to a related question. The source material is always presented in two different formats: written and spoken.

- **Escuchar**

  Each page in this section has two audio passages, each followed by a short activity. The passages allow you to practice your oral comprehension of Spanish.

- **Leer**

  This section contains short readings accompanied by **¿Comprendiste?** and **¿Qué piensas?** questions.

- **Escribir**

  In this section you are asked to write a short composition. A pre-writing activity will help you prepare to write your composition.

- **Cultura**

  Activities in this section focus on the cultural information found throughout each lesson.

Vocabulario A

Level 1, pp. 32-36

¡AVANZA! **Goal:** Talk about activities.

---

1 Put an X next to each activity that you do in your Spanish classroom.

1. _____ andar en patineta

2. _X_ leer un libro

3. _X_ estudiar

4. _____ comprar un helado

5. _X_ aprender el español

2 Talk about what you like to do. Complete the following sentences with a word or expression from the vocabulary.

1. A ti ¿qué _te gusta_ hacer?

2. A mí me gusta montar en _bicleta_ .

3. Me gusta preparar la _comida_ .

4. Los sábados me gusta _alquilar_ un DVD.

3 Ask the following people if they like to do the activities in parentheses.

modelo: Camila (dibujar): **Camila, ¿te gusta dibujar?**

1. Felipe (tocar la guitarra) _Felipe, ¿te gusta tocar la guitarra?_

2. Mayra (hablar por teléfono) _Mayra, te gusta hablar por telefono_

Vocabulario B

¡AVANZA! **Goal:** Talk about activities.

1 Describe what you like to do. Choose the best word or expression from the vocabulary.

1. Después de las clases me gusta (practicar / escuchar) deportes.

2. Me gusta más escuchar (bicicleta / música).

3. ¿Te gusta (escribir / jugar) correos electrónicos?

4. A mí me gusta (descansar / mirar) la televisión.

2 Look at the images below. Then, write what they are under the appropriate category.

Comer	Beber
1. Pizza	1. Agua
2. Galletas	2. Jugo
3. Helado	3. Refresco
4. Fruta	

3 Answer the following questions in complete sentences.

1. ¿Te gusta más escuchar música o leer un libro?

A mi me gusta escuchar musica mas que leer.

2. ¿Te gusta practicar deportes después de las clases?

No me gusta practicar deportes despues de clase

3. ¿Qué te gusta hacer más, alquilar un DVD o andar en patineta?

Me gusta alquilar un DVD Mas

4. ¿Qué te gusta hacer más, pasear o trabajar?

A mi me gusta pasear, mas que trabajar

Vocabulario C

Level 1, pp. 32-36

> ¡AVANZA! **Goal:** Talk about activities.

1 **¿Qué te gusta hacer?** Complete these sentences using the appropriate words from the vocabulary.

1. Después de las clases me gusta _____ música.

2. Los sábados y domingos no me gusta estudiar o hacer _____ .

3. Antes de practicar deportes me gusta beber _____ .

4. Los sábados me gusta _____ un rato con los amigos.

2 Make a list of six things that you like or do not like to eat and drink.

Comer	**Beber**

modelo: (No) Me gusta comer
papas fritas.

1. _____   1. _____

2. _____   2. _____

3. _____   3. _____

3 Write two sentences about what you like to do, and two sentences about what you do not like to do during Saturday and Sunday. Use **Me gusta...** and **No me gusta...**

_____

_____

_____

_____

Gramática A *Subject Pronouns and* ser

Level 1, pp. 37-41

> ¡AVANZA! **Goal:** Use the subject pronouns and the verb **ser**.

1 Some friends talk about themselves. Complete the sentences using the subject pronouns from the box.

Ustedes	Tú	Yo	Ella	Nosotros

1. _____Tú_____ eres estudiante.

2. _____Ella_____ es de Colombia.

3. _____Nosotros_____ somos de México.

4. _____Ustedes_____ son de Argentina.

5. _____Yo_____ soy de España.

2 Underline the correct form of the verb ser in parentheses to tell where everyone is from.

1. Yo (soy / son) de Miami.

2. Tú (eres / es) de Honduras.

3. Nosotros (sois / somos) de Los Ángeles.

4. ¿Usted (es / son) de Buenos Aires, señor Calvo?

5. ¿Ustedes (son / sois) de España, chicos?

3 Write the correct form of the verb **ser** to complete the sentences and tell where everyone is from.

1. Mi amiga _____es_____ de Nueva York.

2. Yo _____soy_____ de Los Ángeles.

3. Tú _____eres_____ de Boston.

4. Sonia _____es_____ de Miami.

5. Nosotros _____somoy_____ de Estados Unidos.

6. Ustedes _____son_____ de Estados Unidos.

Gramática B *Subject Pronouns and* **ser**

Level 1, pp. 37-41

¡AVANZA! **Goal:** Use the subject pronouns and the verb **ser**.

---

1 Choose the correct subject pronoun to talk about where people are from.

1. _____ somos de Buenos Aires.

   a. Yo   **b.** Nosotros   **c.** Ustedes   **d.** Él

2. _____ son de México.

   a. Él   **b.** Tú   **c.** Ellas   **d.** Usted

3. _____ son de Valencia.

   a. Ellos   **b.** Yo   **c.** Ella   **d.** Tú

4. _____ eres de Valladolid.

   a. Él   **b.** Usted   **c.** Tú   **d.** Ellos

2 Two friends talk about where they are from. Complete the dialog using the verb **ser** .

   Claudia: Yo **1.** _soy_ de Panamá. Y tú, ¿de dónde **2.** _son_ ?

   Andrés: Yo **3.** _soy_ de Colombia, pero mi hermano **4.** _soy_

   de Costa Rica y mis padres **5.** _son_ de Venezuela.

   Claudia: Una amiga también **6.** _es_ de Venezuela. ¿De dónde

   7. _son_ tus amigos?

   Andrés: ¡De muchos países!

3 Tell where the following people are from. Use the correct subject pronouns. Write your answers in complete sentences.

   modelo: María y Patricia (Panamá): **Ellas son de Panamá.**

1. Leila y Javier (Colombia)

   Ellos son de colombia

2. Susana (Nueva York)

   Ellos es de Nueva York

3. Marcos (República Dominicana)

   Él es de Republica Dominicana

Gramática C *Subject Pronouns and* **ser**

Level 1, pp. 37-41

> ¡AVANZA! **Goal:** Use the subject pronouns and the verb **ser**.

1 Write the correct form of the verb **ser**.

1. ¿Tú _____ de Bariloche?

2. ¿Profesora Loreto, usted _____ de Texas?

3. Mis hermanas y yo _____ de Nicaragua.

4. ¿Tú y tus padres _____ de Puerto Rico?

2 Ask where these people are from and then write the correct answer.

modelo: Carmela / Bolivia

¿De dónde es Carmela? (Ella) es de Bolivia.

1. Señora Luna y señora Varita / Honduras

_____

2. Vicente / Perú

_____

3. Señor González / Cuba

_____

4. tú / México

_____

3 Write about where you and people you know are from. Use three different subject pronouns.

1. _____

2. _____

3. _____

Gramática A   *The verb gustar*

> **¡AVANZA!** **Goal:** Express what people like to do using the verb **gustar**.

1 **¿Qué les gusta hacer?** Complete these sentences by underlining the correct pronoun in parentheses.

1. A ellas (les / le) gusta escribir correos electrónicos.

2. A nosotros (nos / les) gusta aprender el español.

3. A ustedes (les / le) gusta pasar un rato con los amigos.

4. ¿ A ti (te / les) gusta trabajar los sábados y domingos?

5. A mí (te / me) gusta pasar un rato con los amigos.

2 Complete the sentences with an appropriate form of **gustar** and the correct pronoun.

1. A mis amigas no _____ comer papas fritas.

2. A Napoleón _____ pasar un rato con los amigos.

3. ¿A ellas _____ tocar la guitarra?

4. A mí _____ estudiar.

5. ¿A ustedes _____ alquilar un DVD?

6. A ti _____ comprar fruta.

3 Look at the drawings and write complete sentences to say what these people enjoy doing.

1. **2.** **3.**

1. A ellos _____ .

2. A ella _____ .

3. A él _____ .

Gramática B *The verb gustar*

> **¡AVANZA!** **Goal:** Express what people like to do using the verb **gustar**.

1 To tell what people enjoy doing, choose the correct expression from the word box.

a. A nosotros	**b.** A Paulina	**c.** A ustedes	**d.** A ti

1. _____ nos gusta preparar la comida.

2. _____ te gusta más andar en patineta.

3. _____ le gusta montar en bicicleta.

4. ¿ _____ no les gusta escuchar música?

2 Write sentences with the following words in order to say what each person enjoys or doesn't enjoy doing. Use the verb **gustar**.

1. A Marcos y Marisela / comer papas fritas _____

_____

2. ¿A ustedes / preparar la comida? _____

3. A mis amigas y a mí / practicar deportes _____

_____

4. ¿A ti / pasear los sábados? _____

3 Answer the questions in complete sentences using **a + pronoun**.

modelo: ¿Le gusta comer pizza a Juan?

Sí, (No) **a él** (no) **le gusta** comer pizza.

1. ¿Le gusta tocar la guitarra a la maestra?

_____

2. ¿Les gusta comer fruta a ustedes?

_____

3. ¿Te gusta beber jugo?

_____

4. ¿Les gusta leer libros a ellas?

_____

Gramática C *The verb gustar*

> **¡AVANZA!** **Goal:** Express what people like to do using the verb **gustar**.

1 **¿Qué cosas no les gusta hacer?** Write an appropriate subject pronoun to complete each sentence.

1. A _____ no nos gusta comprar refrescos.

2. A _____ no me gusta hacer la tarea.

3. A _____ no te gusta comer galletas.

4. A _____ no les gusta pasear.

2 Complete the sentences using the verb **gustar** + **infinitive** to tell what people like and dislike doing.

1. A mí _____ un DVD.

2. A nosotros _____ la televisión.

3. A Martín y a Sofía no _____ la tarea después de las clases.

4. ¿A usted _____ jugo de naranja?

5. A Carlos no _____ al fútbol.

3 Write three questions and answers about people you know and the activities they enjoy. Follow the model.

modelo: ¿Qué **les gusta hacer** a Susana y a ti? **A Susana y a mí nos gusta** jugar al fútbol.

1. _____

_____

2. _____

_____

3. _____

_____

Integración: Hablar

Level 1, pp. 49-51
WB CD 01 Track 01

Sofía's homework was to create a Web page that includes what she likes and dislikes doing on Saturdays. But wait! Sofía does not include the things she dislikes, and her mother mentions those during a voice mail she left for Sofía's teacher.

Fuente 1 Leer

Read what Sofía likes to do on Saturdays...

Mi nombre es: Sofía Marcano

Fecha: 23 de noviembre

Los sábados me gusta tocar la guitarra y escuchar música. Me gusta pasar un rato con los amigos. Me gusta montar en bicicleta, ¡ah! y también me gusta mucho descansar. Me gusta hacer muchas actividades los sábados.

Fuente 2 Escuchar   *CD 01 track 02*

Listen to what Sofía's mother says about her. Take notes.

_____

_____

_____

Hablar

What activities does Sofía like and dislike doing on Saturdays?

modelo: Los sábados, a Sofía le gusta... Pero a Sofía no le gusta...

Integración: Escribir

Lisa, your new pen pal in Uruguay, is very organized. She wrote an email to you saying what she likes to do on weekdays. She preferred to tell you all the fun things she likes doing on weekends by recording herself in a video message.

Fuente 1 Leer

Read Lisa's e-mail...

De: Lisa   A: David
Tema: Me gusta hacer...

Me llamo Lisa y soy de Montevideo, Uruguay. Soy organizada. Me gusta hacer cosas todos los días después de las clases. Los lunes, me gusta hacer la tarea; los martes, me gusta alquilar un DVD; los miércoles y los jueves, me gusta hacer más tarea. Hoy es viernes, y los viernes me gusta mucho escribir correos electrónicos y hablar por teléfono.

¡Adiós!

Lisa

Fuente 2 Escuchar   *CD 01 track 04*

Listen to what Lisa says about her weekend activities. Take notes.

_____

_____

_____

Escribir

Explain what Lisa likes to do each day of the week.

modelo: Los lunes a Lisa le gusta...
          Los martes a Lisa le gusta...
          Los sábados a Lisa le gusta...

_____

_____

_____

_____

_____

_____

_____

_____

Escuchar A

Level 1, pp. 52-53
WB CD 01 Tracks 05-06

¡AVANZA! **Goal:** Listen to find out what Carolina and her friends like to do and where they are from.

1 Listen to the conversation about what these friends like to do. Match each name with the appropriate picture.

Ángela

Antonio

Clara

Roberto

2 Listen to each person say what she or he likes to do. Then read each statement below and say if it is true **(cierto)** or false **(falso)**.

C   F   **1.** A Carolina le gusta escuchar música antes de las clases.

C   F   **2.** A Carlos y a Carlota les gusta practicar deportes después de las clases.

C   F   **3.** A Norberto le gusta preparar la comida.

C   F   **4.** A Gabriel le gusta hacer la tarea los sábados y los domingos.

Escuchar B

¡AVANZA!	**Goal:** Listen to find out what Carolina and her friends like to do and where they are from.

1 Listen to each statement and take notes. Then complete the sentences with the activities they like to do.

1. A Carlos y a Carlota les gusta _____ deportes.

2. A Carolina le gusta _____ música.

3. A Gabriel le gusta _____ .

4. A Norberto le gusta _____ la comida.

2 Listen to the conversation and take notes. Then complete the following sentences based on what you heard.

de México	de Honduras
de Estados Unidos	de Chile

1. Ricardo _____ .

2. Laura _____ .

3. Los amigos de Laura _____ .

4. Felipe y Julia _____ .

Escuchar C

¡AVANZA! **Goal:** Listen to find out what Carolina and her friends like to do and where they are from.

1 **¿Qué les gusta hacer?** Listen to the conversation between two friends. Take notes and then complete the sentences.

1. A Ricardo _____ gusta más _____ .

2. A Laura _____ gusta _____ después de la escuela.

3. A Ricardo _____ gusta más _____ y correr después de la escuela.

4. A Laura _____ gusta dibujar y a Ricardo _____ gusta más _____ música.

2 Listen to each person's statement. Take notes and then answer the questions in complete sentences.

1. ¿Qué le gusta a Gabriel?

_____

2. ¿Qué no le gusta a Gabriel?

_____

3. ¿De dónde es Gabriel?

_____

4. ¿De dónde es Carlota?

_____

5. ¿Qué no le gusta hacer a Carlota?

_____

Leer A

DIA DE ACTIVIDADES CON AMIGOS

¿Te gusta...

❂ *pasar un rato con los amigos*

❂ *dibujar*

❂ *escuchar música*

❂ *tocar la guitarra*

❂ *practicar deportes?*

Actividades después de las clases _____

¿Comprendiste? Did you understand the reading? Answer the following questions true **(cierto)** or false **(falso)**.

C   F   **1.** El día de actividades es para practicar deportes.

C   F   **2.** El día de actividades es para pasear con amigos.

C   F   **3.** El día de actividades es para tocar la guitarra.

C   F   **4.** Las actividades son antes de las clases.

¿Qué piensas?

1. ¿A ti te gusta pasar un rato con los amigos?

_____

2. ¿Qué te gusta hacer en el día de actividades con amigos?

_____

3. ¿Qué otras (*others*) actividades te gustan?

_____

Leer B

¡Buenos días! Me llamo Graciela y soy de la ciudad de Panamá, en la República de Panamá. Es un país muy bonito. Mi escuela es muy buena. Se llama Instituto Cultural. Me gusta estudiar. Muchos estudiantes son internacionales. Mi amigo Juan es de Lima, Perú. A Juan le gusta jugar al fútbol. A mi me gusta más andar en patineta. Mi amiga Silvia es de Buenos Aires, Argentina. A ella le gusta dibujar y leer. A nosotros nos gusta pasar un rato con los amigos y escuchar música o mirar la televisión. Los sábados nos gusta alquilar DVDs y comprar pizzas.

¿Comprendiste?

Did you understand the reading? Complete the following sentences.

1. A Graciela le gusta _____ .

2. Juan es de _____ .

3. A los amigos de Graciela les gusta _____ .

4. Los sábados les gusta _____ .

5. A Silvia le gusta _____ .

¿Qué piensas?

1. ¿De dónde eres?

   _____

2. ¿De dónde es el (la) maestro (a) de español?

   _____

3. ¿Qué les gusta hacer a ustedes los sábados y domingos?

   _____

   _____

Leer C

Me llamo Valeria: ¿Qué nos gusta hacer?

Lucas es de Nicaragua. *A Lucas le gusta escribir y leer libros. También le gusta comer helado los domingos por la tarde. Lucas es mi amigo. A nosotros nos gusta alquilar un DVD los sábados y practicar deportes después de las clases.*

Araceli es de México. *A ella le gusta preparar la comida. A mí me gusta comer la comida que ella prepara. A Araceli y a mí nos gusta comprar y comer helado los domingos. También nos gusta hacer la tarea después de las clases.*

Simón es de Texas, Estados Unidos. *A él le gusta aprender el español en la escuela. A nosotros nos gusta estudiar el español después de las clases. También le gusta andar en patineta y comer helado los sábados y domingos.*

¿Comprendiste?

Did you understand the reading? Answer the following questions in complete sentences.

1. ¿De dónde son Lucas, Araceli y Simón?

   _____

2. ¿Qué les gusta hacer a Valeria y a Lucas los sábados?

   _____

   _____

3. ¿Qué le gusta hacer a Araceli? ¿Qué le gusta comer a Valeria?

   _____

   _____

4. ¿Qué les gusta hacer a Valeria y a Simón después de las clases?

   _____

5. ¿Qué les gusta a todos?

   _____

¿Qué piensas?

1. ¿A ti te gusta comer helado? ¿Qué te gusta comer?

   _____

   _____

2. ¿Qué actividades les gusta hacer a ti y a tus amigos después de las clases?

   _____

   _____

Escribir A

> **¡AVANZA!** **Goal:** Write about activities that you like and don't like to do.

Step 1

Make a list of four activities you like and don't like to do.

_____

_____

_____

_____

Classify your list in the chart.

Me gusta…	No me gusta…
1.	1.
2.	2.

Step 2

Write four sentences using the information above about what you like to do .

_____

_____

Step 3

Evaluate your writing using the information in the table.

Writing Criteria	Excellent	Good	Needs Work
Content	Your sentences state four things that you like and don't like to do.	Your sentences state three things that you like and don't like to do.	Your sentences state less than three things that you like and don't like to do.
Communication	Most of your responses are clear.	Some of your responses are clear.	Your message is not very clear.

Escribir B

Level 1, pp. 52-53

> ¡AVANZA! **Goal:** Write about activities that you and others like and don't like to do.

Step 1

Make a list of three things your friend likes to do, and three things she/he doesn't like to do.

Nombre de mi amigo(a): _____

Le gusta…	No le gusta…
1.	1.
2.	2.
3.	3.

Step 2

Write a paragraph about what your friend likes and doesn't like to do.

_____

_____

Step 3

Evaluate your writing using the information in the table.

Writing Criteria	Excellent	Good	Needs Work
Content	You state six things your friend likes and doesn't like to do.	You state four or five things that your friend likes and doesn't like to do.	You state fewer than four things that your friend likes and doesn't like to do.
Communication	Most of your responses are clear.	Some of your responses are clear.	Your message is not very clear.
Accuracy	You make few mistakes in grammar and vocabulary.	You make some mistakes in grammar and vocabulary.	You make many mistakes in grammar and vocabulary.

Escribir C

Level 1, pp. 52-53

> **¡AVANZA!** **Goal:** Write about activities that you and others like and don't like to do.

Step 1

Fill in the chart with information about yourself.

Me gusta...	1.	2.	3.
No me gusta...	1.	2.	3.
Soy de...			

Step 2 Now write a short letter to a pen pal with the information from above.

_____

_____

_____

_____

Step 3

Evaluate your writing using the information in the table.

Writing Criteria	Excellent	Good	Needs Work
Content	Your letter includes what you like and don't like to do.	Your letter includes most of what you like and don't like to do	Your letter does not include what you like and don't like to do.
Communication	Your letter is clear and easy to follow.	Parts of your letter are clear and easy to follow.	Your letter is not very clear.
Accuracy	You make few mistakes in grammar and vocabulary.	You make some mistakes in grammar and vocabulary.	You make many mistakes in grammar and vocabulary.

Cultura A

> **¡AVANZA!** **Goal:** Review cultural information about the Hispanic community in the United States.

1 **United States** Read the following statements about the United States and answer *true* or *false*.

T   F   **1.** There are almost 40 million Hispanics in the United States.

T   F   **2.** The city with the largest Hispanic population in the United States is San Francisco.

T   F   **3.** Xavier Cortada is a Cuban American artist.

T   F   **4.** San Antonio's oldest neighborhood is called La Villita.

2 **In the community** Complete the following sentences with a word from the box.

Calle Ocho	Freedom Tower
Hispanic Heritage Month	Fiesta San Antonio

1. The _____ celebrates the cultural diversity of Americans.

2. _____ is famous for its Cuban restaurants, cafés, and shops.

3. The _____ honors the heroes of the Álamo.

4. The _____ is the building that houses the Cuban-American Museum.

3 **Los Premios Juventud** Write a few lines to describe **los Premios Juventud.** Then, if you were to vote for some nominees, who would you choose? Write a name for each category listed below.

_____

_____

_____

Best Actor: _____

Best Actress: _____

Best Female Vocalist: _____

Best Male Vocalist: _____

Best Sports Player: _____

> **¡AVANZA!** **Goal:** Review cultural information about Hispanic communities in the United States.

1 **Awards** Complete the following sentences with the words from the box.

teens	Spanish-language	actors	Juanes	Juventud

1. Los Premios _____ are awarded in Miami.

2. _____ nominate and vote for their favorite artists.

3. _____ was a past nominee.

4. The event is shown on _____ television.

5. The winners of these awards can be famous sports stars, singers, and _____ .

2 **In the U. S.** Choose a multiple-choice item to complete the following sentences.

1. The number of Hispanics living in the United States is ____

   a. 40 million   **b.** 20 million   **c.** 30 million

2. The Fiesta San Antonio honors the heroes of the Álamo and the Batalla de ____

   a. San Jorge   **b.** San Jacinto   **c.** San Luis

3. The street in Miami renowned for its Cuban restaurants, cafés, and shops is called ____

   a. Calle Siete   **b.** Calle Ocho   **c.** Calle Nueve

4. Miami's Cuban American Museum is located in the ____

   a. University of Miami   **b.** public library   **c.** Freedom Tower

3 **Describing art** Look at the picture of Xavier Cortada's *Music* on page 44 of your book. Describe it. What feelings does it evoke? What message do you think the artist wants to convey?

_____

_____

_____

_____

_____

_____

Cultura C

> ¡AVANZA! **Goal:** Review cultural information about Hispanic communities in the United States.

1 **Celebrities** Do you know where the following celebrities come from? Write the name of the country of origin of each person listed below.

Name	Where is he/she from?
Juanes	
Gael García Bernal	
Jennifer Lopez	

2 **Hispanic community in the U. S.** Answer the following questions.

1. What is San Antonio's oldest neighborhood called? _____

_____

2. What do people celebrate in the United States between September 15 and October 15?

_____

_____

3. What is something that influences Xavier Cortada's artwork?

_____

3 **Los Premios Juventud** Create a poster advertising **Los Premios Juventud.** Your poster should explain what the event is and where it is held. Also include a date and time for the event.

Vocabulario A

Level 1, pp. 56–60

┃**¡AVANZA!**┃ **Goal:** Describe yourself and others.

1 **¿Cómo eres?** Match the adjective in the first column with an adjective that means the opposite in the second column. .

seria   alto

bajo   cómica

malo   pequeño

trabajadora   perezosa

grande   bueno

2 Describe these people by completing the following sentences with an adjective from the word bank.

| estudiosa | atlética | organizado | artístico |

1. A Julio le gusta dibujar. Julio es _____ .

2. A Julieta le gusta estudiar. Julieta es _____ .

3. El señor Gustavo no es desorganizado; es muy _____ .

4. A la señora Ponce le gusta practicar deportes; es muy _____ .

3 **¿Cómo eres tú?** Make a list of words that describe your personality. and then write one sentence using them. Follow the model.

modelo: Lista de palabras: _____ *cómica, joven, baja, pelo castaño* _____

Oración: **Soy cómica, joven, baja y tengo pelo castaño**.

1. Lista de palabras: _____

2. Oración: _____

Nombre _____ Clase _____ Fecha _____

Vocabulario B

Level 1, pp. 56–60

> **¡AVANZA!** **Goal:** Describe yourself and others.

1 **¿Cómo son?** Choose the word or expression from the vocabulary that best describes the people in the following sentences.

1. A Samuel no le gusta trabajar los domingos. Es un chico (perezoso / trabajador).

2. A Rebeca y a Marta no les gusta hacer la tarea. No son estudiantes muy (simpáticas / buenas).

3. Gustavo tiene pelo (estudioso / castaño).

4. La clase de español tiene tres estudiantes. Es una clase (grande / pequeña).

2 **¿Quién es?** Choose the word from the word bank that best completes each sentence.

1. A Víctor le gusta estudiar. Es un _____ muy bueno.

2. La señora García es una _____ muy buena.

3. Arturo tiene una _____ muy guapa. Se llama Beatriz.

4. Al señor Gómez le gusta pasar un rato con los amigos. Es un _____ muy simpático.

> estudiante
> persona
> amiga
> hombre

3 **¿Cómo son ustedes?** Write two complete sentences describing yourself and one of your friends. Follow the model.

modelo: Yo soy alto y tengo pelo castaño.

Mi amigo Daniel es grande y tiene pelo rubio.

1. _____

2. _____

Vocabulario C

> **¡AVANZA!** **Goal:** Describe yourself and others.

1 Choose the correct word to complete each description.

1. Anita es una chica muy (guapa / un poco / malo).

2. Danilo es (trabajador / un poco / amigo) desorganizado.

3. Aníbal, Darío, Facundo y Sergio son (guapo / un poco / todos) estudiantes.

4. Diana y Adela tienen pelo (rubio / pelirrojas / viejo).

2 **¿Cómo son?** Look at each drawing and write a complete sentence that describes the people in them. The first one is done for you.

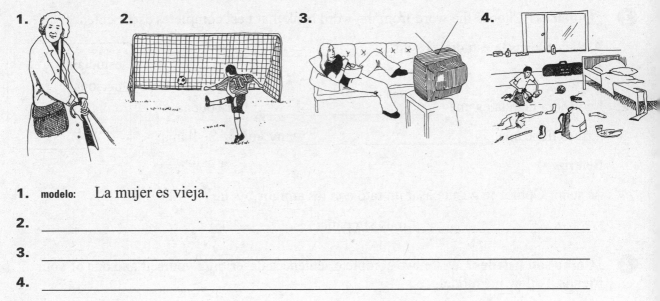

1. 2. 3. 4.

1. **modelo:** La mujer es vieja.

2. _____

3. _____

4. _____

3 **Te presento a…** Complete this dialog. Each friend introduces another friend to someone else. Each friend should describe herself and say what she likes to do.

Antonia: ¡Hola Patricia! Ella es mi amiga Begoña. Es de España.

Patricia: Encantada. Begoña, ¿te gusta mirar la televisión o correr? Me gusta correr porque soy muy atlética.

Begoña: _____

Antonia: _____

Patricia: _____

Gramática A *Definite and Indefinite Articles*

> ¡AVANZA! **Goal:** Use definite and indefinite articles to identify people and things.

1 Match the noun on the left with the correct indefinite article on the right.

chico   unos

persona   un

amigas   unas

hombres   una

2 **¿Qué les gusta comer?** Underline the correct article in parentheses to complete the sentences describing what these people like to eat.

1. A Eva le gustan (las / unos) galletas.

2. A Sebastián y Celestino les gustan más (una / las) papas fritas.

3. A nosotros nos gusta beber (el / los) refresco.

4. ¿A usted le gusta (unas / la) pizza?

5. ¿A ustedes les gustan (unos / unas) helados?

3 Use the verb **ser** to describe what these people are like in three complete sentences. You may use the adjectives from the box.

| organizado(a)   simpáticos(as)   atléticos(as)   perezosos(as)   trabajador(a) |

modelo: Mis padres **son muy trabajadores**.

Los futbolistas _____

Pablo y Luis _____

El maestro _____

Gramática B *Definite and Indefinite Articles*

Level 1, pp. 61–65

> ▶ ¡AVANZA! **Goal:** Use definite and indefinite articles to identify people and things.

1 **Somos…** Write **un, una, unos,** or **unas** to complete the sentences.

Hola, me llamo Dolores y soy **1.** _____ chica de

La Habana. Las amigas, Isabel y Rosita, son **2.** _____

personas muy inteligentes y buenas. Ellas son estudiosas. Les gusta

más leer **3.** _____ libro que descansar. Yo soy perezosa.

Me gusta más alquilar **4.** _____ DVD. Nuestros

vecinos (*Our neighbors*), el señor Valdés y el señor León, son **5.**

_____ señores artísticos. Les gusta mucho dibujar.

2 Change each noun from singular to plural. Then, write the appropriate plural definite article for each. Follow the model.

modelo: una persona
dos **personas**
las personas

1. un amigo   **2.** una mujer   **3.** un hombre

_____cuatro_____   _____ocho_____   _____siete_____

_____   _____   _____

3 **¿Cómo es?** These friends are different. Tell how. Use **ser.** Follow the model.

modelo: María / estudiante organizada   Katy / chica desorganizada

María es una estudiante organizada. Katy es una chica desorganizada.

1. Roberto / hombre trabajador   Alejandro /chico perezoso

_____

2. Julia / mujer alta   Guadalupe / chica baja

_____

Gramática C *Definite and Indefinite Articles*

| ¡AVANZA! | **Goal:** Use definite and indefinite articles to identify people and things. |

1 Fill in the blanks with a correct definite or indefinite article.

1. Nosotros somos _____ estudiantes de Buenos Aires.

2. Ellos son _____ amigos de Gisela.

3. Ustedes son _____ personas estudiosas e inteligentes.

4. Tú eres _____ hombre de Valladolid.

2 Rewrite these sentences changing the words underlined to the plural.

1. Él es un hombre de Bariloche.

_____

2. ¿Ella es la amiga de Texas?

_____

3. Me gusta beber el jugo.

_____

4. ¡Tú eres un estudiante atlético!

_____

3 Write three sentences describing people you know. Use the verb **ser** and the indefinite articles **un, una, unos, unas**.

1. _____

2. _____

3. _____

Gramática A *Noun-Adjective Agreement*

Level 1, pp. 66–68

> **¡AVANZA!** **Goal:** Use adjectives with nouns.

1 Underline the adjective in parentheses that agrees with the noun on the left.

1. las chicas (bajos / bajas)

2. una persona (buena / bueno)

3. un estudiante (trabajador / trabajadora)

4. los hombres (ancianas / ancianos)

2 Write the correct ending that completes these adjectives. Remember to match the gender and number of the noun.

1. A Eva le gusta comer unas galletas buen_____ .

2. A Samuel y a Carlos les gusta dibujar. Son unos chicos artístic_____ .

3. Natalia es una chica guap_____ .

4. ¿A ustedes les gusta comer las pizzas grand_____ ?

5. Ignacio e Isabela son unos estudiantes organizad_____ .

3 Complete these sentences with an appropriate adjective. Use different adjectives in each sentence. Follow the model.

modelo   David es un chico **trabajador** porque le gusta trabajar los sábados y
         domingos.

1. El señor Moreno es un maestro de español muy _____ .

2. Nosotros somos los estudiantes más _____ del señor

   Unamuno.

3. Vosotros sois estudiantes buenos porque sois _____ .

4. La señora Márquez es una maestra muy _____ .

Gramática B *Noun-Adjective Agreement*

Level 1, pp. 66–68

> **¡AVANZA!** **Goal:** Use adjectives with nouns.

1 We are all different. Choose the correct adjective that best completes these sentences about different people.

1. Nosotros somos unos estudiantes _____ .

  a) guapo   **b)** guapa   **c)** guapos

2. A él le gusta pasar un rato con amigos porque es _____ .

  a) simpáticas   **b)** simpáticos   **c)** simpático

3. Vosotros sois unas personas _____ .

  a) inteligentes   **b)** inteligente

4. Las chicas de la clase de la señora García son muy _____ .

  a) trabajador   **b)** trabajadoras   **c)** trabajadores

2 Write the correct form of an adjective to complete the following sentences:

1. A los amigos les gusta leer y hacer la tarea. Son _____ .

2. María y Carla son unas mujeres _____ .

3. Los chicos no son altos, son _____ .

4. Las mujeres no son viejas, son _____ .

3 In three complete sentences, describe the people you see in the drawings below.

1. _____

2. _____

3. _____

Gramática C *Noun-Adjective Agreement*

> ¡AVANZA! **Goal:** Use adjectives with nouns.

1 Change each phrase from plural to singular. Follow the model.

modelo: las personas inteligentes

la persona inteligente

1. los chicos atléticos _____

2. las mujeres trabajadoras _____

3. los hombres pelirrojos _____

2 Complete these descriptions with the appropriate word.

1. Miguel es _____ porque le gusta practicar deportes.

2. Elisa es buena estudiante porque _____ .

3. Laura es muy _____ porque no es mala.

4. Mario es un chico muy _____ porque no es desorganizado.

3 In complete sentences, describe three of your friends. Say where each one is from, what each one looks like, and write two adjectives that describe them. Follow the model.

modelo: Andrea es de Texas. Andrea es una chica alta y tiene pelo rubio. Andrea es atlética.

1. _____

_____

2. _____

_____

3. _____

_____

Integración: Hablar

Arthur moved from Denver, Colorado, to Mexico City. He is going to study Spanish for a year abroad at a local High School. The high school's principal is very happy because Arthur is a talented soccer player who can help the school's soccer team win the city championship. Arthur writes about himself for the high school newspaper. The Principal introduces Arthur to everybody at the first soccer match of the year.

Fuente 1 Leer

   Read what Arthur wrote in the school's newspaper...

¡HOLA!

   Me llamo Arthur. Arturo en español. Yo soy de los Estados Unidos. Soy de Colorado. En Colorado hace frío y nieva.
Soy atlético y me gusta practicar deportes .
También me gusta jugar al fútbol. Soy inteligente pero un poco desorganizado.

Fuente 2 Escuchar   *CD 01 track 12*

   Listen to the principal's description of Arthur over the loudspeaker before his first soccer game. Take notes.

_____

_____

_____

_____

Hablar

What is Arthur like? Describe his personality and appearance.

modelo: Arthur es... Y también es... Pero no es...

_____

_____

_____

Integración: Escribir

Escuela González, a soccer foundation in Ecuador, is looking for international participants for its programs. On their Web page there is a letter from the director of the foundation who is looking for volunteers.

Fuente 1 Leer

Read the letter from the director.

> ¡Hola! Me llamo Gustavo González y soy el director de la Escuela González. La escuela tiene muchas personas trabajadoras. ¿Te gusta practicar deportes? La escuela tiene seis maestros de fútbol de lunes a viernes y nueve maestros los sábados y domingos. Tenemos clases de hombres y mujeres, y también tenemos clases de chicos y chicas.

Fuente 2 Escuchar   *CD 01 track 14*

Listen to the audioclip of a testimonial from Escuela González's Web site. Take notes.

_____

_____

_____

_____

Escribir

Why would you choose Escuela González to learn soccer? Remember to include information from both the Web page and the audioclip for your answer.

Modelo: Escuela González tiene... También, es...

_____

_____

_____

_____

_____

_____

Escuchar A

> ¡AVANZA! **Goal:** Listen to students at an international school as they describe themselves and each other.

1 Listen to each statement and take notes. Then choose who fits each description below.

_____ **1.** trabajador(a)

_____ **2.** estudioso(a)

_____ **4.** artístico(a)

a. Claribel
b. Gustavo
c. Mario

2 Listen to each person describe him/herself. Then read each statement below and say if it is true (**Cierto**) or false (**Falso**).

C   F   **1.** Julio y Araceli son unos chicos simpáticos.

C   F   **2.** Araceli es una chica artística.

C   F   **3.** A Julio le gusta jugar al fútbol.

C   F   **4.** A Julio le gusta dibujar.

Escuchar B

> **¡AVANZA!** **Goal:** Listen to students at an international school as they describe themselves and each other.

1 Listen and then draw a line from the people to the adjectives that describe them.

Ramón es   muy simpática

María es   muy bonita y tiene pelo castaño

Simón es   ,   muy desorganizado

Enriqueta es   alto y pelirrojo

2 Listen to how each person is described. Then complete the following sentences.

1. Iván es _____ .

2. Nancy es _____ .

3. Melvin es _____ .

4. Iván y Melvin son _____ .

Escuchar C

¡AVANZA! **Goal:** Listen to students at an international school describe themselves and   each other.

1 Listen to the dialog and then write three adjectives to describe each of the following people:

1. La señora Guadalupe: _____

_____

2. Mauricio: _____

_____

3. Marta y Tania: _____

2 Take notes while you listen to the conversation. Then answer the questions in complete sentences.

1. ¿Cómo es Esperanza?

_____

2. ¿Quiénes son estudiosas?

_____

3. ¿Quién tiene pelo rubio?

_____

4. ¿Cómo es Luisa?

_____

5. ¿Cómo eres tú?

_____

> **¡AVANZA!** **Goal:** Read how people describe themselves and others.

¡Hola! Me llamo Rocío. Tengo pelo rubio y soy estudiosa. El señor Cruz, es un poco viejo y es muy bueno. Nora y Lidia, son muy inteligentes. Les gusta mucho leer. Nora tiene un hermano. Se llama Norberto. Es bajo. Nora es alta y tiene pelo rubio, pero su hermano es pelirrojo. Nora, Norberto y Lidia son simpáticos.

¿Comprendiste?

Answer the following questions true **(Cierto)** or false **(Falso).**

C   F   **1.** A Rocío no le gusta estudiar.

C   F   **2.** El señor Cruz es joven.

C   F   **3.** Las amigas de Rocío son chicas muy inteligentes.

C   F   **4.** Norberto es un chico alto.

C   F   **5.** Norberto, Nora y Lidia son simpáticos.

¿Qué piensas?

1. ¿Tienes pelo castaño?

_____

2. ¿Cómo son tus amigos(as)?

_____

3. ¿Eres un chico o una chica organizado(a)?

_____

4. Describe a un amigo.

_____

Leer B

> **¡AVANZA!** **Goal:** Read how people describe themselves and others.

¡Hola! Me llamo Pedro. Tengo pelo castaño. Rafael tiene pelo rubio.
Laura y Raquel tienen pelo castaño. Son muy altas, también son muy
inteligentes. La persona de pelo rubio es muy perezosa, seria y un poco
mala.

¿Comprendiste?

Answer the following questions in complete sentences, based on the information in the reading.

1. ¿Cómo es Rafael?

_____

_____

2. ¿Cómo son Laura y Raquel?

_____

_____

3. ¿Es Rafael trabajador?

_____

¿Qué piensas?

1. ¿Cómo eres tú?

_____

2. ¿Te gustan las personas rubias?

_____

3. ¿Te gustan las personas altas?

_____

Leer C

| ¡AVANZA! | **Goal:** Read how people describe themselves and others. |

¡Hola! Somos estudiantes. Yo me llamo Alberto y soy de España. Tengo unos amigos de los Estados Unidos y otros (*others*) de Colombia. La maestra es una mujer joven de Paraguay. Yo soy una persona organizada y un estudiante bueno porque me gusta estudiar. A Andrés no le gusta hacer la tarea, pero es muy artístico. A él le gusta dibujar. Felipe es un poco desorganizado, pero es muy simpático. Sandro es un estudiante bueno y es muy atlético. Le gusta correr y jugar al fútbol. Andrés tiene pelo castaño y es alto. Felipe es grande y tiene pelo rubio. Yo soy pelirrojo y un poco bajo. ¡Todos somos amigos muy simpáticos!

¿Comprendiste?

Answer the following questions in complete sentences.

1. ¿Cómo es la maestra?

   _____

2. ¿Es Alberto un estudiante bueno? ¿Por qué?

   _____

3. ¿Cómo es Andrés?

   _____

4. ¿Cómo es Felipe?

   _____

¿Qué piensas?

1. ¿Son los chicos buenos amigos? ¿Por qué? (Why?)

   _____

2. ¿Cómo son los amigos de tu (your) clase?

   _____

   _____

Escribir A

> **¡AVANZA!** **Goal:** Write descriptions of people you know.

Step 1

Write the name of one person you admire. Then, make a list of adjectives that describe him or her.

1. **Nombre:** _____

2. **¿Cómo es?:** _____

Step 2

Refer back to your list in Step 1, and write two sentences about the person you chose and one sentence about why (s)he is that way.

_____

_____

Step 3

Evaluate your writing using the information in the table.

Writing Criteria	Excellent	Good	Needs Work
Content	You have included three sentences to write your description about the person you chose.	You have included two sentences to write your description about the person you chose.	You have included one or less sentences to write your description about the person you chose.
Communication	Most of your description is clear.	Some of your desription is clear.	Your description is not very clear.
Accuracy	You make few mistakes in grammar and vocabulary.	You make some mistakes in grammar and vocabulary.	You make many mistakes in grammar and vocabulary.

Escribir B

Level 1, pp. 76–77

> **¡AVANZA!** **Goal:** Write descriptions of people you know.

Step 1

Fill out this chart with information about yourself.

Nombre	
Soy	
No soy	
Tengo	
Me gusta	

Step 2

Now, tell why you chose the words above to describe yourself. Write three complete sentences about yourself. Follow the model.

modelo: Soy una estudiante buena porque me gusta hacer la tarea. No soy perezosa porque me gusta trabajar. Me gusta tocar la guitarra porque soy artística.

_____

_____

Step 3

Evaluate your writing using the information in the table.

Writing Criteria	Excellent	Good	Needs Work
Content	You have included three sentences in your explanation.	You have included two sentences in your explanation.	You have included one of fewer sentences in your explanation.
Communication	Most of your explanation is clear.	Some of your explanation is clear.	Your explanation is not very clear.
Accuracy	You make few mistakes in grammar and vocabulary.	You make some mistakes in grammar and vocabulary.	You make many mistakes in grammar and vocabulary.

Escribir C

> [¡AVANZA!] **Goal:** Write descriptions of people you know.

Step 1

List one person you know. Then, write as many nouns, adjectives and other expressions as you can to describe him or her.

Nombre: _____

_____

_____

_____

Step 2

Now, in four sentences, tell why you like the person you chose in Step 1. Begin your paragraph with "Me gusta…" and the name of the person you described.

_____

_____

_____

Step 3

Evaluate your writing using the information in the table.

Writing Criteria	Excellent	Good	Needs Work
Content	You have included four sentences to write your explanation.	You have included three sentences to write your explanation.	You have included two or less sentences to write your explanation.
Communication	Most of your explanation is clear.	Some of your explanation is clear.	Your explanation is not very clear.
Accuracy	You make few mistakes in grammar and vocabulary.	You make some mistakes in grammar and vocabulary.	You make many mistakes in grammar and vocabulary.

Cultura A

> **¡AVANZA!** **Goal:** Review the importance of the Hispanic community in the United States.

1 **The United States** Complete the following sentences with one of the multiple choice phrases.

1. This city has the highest percentage of Latinos (77%) in the United States. _____

   a. San Antonio   **b.** Houston   **c.** El Paso

2. Miami's Little Havana is home to the famous _____

   a. Calle Ocho   **b.** Calle Nueve   **c.** Calle Cuatro

3. One of San Antonio's main attractions is _____

   a. the Freedom Tower   **b.** the Paseo del Río   **c.** the Cuban American Museum

2 **Florida and Texas** Complete the following sentences.

1. Carmen Lomas Garza is a painter who grew up in _____ .

2. _____ are eggshells filled with confetti.

3. Many people go to _____ in Miami to enjoy Cuban sandwiches and mango juice.

4. It is possible to hear _____ music played in San Antonio's El Mercado.

3 **Regional cuisine** Fill out the chart below to list typical dishes or ingredients of Tex-Mex and Mexican cuisine. Then, describe the foods you listed. Have you ever eaten any of these dishes (or dishes made with these ingredients)? Tell where you have eaten them and whether or not you like the dish.

Tex-Mex	Mexican

_____

_____

_____

_____

Cultura B

 Goal: Review the importance of the Hispanic community in the United States.

1 **The United States** Read the following sentences and answer *true* or *false*.

T   F   **1.** Tex-Mex is a mix of Mexican and Cuban food.

T   F   **2.** *Cascarones* are eggshells filled with rice.

T   F   **3.** **Chile con carne** is a Tex-Mex dish.

T   F   **4.** Black beans are typical of traditional Mexican cuisine.

T   F   **5.** The Alamo is located in San Antonio.

2 **Popular places** Write where you can find the following places.

Places to visit	In which city are they located?
Little Havana	
The Paseo del Río	
Calle Ocho	
La Villita	

3 **Cascarones** Write a simple, step-by-step guide for making *cascarones*. Tell what they are, how to make them, and what to do with them.

_____

_____

_____

_____

_____

_____

Cultura C

> **¡AVANZA!** **Goal:** Review the importance of the Hispanic community in the United States.

1 **Hispanic culture** Complete the following sentences.

1. _____ are eggshells filled with confetti.

2. Carmen Lomas Garza is a painter who grew up in _____ .

3. The Paseo del Río and the Alamo are located in _____ .

4. Little Havana is located in _____ .

2 **In the U. S.** Answer the following questions about the Hispanic community in the United States.

1. Where in the United States can you hear mariachi music?

_____

2. What is Tex-Mex food? Give two examples.

_____

_____

3. Where is Calle Ocho located and what can people do there?

_____

_____

3 **Visiting San Antonio** Write a postcard to a friend describing a trip to San Antonio. What did you see and do there? What foods did you try?

_____

_____

_____

_____

_____

_____

_____

Comparación cultural: Me gusta...

Level 1, pp. 78–79

Lectura y escritura

After reading the paragraphs about how José, Manuel, Martina, and Mónica describe themselves and their favorite activities, write a short paragraph about yourself. Use the information on your personal chart to write sentences and then write a paragraph that describes yourself.

Step 1

Complete the personal chart describing as many details as you can about yourself.

Categoría	Detalles
país de origen	
descripción física	
personalidad	
actividades favoritas	
comidas favoritas	

Step 2

Now take the details from your personal chart and write a sentence for each topic on the chart.

_____

_____

_____

_____

_____

_____

_____

_____

Comparación cultural: Me gusta...

Lectura y escritura (continued)

Step 3

Now write your paragraph using the sentences you wrote as a guide. Include an introduction sentence and use the verbs **ser** and **gustar** to write about yourself.

_____

_____

_____

_____

_____

_____

_____

Checklist

Be sure that...

☐ all the details about yourself from your chart are included in the paragraph;

☐ you use details to describe, as clearly as possible, the activities you like the most;

☐ you include new vocabulary words and the verbs **ser** and **gustar.**

Rubric

Evaluate your writing using the rubric below.

Writing criteria	Excellent	Good	Needs Work
Content	Your paragraph includes many details about yourself.	Your paragraph includes some details about yourself.	Your paragraph includes little information about yourself.
Communication	Most of your paragraph is organized and easy to follow.	Parts of your paragraph are organized and easy to follow.	Your paragraph is disorganized and hard to follow.
Accuracy	Your paragraph has few mistakes in grammar and vocabulary.	Your paragraph has some mistakes in grammar and vocabulary.	Your paragraph has many mistakes in grammar and vocabulary.

Comparación cultural: Me gusta...

Compara con tu mundo

Now write a comparison about yourself and one of the three students from page 79. Organize your comparison by topics. First, compare where you are from, then your personality and physical description, and lastly your favorite activities and food.

Step 1

Use the chart to organize your comparison by topics. Write details for each topic about yourself and the student you chose.

Categoría	Mi descripción	La descripción de _____
país de origen		
descripción física		
personalidad		
actividades favoritas		
comidas favoritas		

Step 2

Now use the details from your personal chart to write a comparison. Include an introduction sentence and write about each topic. Use the verbs **ser** and **gustar** to describe yourself and the student you chose.

_____

_____

_____

_____

_____

_____

Vocabulario A

> **¡AVANZA!** **Goal:** Talk about daily schedules.

1 What are your classes this year? Read the following list and mark with an X next to each subject you are taking.

1. ____ el español
2. ____ el inglés
3. ____ el arte

7. ____ la historia
8. ____ las matemáticas
9. ____ las ciencias

2 **¿A qué hora son las clases?** Look at Wednesday's class schedule and complete the sentences with the time each class meets.

Horario de clases	
Hora	**miércoles**
8:30	historia
9:15	inglés
10:00	español
12:50	ciencias

1. La clase de historia es _____ .

2. La clase de inglés es _____ .

3. La clase de español es _____ .

4. La clase de ciencias es _____ .

3 In a complete sentence, answer the following questions about yourself:

1. ¿A qué hora es la clase de matemáticas?

_____

2. ¿Cuántos exámenes hay en la clase de español?

_____

Vocabulario B

> **¡AVANZA!** **Goal:** Talk about daily schedules.

1 Choose the correct word or phrase in parentheses to complete each sentence.

1. Hay (veinticuatro / veintiún) horas en un día.

2. Hay (setenta / sesenta) minutos en una hora.

3. Tengo que estudiar para (sacar una buena nota / sacar una mala nota).

4. Estudiar a las diez de la noche es estudiar (tarde / temprano).

5. El maestro tiene que (aprender / enseñar) el español.

6. La estudiante tiene que (llegar/ contestar) la pregunta.

2 Look at María's schedule and tell when she has the following classes. Use the words in the box.

Hora	lunes	martes	miércoles	jueves	viernes
8:30	historia	historia	historia	historia	historia
10:15	matemáticas	matemáticas	matemáticas	matemáticas	matemáticas
12:00	inglés	español	ciencias	español	español

1. ¿La clase de historia?

_____

2. ¿La clase de arte?

_____

3. ¿La clase de ciencias?

_____

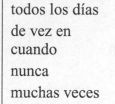

todos los días
de vez en
cuando
nunca
muchas veces

3 Describe your schedule of morning classes in complete sentences. Follow the model:

modelo: A las siete y media de la mañana tengo clase de inglés. La clase de matemáticas es a las nueve. A las once tengo clase de arte.

_____

_____

_____

Vocabulario C

> ¡AVANZA! **Goal:** Talk about daily schedules.

1 Describe what you have to do in each class in order to get a good grade. Use complete sentences.

1. (la clase de español) _____

2. (la clase de matemáticas) _____

3. (la clase de ciencias) _____

4. (la clase de inglés) _____

2 Answer the following questions with complete sentences:

1. ¿Te gusta usar la computadora en la clase de español?

_____

2. ¿Te gusta hablar en la clase de español?

_____

3. ¿Te gusta dibujar en la clase de arte?

_____

4. ¿ A qué hora es tu clase de matemáticas?

_____

5. ¿Te gusta leer libros en la clase de inglés?

_____

6. ¿Cómo es el(la) maestro(a) de ciencias?

_____

3 Describe your schedule of afternoon classes in complete sentences. Explain what you like to do in each class.

_____

_____

_____

_____

_____

Gramática A   *The Verb tener*

> ¡AVANZA! **Goal:** Use **tener** to say what people have and have to do.

1 Underline the correct form of **tener** that completes the sentence.

1. Nosotros (tienen / tenemos) patinetas.

2. Tú (tienes / tengo) una computadora.

3. Laura y Tomás (tiene / tienen) clase a las nueve y cuarto.

4. Yo (tiene / tengo) mucha tarea de ciencias.

2 Complete the following sentences with an expression of frequency from the word bank:

nunca	siempre	de vez en cuando	mucho

1. Rodrigo y Trina son muy inteligentes; _____ les gusta contestar las preguntas del maestro.

2. No me gusta sacar una mala nota; tengo que estudiar _____ .

3. Teresa es muy perezosa; _____ le gusta hacer la tarea.

4. La clase de inglés es muy fácil; tenemos tarea _____ .

3 **Para sacar una buena nota en el examen...** Look at the drawings and write two complete sentences about what the following people have to do.

1.   **2.**   **3.**

1. _____

2. _____

3. _____

Gramática B   *The Verb tener*

> **¡AVANZA!** **Goal:** Use **tener** to say what people have and have to do.

1 Choose the form of **tener** that best completes each sentence.

1. Javier _____ clase de español los martes a las once menos cuarto.

   a. tienen   **b.** tienes   **c.** tenemos   **d.** tiene

2. Muchas veces, Raúl y Aída _____ que tomar apuntes en la clase de historia.

   a. tiene   **b.** tienen   **c.** tenemos   **d.** tienes

3. Lorena, Paloma y yo _____ que trabajar los sábados y domingos.

   a. tenéis   **b.** tengo   **c.** tenemos   **d.** tienen

4. Carolina, ¿tú _____ un lápiz?

   a. tiene   **b.** tengo   **c.** tienes   **d.** tenéis

2 Tell what the following people have to do in order to get good grades. Write complete sentences.

   modelo: Jorge / tomar apuntes (siempre)
   Jorge siempre tiene que tomar apuntes.

1. María Elena y Nora / estudiar (mucho)

   _____

2. nosotros / usar la computadora (siempre)

   _____

3. yo / hablar con la maestra (de vez en cuando)

   _____

4. Alejandro / hacer la tarea (muchas veces)

   _____

5. tú / leer el libro / (todos los días)

   _____

3 Write three sentences to explain what you have to do in Spanish class today.

   _____

   _____

Gramática C *The Verb Tener*

> **¡AVANZA!** **Goal:** Use **tener** to say what people have and have to do.

1 Write the correct form of the verb **tener**.

1. Manuel y Norberto _____ un examen de ciencias mañana.

2. Yo _____ que estudiar todos los días para el examen de historia.

3. Nosotros siempre _____ que tomar apuntes en la clase de inglés.

4. Muchas veces Nadia _____ que trabajar los sábados.

2 Answer the following questions in complete sentences.

1. ¿A qué hora y qué días tienes clase de español?

_____

_____

2. ¿Qué tienes que hacer para sacar buenas notas?

_____

_____

3. ¿Qué tienes que hacer siempre en la clase de español?

_____

_____

4. ¿Cuántas clases tienes los martes?

_____

_____

3 Write four sentences about what you have to do in a regular week at school. Use expressions of frequency.

_____

_____

_____

_____

_____

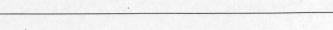
Gramática A *Present tense of –ar verbs*

Level 1, pp. 96-98

> **¡AVANZA!** **Goal:** Use the present tense to say what people do.

1 Underline the verb that best completes each sentence below.

1. Sara (mira/ miran / miro) la televisión por la tarde.

2. Alicia y yo (escucho / escuchamos / escucha) música todos los días.

3. Muchas veces, tú (contestamos / contesta/ contestas) las preguntas.

4. Ustedes (trabaja / trabajamos / trabajan) todos los días.

2 Complete the following sentences with the appropriate form of the verb in parentheses.

1. Todos los días, Sandra, Eduardo y yo _____ la guitarra. (tocar)

2. Sandra y sus amigas _____ por las tardes. (dibujar)

3. Yo _____ las preguntas del maestro. (contestar)

4. Sandra, tú siempre _____ temprano a casa. (llegar)

3 Write complete sentences to say what each person is doing. Follow the model:

modelo: nosotros / estudiar mucho: Nosotros estudiamos mucho.

1. tú / siempre / tomar apuntes

_____

_____

2. Fernando y Clara / casi nunca / montar en bicicleta

_____

_____

3. Yaliza y yo / nunca / sacar malas notas

_____

_____

4. Usted / enseñar matemáticas

_____

_____

Gramática B   *Present Tense of –ar Verbs*

> ¡AVANZA! **Goal:** Use the present tense to say what people do.

1 Sandra and Eduardo do many things. Choose the verb that best completes each sentence.

1. Sandra ____ televisión por la tarde.

   a. miras   **b.** miran   **c.** miramos   **d.** mira

2. Eduardo ____ música todos los días.

   a. escuchan   **b.** escuchas   **c.** escucha   **d.** escuchamos

3. Eduardo y Sandra casi nunca ____ por la tarde.

   a. descansas   **b.** descansan   **c.** descanso   **d.** descansamos

4. Yo siempre ____ un DVD.

   a. alquila   **b.** alquilo   **c.** alquilas   **d.** alquilan

2 Write the correct form of the verbs in parentheses to complete the following conversation.

Sandra: Hola, Eduardo. ¿**1.** _____ (descansar) en la tarde?

Eduardo: Nunca. Mis amigos y yo siempre **2.** _____ (tocar) la guitarra. ¿Y tú?

Sandra: Yo **3.** _____ (practicar) deportes casi todas las tardes. ¿Tú **4.** _____ (estudiar) en la mañana o en la tarde?

Eduardo: En la tarde **5.** _____ (montar) en bicicleta.

      6. _____ (Estudiar) en la mañana, a las seis.

3 Answer the following questions in complete sentences.

1. ¿Preparas la comida todos los días?

_____

2. ¿Estudias mucho en la clase de español?

_____

3. ¿Miras la televisión después de las clases?

_____

Gramática C *Present Tense of –ar Verbs*

> **¡AVANZA!** **Goal:** Use the present tense to say what people do.

1 Complete these sentences with the correct form of the verb **llegar**.

Martín y yo **1.** _____ a la escuela antes de las ocho.

Somos estudiantes en la escuela de Miami. Martín siempre

2. _____ temprano a clase, pero yo casi siempre

3. _____ tarde porque hablo mucho con los amigos. Y

tú, ¿ **4.** _____ tarde o temprano a clase?

2 Look at the drawings below and write what each person is doing.

1.   **2.**   **3.**   **4.**

1. Soraya y yo _____

2. Manuel _____

3. los maestros _____

4. yo _____

3 Write four sentences describing what you do after school.

_____

_____

_____

_____

_____

_____

_____

Integración: Hablar

The Rodríguez' go to a family summer camp in México. There are many recreational and educational activities, and kids and parents need to come to terms with their schedules. The parents and kids want to participate in different activities, but they also want to be together. Señora Rodríguez calls the camp's Automated Information Center to get help with everybody's schedules.

Fuente 1 Leer

Read the ad for the family summer camp...

CAMPAMENTO FAMILIAR GUADALAJARA

HAY ACTIVIDADES TODOS LOS DÍAS.

- Los lunes, miércoles y viernes tenemos clases de la historia y el arte de México. Las clases son de hombres y mujeres. Son de las nueve y media a las diez y cuarto de la mañana.

- ¿Les gusta practicar deportes? Los martes y jueves tenemos fútbol de hombres y mujeres, de las diez y cuarto a las once de la mañana.

El horario del sábado y domingo es muy bueno; siempre hay actividades de grandes y pequeños ¿La familia tiene chicos y chicas? ¿Tienen preguntas? **El número de teléfono es 723-888-2479.**

Fuente 2 Escuchar   *CD 01 track 22*

Listen to the students' schedule recorded on the automated information center. Take notes.

_____

_____

_____

Hablar

How are the kids' schedules different from the parents'? Include information from both the camp ad and the automated information center in your answer.

modelo: Los hombres y mujeres tienen actividades en la...El horario de los chicos y chicas...Pero los sábados y domingos...

Integración: Escribir

Joaquín writes an editorial about his history teacher. He describes him in such good terms that now everybody calls señor Ortiz's office to get into his class. Señor Ortiz records an automated answer with frequently asked questions.

Fuente 1 Leer

Read Joaquín's editorial in the school's newspaper about his history teacher...

El señor Ortiz: un maestro de historia muy bueno

En la clase de historia me gusta aprender. ¿Por qué? Porque el señor Ortiz es bueno. Él siempre contesta las preguntas de los estudiantes. A veces la tarea es difícil. Pero soy organizado y tomo apuntes todos los días. Tengo que sacar una buena nota, porque me gusta aprender con el señor Ortiz.

Fuente 2 Escuchar   *CD 01 track 24*

Listen to señor Ortiz's recorded message. Take notes.

_____

_____

_____

_____

Escribir

What do you need to do to get a good grade in señor Ortiz's history class?

modelo: Tengo que ser organizado y también tengo que llegar temprano, nunca llegar tarde. De vez en cuando está bien, pero no siempre.

_____

_____

_____

_____

_____

_____

Escuchar A

Level 1, pp. 106-107
WB CD 01 tracks 25-26

> **¡AVANZA!** **Goal:** Listen to find out about the activities that some kids do.

1 Listen to Pablo and take notes. Then, read each sentence and answer **cierto** (true) or **falso** (false).

C F **1.** El examen de ciencias es el martes.

C F **2.** Claudia nunca saca buenas notas.

C F **3.** A Pablo no le gusta estudiar.

C F **4.** Pablo y sus amigos siempre tocan la guitarra.

C F **5.** Hoy, Pablo llega tarde.

2 Listen to Adriana and take notes. Then, complete the sentences below.

1. Adriana es muy _____ .

2. A Saúl no le gusta _____ .

3. A Saúl le gusta más _____ .

4. Saúl necesita _____ el viernes.

5. Hoy, Saúl _____ con Adriana.

Escuchar B

> **¡AVANZA!** **Goal:** Listen to find out about the activities that some kids do.

1 Listen to Luciana talk about different people. Take notes. Then match the activities below with the correct name in the box.

1. Monta en bicicleta. _____

2. Tiene que sacar una buena nota en la clase de ciencias. _____

3. Enseña la clase de ciencias. _____

4. Tienen un examen de ciencias el viernes. _____

a. Luciana y Rubén
b. la señora Burgos
c. Luciana
d. Rubén

2 Listen to Rubén and take notes. Then, write about what people are doing in complete sentences.

1. _____

2. _____

3. _____

4. _____

UNIDAD 2 • Escuchar B
Lección 1

62
Escuchar B

Unidad 2, Lección 1
Escuchar B

¡Avancemos! 1
Cuaderno: Práctica por niveles

Escuchar C

> ¡AVANZA! **Goal:** Listen to find out about the activities that some kids do.

1 Listen to señora Domínguez and take notes. Then, complete the following sentences.

1. Los estudiantes de la señora Domínguez casi siempre _____ .

2. Los estudiantes llegan _____ a clase.

3. De vez en cuando, Mercedes no _____ mucho.

4. Todos los estudiantes de la señora Domínguez _____ .

5. Los chicos nunca _____ a casa.

2 Listen to señora Pérez describe her class. Then answer the questions below in complete sentences.

1. ¿Cómo son los estudiantes de la señora Pérez?

_____

_____

2. ¿Llegan tarde a clase?

_____

_____

3. ¿Qué tiene que hacer Iván?

_____

_____

4. ¿Quién *(who)* toma muchos apuntes?

_____

_____

Leer A

> **¡AVANZA!** **Goal:** Read about what students do and what they have to do.

En la clase de ciencias hay muchos estudiantes. A Irene siempre le gusta estudiar y hacer la tarea. En todos los exámenes saca cien. Pablo nunca estudia y no le gusta tomar apuntes. En los exámenes saca cuarenta, cincuenta y treinta. Muchas veces, a Sandra le gusta hacer la tarea. En los exámenes saca noventa, cuarenta y cien. A Eduardo a veces le gusta estudiar y hacer la tarea. En los exámenes saca noventa, noventa y noventa. A Javier nunca le gusta leer libros. En los exámenes saca cuarenta, cincuenta y cuarenta. Todos los estudiantes son diferentes y me gusta enseñar ciencias a todos.

¿Comprendiste?

Read the note from señor Ortiz. Then, read each sentence and answer **cierto** (true) or **falso** (false).

C F **1.** Irene siempre saca buenas notas.

C F **2.** De vez en cuando, Sandra saca una mala nota.

C F **3.** En todos los exámenes, Javier saca buenas notas.

C F **4.** Muchas veces, Pablo saca una buena nota.

C F **5.** Eduardo nunca saca una mala nota.

¿Qué piensas?

1. ¿Piensas que Javier tiene que estudiar más?¿Por qué?

_____

_____

_____

2. ¿Tú sacas buenas notas en la clase de ciencias?

_____

_____

_____

Leer B

> ![AVANZA!] **Goal:** Read about what students do and what they have to do.

Señores Rodríguez,

Soy la maestra de ciencias y Javier es estudiante en la
clase. Javier saca malas notas en los exámenes de ciencias. Él siempre toma apuntes en clase y prepara la tarea todos los días, pero necesita estudiar más. A Javier
no le gusta contestar preguntas en clase. Es inteligente
pero no trabaja mucho en clase. Por favor, necesitan
hablar con Javier antes del exaámen en mayo.

Señora Burgos

¿Comprendiste?

Read the letter Javier's teacher has written to his parents. Then, complete the following sentences:

1. Javier saca _____ en ciencias.

2. Javier siempre _____ en clase.

3. Javier _____ la tarea todos los días.

4. Javier _____ estudiar más.

5. Javier no _____ mucho en la clase.

¿Qué piensas?

1. ¿Necesitas estudiar mucho en todas las clases? Explica.

_____

_____

_____

2. ¿En qué clases no tomas apuntes?

_____

_____

_____

Leer C

> **¡AVANZA!** **Goal:** Read about what students do and what they have to do.

Mario:	¡Hola Leonor! ¿Cómo estás?
Leonor:	Bien. ¿Tienes que llegar a clase temprano?
Mario:	Sí. La clase de español es a las ocho y diez de la mañana.
Leonor:	¿Qué tienes que hacer después de las clases?
Mario:	Después de las clases tengo que hacer la tarea. Necesito leer un libro de inglés. ¿Y tú?
Leonor:	Yo tengo que tocar la guitarra. Tengo una clase de música a las cinco y media. Toco la guitarra casi todos los días.
Mario:	También dibujo o escucho música en la tarde.
Leonor:	Mario, ¡son las ocho menos diez!
Mario:	¡Tengo que ir a clase! Adiós.
Leonor:	¡Hasta luego!

¿Comprendiste?

Read the conversation between two friends, Mario and Leonor. Then, answer **cierto** (true) or **falso** (false).

C F **1.** Mario tiene que ir temprano a la clase de español.

C F **2.** Leonor toca la guitarra de vez en cuando.

C F **3.** A Mario le gusta mucho tocar la guitarra.

C F **4.** Leonor tiene que ir a la clase de música por la tarde.

C F **5.** Mario dibuja y toca música.

¿Qué piensas?

1. ¿Qué tienes que hacer antes de las clases?

_____

2. ¿Qué tienes que hacer después de las clases?

_____

Escribir A

> **¡AVANZA!** **Goal:** Write about your daily schedule.

Step 1

Write Carolina's schedule in order in the chart using the list in the box. Write the class times in numbers.

nueve menos diez: ciencias	diez y cuarto: español	doce y media: historia	dos y diez: arte

Hora				
Lunes				

Step 2

Write three sentences telling when Carolina has class on Monday.

_____

_____

_____

Step 3

Evaluate your writing using the information in the table.

Writing Criteria	Excellent	Good	Needs Work
Content	You included three sentences telling when Carolina has class on Monday.	You included two sentences telling when Carolina has class on Monday.	You include one sentence telling when Carolina has class on Monday.
Communication	Most of your message is organized and easy to follow.	Parts of your message are organized and easy to follow.	Your message is disorganized and hard to follow.
Accuracy	You make few mistakes in grammar and vocabulary.	You make some mistakes in grammar and vocabulary.	You make many mistakes in grammar and vocabulary.

Escribir B

> **¡AVANZA!** **Goal:** Write about your your daily schedule.

Step 1

Write out in words the times of the classes in Laura's schedule:

Hora	lunes	martes	miércoles	jueves
8:30 _____	matemáticas	historia	matemáticas	matemáticas
11:15 _____	ciencias	ciencias	historia	ciencias
1:20 _____	español			español

Step 2

Look at Laura's schedule and write about her week at school:

_____

_____

_____

_____

Step 3

Evaluate your writing using the information in the table.

Writing Criteria	Excellent	Good	Needs Work
Content	You have described Laura's schedule at school completely.	You have described most of Laura's schedule at school.	You have not described much of Laura's schedule at school.
Communication	Most of your response is clear.	Some of your response is clear.	Your message is not very clear.
Accuracy	You make few mistakes in grammar and vocabulary.	You make some mistakes in grammar and vocabulary.	You make many mistakes in grammar and vocabulary.

Escribir C

> **¡AVANZA!** **Goal:** Write about your daily schedule.

Step 1

Read what Julio says and write his class schedule in order. Write the subjects and times of the classes in the table below.

Julio: Los lunes, miércoles y viernes tengo clase de matemáticas a las doce y cuarto de la tarde. Los martes y jueves tengo clase de español a las nueve y media de la mañana. Los lunes y miércoles tengo clase de inglés a las ocho menos diez de la mañana. Tengo clase de ciencias los martes y jueves a las dos y veinte de la tarde.

Hora	lunes	martes	miércoles	jueves	viernes

Step 2

Using Julio's schedule above, and the words **siempre, muchas veces, de vez en cuando,** write about what Julio has to do in three of his classes.

_____

_____

_____

Step 3

Evaluate your writing using the information in the table.

Writing Criteria	Excellent	Good	Needs Work
Content	You described what Julio has to do in three classes.	You described what Julio has to do in two classes.	You described what Julio has to do in one class.
Communication	Most of your message is organized and easy to follow.	Parts of your message are organized and easy to follow.	Your message is disorganized and hard to follow.
Accuracy	You make few mistakes in grammar and vocabulary.	You make some mistakes in grammar and vocabulary.	You make many mistakes in grammar and vocabulary.

Cultura A

> **¡AVANZA!** **Goal:** Review cultural information about Mexico.

1 **Mexican culture** Choose the multiple choice item that completes each sentence.

1. The currency of Mexico is the ____

    a. Mexican dollar   **b.** Mexican peso   **c.** Mexican bolívar

2. A **zócalo** is a ____

    a. town square   **b.** garden   **c.** temple

3. Three typical Mexican foods are ____

    a. pizzas, pasta and sausages   **b.** hamburgers, French fries, and malts   **c.** tortillas, tacos, and enchiladas

2 **Mexico** Choose the correct word to complete the following sentences.

1. UNAM is Mexico's largest (airport / university).

2. The pyramid of Kukulcán was used as a (tomb / temple).

3. Salma Hayek is a Mexican (actress / writer).

4. The Jardín Principal in San Miguel de Allende, Mexico is a (temple / park).

5. It is common for students in Mexico to wear (jeans / uniforms) to school.

3 **Arte mexicano** Look at the image from the mural on page 97 of your book. Who painted it, and what ideas does it reflect? Describe what you see in the mural.

_____

_____

_____

_____

_____

_____

Cultura B

> ¡AVANZA! **Goal:** Review cultural information about Mexico.

1 **Mexico** Read the following statements about Mexico and circle *true* or *false*.

T F **1.** The capital of Mexico is San Luis.

T F **2.** Tacos are an example of typical Mexican food.

T F **3.** The Mexican currency is the euro.

T F **4.** Diego Rivera created many murals reflecting Mexico's history.

T F **5.** Mexico has the largest Spanish-speaking population in the world.

T F **6.** Only private school students in Mexico wear uniforms.

2 **Identify places** Match each place with the corresponding description.

The pramid of Kukulcán

The **Jardín Principal**

UNAM

Chichén Itzá

zócalo

One of the oldest universities in
   Latin America

Used as a temple

A town square or plaza

A park located in San Miguel de Allende

An ancient Mayan city

3 **School requirements** Write a comparison of your school and the Colegio Americano in Guadalajara, Mexico. What subjects do you have to study at school? What do you have to do to graduate from high school? How is this similar or different from the requirements at the Colegio Americano?

_____

_____

_____

_____

_____

_____

Cultura C

¡AVANZA! **Goal:** Review cultural information about Mexico.

1 **Mexico** Complete the following sentences.

1. The _____ is the official currency of Mexico.

2. The _____ of Kukulcán was used as a temple.

3. _____ are commonly worn by students in Mexican schools.

4. The _____ de México has almost 270,000 students.

5. Many Mexican cities have town squares known as _____

2 **Mexican culture** Answer the following questions about Mexico.

1. What can you do in the **Jardín Principal** in San Miguel de Allende?

_____

2. What languages, other than Spanish, are spoken in Mexico?

_____

3. What appears on the walls of the library at UNAM?

_____

3 **A visit to Mexico** There are many interesting places to visit in Mexico. Write a paragraph about the following places in Mexico: Parque San Miguel de Allende, the Mayan city of Chichén Itzá, and the Universidad Nacional Autónoma de México (UNAM). Describe each place and then tell which place you would like to visit and why.

_____

_____

_____

_____

_____

_____

_____

_____

Vocabulario A

> **¡AVANZA!** **Goal:** Talk about your school.

1 Marcela needs to go to science class. Indicate what she would put in her backpack by placing an X next to the words.

1. _____ el escritorio

6. _____ la pluma

2. _____ el lápiz

7. _____ el papel

3. _____ el cuaderno

8. _____ la silla

4. _____ el pizarrón

9. _____ la puerta

5. _____ la calculadora

10. _____ el mapa

2 Raúl and Graciela are at school. Complete the following sentences with the appropriate word from the box.

1. Raúl practica muchos deportes los lunes. Hoy es martes y él está

_____ .

2. El maestro escribe en el pizarrón. Él necesita

_____ y _____ .

3. Graciela necesita leer un libro. Ella está en _____ .

4. Pasar un rato con amigos en la cafetería es _____ .

5. Hoy hay un examen de matemáticas muy difícil. Los estudiantes están

_____ .

| la biblioteca |
| nerviosos |
| tiza |
| divertido |
| cansado |
| un borrador |

3 List three items you have in your backpack for your morning classes.

En la mochila tengo:

_____

_____

_____

_____

Vocabulario B

| ¡AVANZA! | **Goal:** Talk about your school. |

1 The following students are at school. Choose the word that best completes the sentence:

1. Raúl está ____ porque tiene examen de ciencias. Es muy difícil.

   a. contento   **b.** interesante   **c.** nervioso   **d.** aburrido

2. Cristina necesita libros de ciencias. Ella está en ____ .

   a. el gimnasio   **b.** el pasillo   **c.** el baño   **d.** la biblioteca

3. Muchos estudiantes compran refrescos en ____ .

   a. casa   **b.** la cafetería   **c.** la biblioteca   **d.** el baño

4. Susana tiene mucha tarea; está muy ____ .

   a. aburrida   **b.** ocupada   **c.** difícil   **d.** tranquila

5. La clase de música no es aburrida porque el maestro es ____ .

   a. interesante   **b.** emocionada   **c.** enojado   **d.** deprimido

2 Roberto is the opposite of his friend Lorena. Complete the following sentences.

1. Cuando Roberto está deprimido, o triste, Lorena está _____ .

2. Lorena es divertida, pero Roberto es _____ .

3. Cuando Roberto está nervioso, Lorena está _____ .

4. Cuando Lorena tiene tarea fácil, Roberto tiene tarea _____ .

3 Answer the following questions about yourself and your classroom in complete sentences.

1. ¿Cómo estás cuando sacas una buena nota?

_____

2. ¿Cómo estás cuando tienes un examen difícil?

_____

3. ¿Cuántas ventanas hay en tu clase?

_____

Vocabulario C

Level 1, pp. 110-114

> ¡AVANZA! **Goal:** Talk about your school.

1 Margarita and Marcelo are at school. Complete the following text using the words from the box.

Margarita y Marcelo compran refrescos en **1.** _____

de la escuela. Luego, leen libros en **2.** _____

para el examen de ciencias del viernes. El examen no es

3. _____ , es difícil. Por eso, Marcelo está

4. _____ . Margarita no está nerviosa, ella está

muy **5.** _____ porque siempre saca buenas notas en

ciencias. A Margarita le gusta mucho estudiar ciencias porque es

6. _____ .

tranquila
la biblioteca
interesante
la cafetería
fácil
nervioso

2 Complete the following sentences describing a school.

1. En la escuela de El Valle, hay _____ para practicar deportes.

2. Los estudiantes dibujan en _____ con la tiza.

3. No hay _____ en la clase. ¿Qué hora es?

4. Antes de las clases, los estudiantes están en _____ .

5. Cuando hay problemas muy difíciles en la clase de matemáticas, usamos

_____ .

3 You have just transferred to a new school. Send an e-mail to your best friend and describe what it looks like and your feelings about it.

_____

_____

_____

_____

_____

Gramática A   *The Verb estar*

> **¡AVANZA!** **Goal:** Use the verb **estar** to talk about location and condition.

1 Cristina and Sergio are talking in the hall. Re-create their conversation below.

Hola, Sergio. ¿Cómo _____ ? (están / estás)

Hola Cristina. _____ un poco nervioso. (Estamos / Estoy)

¿Por qué _____ nervioso? (estás / estoy)

_____ nervioso por el examen de ciencias. (Estoy / Están) Es difícil.

No, es fácil. Yo _____ tranquila. (estamos / estoy) En mi cuaderno tengo

todos los apuntes. ¿Dónde _____ tu cuaderno? (está / están)

_____ en mi mochila, encima de mi escritorio. (Estoy / Está)

2 Write the correct form of **estar** to complete the description of where these people are.

1. Sarita _____ en la clase de inglés.

2. Yo _____ en la biblioteca.

3. Ana, Claudia y yo _____ en la cafetería.

4. ¿Dónde _____ Sarita y Pablo?

5. El señor Ramírez _____ en la oficina del director.

3 Write questions about Guillermo and his friends. Follow the model.

modelo: Guillermo está en la oficina. ¿Está Guillermo en la oficina?

Jorge está en el pasillo. _____

Luisa está muy contenta. _____

Ramón está nervioso. _____

Gramática B *The Verb estar*

> **¡AVANZA!** **Goal:** Use the verb **estar** to talk about location and condition.

1 Choose the correct form of the verb to complete the following statements about location.

1. Mi cuaderno ____ encima de mi escritorio.

   a. estás   **b.** están   **c.** está   **d.** estamos

2. Las ventanas ____ al lado de la puerta.

   a. estamos   **b.** están   **c.** estoy   **d.** está

3. Milagros y yo ____ detrás de la puerta.

   a. estoy   **b.** estás   **c.** están   **d.** estamos

4. La calculadora ____ dentro de la mochila.

   a. están   **b.** está   **c.** estás   **d.** estoy

2 Write sentences to describe some people at school.

1. El maestro / estar en la oficina del director.

   _____

2. Los estudiantes / estar en la cafetería / al lado de la biblioteca.

   _____

3. El director / estar ocupado.

   _____

4. ¿Estar / (tú) cansado?

   _____

3 Esteban has answered his friend's e-mail. Write questions for his responses.

1. _____

   Sí, la oficina del director está cerca del gimnasio.

2. _____

   No, no estoy muy nervioso.

3. _____

   No, el director no está enojado.

Gramática C *The Verb estar*

> **¡AVANZA!** **Goal:** Use the verb **estar** to talk about location and condition.

1 Write complete sentences to find out about the following people in Spanish class.

1. Claudia y yo / estar / cerca de la puerta

_____

2. La maestra / estar / contenta

_____

3. Los estudiantes / estar / ocupados

_____

4. tú / estar / delante de Ana

_____

5. yo / estar / detrás de Miguel

_____

2 Complete the following questions with the correct form of **estar** and the subject. Then, answer each question in complete sentences.

1. ¿ _____ nervioso(a) cuando tienes un examen? (estar / tú)

_____

2. ¿ _____ contentos cuando sacan buenas notas?
(estar / los estudiantes)

_____

3. ¿ _____ cerca de la biblioteca? (estar / los baños)

_____

3 Write three sentences describing people, places, and things at your school. Use the verb **estar** in each of your sentences.

_____

_____

_____

_____

Gramática A *The Verb ir*

> **¡AVANZA!** **Goal:** Use the verb **ir** to say where you and others are going.

1 **¿Adónde van?** Choose the verb that best completes each sentence below.

1. ¿Adónde (va / vamos) Sandra?

2. Nosotras (vamos / van) al gimnasio.

3. ¿Cuándo (vas / van) Sergio y tú a la cafetería?

4. Tú (va / vas) a la clase de inglés los lunes y miércoles.

5. Yo (va / voy) a la biblioteca.

2 Write three complete sentences using the information in the boxes below.

Cristina	ir a	la biblioteca
Sandra y yo		el gimnasio
Tú		la clase de arte

1. _____

2. _____

3. _____

3 Answer the following questions in complete sentences.

1. ¿Adónde vas los lunes a las 8:30 de la mañana?

_____

_____

2. ¿Adónde vas los lunes a las 3:30 de la tarde?

_____

_____

Gramática B *The Verb ir*

> **¡AVANZA!** **Goal:** Use the verb **ir** to say where you and others are going.

1 Three students are going to Spanish class. Complete the text below with words from the box.

voy	van	vamos	va

Sarita, Cristina y yo **1.** _____ a la clase de español. Lucía

también **2.** _____ a la clase de español. A mí me gusta,

pero es un poco difícil. Ustedes **3.** _____ a la clase de

español los lunes y miércoles. **4.** Yo _____ a la clase de

español los martes y jueves.

2 Write complete sentences about the following students.

1. Ana y Sandra / ir / a la cafetería.

_____

2. ¿Cuándo ir / Claudia y yo / al gimnasio?

_____

3. (Yo) / ir / a la clase de música.

_____

4. Ustedes / ir / a España / mañana por la noche.

_____

3 Complete the dialogue by answering Nora's questions

       Nora: ¿Vas a la clase de inglés en la mañana o en la tarde?

        Tú: _____

       Nora: ¿Cuándo vas a la cafetería?

        Tú: _____

       Nora: ¿Adónde vas después de comer?

        Tú: _____

Gramática C

> **¡AVANZA!** **Goal:** Use the verb **ir** to say where you and others are going.

1 Complete the sentences with the correct form of **ir**.

 1. Todos los días, yo _____ a la escuela.

 2. ¿Adónde _____ Sergio y yo cuando estudiamos?

 3. Yo _____ a la escuela cerca de mi casa.

 4. Ustedes _____ a Colombia el miércoles.

 5. ¿Adónde _____ tú a las ocho de la mañana?

2 These students are at school. Put the sentence in the correct order using the correct form of the verb **ir**.

 1. Sandra y Pablo / gimnasio (ir)

 _____

 2. yo / todos los días / a la escuela (ir)

 _____

 3. Sandra, Sarita y yo / ¿Adónde / en la tarde? (ir)

 _____

 4. todas las tardes / tú / a la biblioteca (ir)

 _____

3 Write an e-mail to one of your friends at school about plans you have with another friend. Be sure to explain where you are going.

_____
_____
_____
_____
_____

Integración: Hablar

It's the first day of class at Escuela Monterrey, in Mexico. Señor Amador, the doorman, is handing out welcome flyers to all students. Then, the principal welcomes everybody over the loudspeaker and gives information about school supplies.

Fuente 1 Leer

Read the school's handout for students...

DÍA UNO EN LA ESCUELA MONTERREY

¡Hola! Soy el señor Amador. Siempre estoy en la puerta de la escuela. Siempre estoy contento. Los estudiantes tienen mucho que hacer. Las clases son muy interesantes y el gimnasio es grande. La cafetería es pequeña; a todos les gusta. Cuando estás en clase, siempre necesitas un cuaderno, un lápiz y una pluma. Pero, ¿cuándo necesitas la calculadora y el mapa? Escucha a la directora. Ella habla todos los días a las ocho y diez. Necesitas llegar temprano siempre y escuchar a la directora.

Fuente 2 Escuchar   *CD 01 track 32*

Listen to the principal's loudspeaker message. Take notes.

_____

_____

_____

_____

Hablar

You need to bring many things to school but, when exactly do you need these things? Remember to include information from both señor Amador's handout and the principal's message in your answer.

Modelo: Todos los días hay clases y necesito... Pero cuando no hay clases de...

Integración: Escribir

Level 1, pp.123-125
WB CD 01 track 33

A group of students has created posters to start an afterschool club. They want to help fellow students who are feeling bored. They want to convince everybody to join the club, so they put an ad in their school radio station.

Fuente 1 Leer

Read the poster the students created.

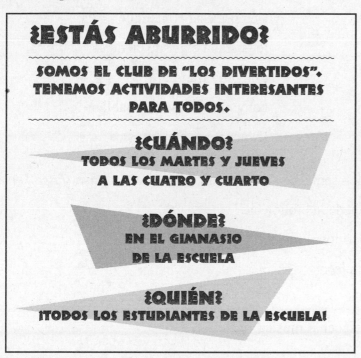

¿ESTÁS ABURRIDO?

SOMOS EL CLUB DE "LOS DIVERTIDOS".
TENEMOS ACTIVIDADES INTERESANTES
PARA TODOS.

¿CUÁNDO?
TODOS LOS MARTES Y JUEVES
A LAS CUATRO Y CUARTO

¿DÓNDE?
EN EL GIMNASIO
DE LA ESCUELA

¿QUIÉN?
¡TODOS LOS ESTUDIANTES DE LA ESCUELA!

Fuente 2 Escuchar *CD 01 track 34*

Listen to the school radio ad. Take notes.

_____

_____

_____

Escribir

Then answer this question: You have to convince your friend to join the club. What can you say? Remember to include information from both the poster as well as the radio ad in your answer.

modelo: ¡Hola! ¿Estás aburrido? Hay...

_____

_____

_____

Escuchar A

> **Goal:** Listen to find out what the kids are doing and what they like to do.

1 Listen to Sandra. Match each person with his or her description.

a. Todos   siempre está contenta.

b. Sergio   le gusta la clase de ciencias.

c. Cristina   está muy tranquilo.

d. David   compran refrescos y hablan.

e. Sandra   le gusta escuchar música.

2 Listen to Miguel. Then, read each sentence and answer **cierto** *(true)* o **falso** *(false)*.

C   F   **1.** El pasillo está cerca de la biblioteca.

C   F   **2.** Tomás está muy nervioso.

C   F   **3.** A Elena no le gusta leer.

C   F   **4.** Mario es aburrido.

C   F   **5.** A Mario le gusta escuchar música.

Escuchar B

> **¡AVANZA!** **Goal:** Listen to find out what the kids are doing and what they like to do.

1 Listen to Sergio. Then complete the sentences below.

1. Los chicos van al pasillo que está al lado _____ .

2. Los chicos van a _____ y compran refrescos.

3. El pasillo está _____ de la biblioteca.

4. Los amigos de Sergio son _____ .

5. Los amigos de Sergio nunca están _____ .

2 Listen to Pablo. Then, answer the questions in complete sentences.

1. ¿Qué tiene que hacer Carolina?

_____

_____

2. ¿Qué actividades practican los amigos de Pablo?

_____

_____

_____

Escuchar C

> **¡AVANZA!** **Goal:** Listen to find out what the kids are doing and what they like to do.

1 Listen to David and take notes. Then, complete the sentences.

1. A David le gusta _____ .

2. David está contento porque _____ .

3. El pasillo está _____ .

4. Los amigos de David son _____ .

5. _____ tiene libros dentro de la mochila.

2 Listen to Fabián and take notes. Then, answer the questions in complete sentences.

1. ¿De qué cosas hablan los amigos de Fabián?

_____

_____

_____

2. ¿De qué están cansados los amigos de Fabián?

_____

_____

_____

_____

Leer A

> ¡AVANZA! **Goal:** Read about a survey made to the students.

Nombre	¿Cómo estás y por qué?
Sandra	Estoy ocupada porque tengo que estudiar ciencias. Es una clase muy interesante.
David	Estoy emocionado porque voy a la clase de música. Toco la guitarra todos los lunes.
Sarita	Estoy contenta porque siempre saco una buena nota en inglés.

¿Comprendiste?

Answer the following questions in complete sentences:

1. ¿Saca Sarita una mala nota en inglés?

   _____

2. ¿Está ocupada Sandra? Explica.

   _____

3. ¿Está David deprimido? Explica.

   _____

¿Qué piensas?

Answer the following questions.

¿Cómo estás cuando vas a...

1. la clase de ciencias? _____

   _____

   _____

2. la clase de español? _____

   _____

   _____

3. la biblioteca? _____

   _____

   _____

Leer B

¡AVANZA! **Goal:** Read a sign with the description of a lost backpack.

¿Dónde está mi mochila?

Dentro de mi mochila hay un cuaderno, una calculadora, lápices, papeles, una pluma y ¡mi examen de matemáticas!

Siempre tengo mi mochila. Voy a la cafetería, al gimnasio y al pasillo que está cerca de la biblioteca. Siempre tengo mi mochila pero ahora ¡no está!

Estoy nervioso: ¡Necesito el examen y está dentro de mi mochila!

–Miguel

¿Comprendiste?

Read Miguel's sign describing the lost backpack. Then, read each sentence below and answer **cierto** (true) or **falso** (false).

C   F   **1.** Dentro de la mochila hay un libro.

C   F   **2.** Miguel nunca tiene su mochila.

C   F   **3.** Miguel siempre va al pasillo cerca de la oficina.

C   F   **4.** Miguel no está tranquilo.

C   F   **5.** Miguel necesita el examen de matemáticas.

¿Qué piensas?

Answer the following question in a complete sentence.

¿Está Miguel nervioso? Explica.

_____

_____

_____

_____

Leer C

Level 1, pp. 130-131

> ¡AVANZA! **Goal:** Read an article from the schools newspaper.

¡Vamos a pasar un rato divertido!

¿Están aburridos?

Los chicos del club pasan un rato divertido con amigos.

Todos los viernes en la tarde, unos estudiantes van a la biblioteca y hablan de los libros. Van a la clase al lado de la oficina del director y hablan de ciencias. ¡Es muy interesante!

Muchos estudiantes van al gimnasio y practican deportes. ¡Es muy emocionante! Después, todos van a la cafetería, compran refrescos y escuchan música. ¡Es muy divertido!

UNIDAD 2
Lección 2

Leer C

¿Comprendiste?

Read the article above and then complete the sentences below.

1. El club es para los chicos que están _____

2. Todos los _____ , los chicos pasan un rato divertido.

3. Los chicos hablan de libros en la _____

4. Hablan de ciencias en la _____

5. Los chicos escuchan música en _____

¿Qué piensas?

Answer the following questions in complete sentences.

1. ¿Vas a un club después de las clases?¿Qué club?

   _____

2. ¿Es divertido hablar de ciencias?¿De libros?

   _____

   _____

Escribir A

> ¡AVANZA! **Goal:** Write about yourself and your school.

Step 1

Respond to the following survey by writing how you feel when certain things happen at school. Use the words from the box.

Cuando...	¿Cómo estás?
Sacas una mala nota	
Practicas mucho deporte	
Estás en la cafetería	

triste
cansado(a)
contento(a)

Step 2

Answer the following question about yourself in a complete sentence:

¿Cuándo estás nervioso?

_____

_____

_____

Step 3

Evaluate your writing using the information in the table.

Writing Criteria	Excellent	Good	Needs Work
Content	You have answered the question completely.	You have partially answered the question.	You have not answered the question.
Communication	Most of your response is clear.	Some of your response is clear.	Your response is not very clear.
Accuracy	You make few mistakes in grammar and vocabulary.	You make some mistakes in grammar and vocabulary.	You make many mistakes in grammar and vocabulary.

Escribir B

> ¡AVANZA! **Goal:** Write about yourself and your school.

Step 1

Respond to the following survey by writing where things are at your school.

¿Dónde está...	Está...
el gimnasio?	
la biblioteca?	
la cafetería?	

Step 2

Write three complete sentences about the location of some things at your school. Use the words from the survey above.

_____

_____

_____

Step 3

Evaluate your writing using the information in the table.

Writing Criteria	Excellent	Good	Needs Work
Content	You have written three complete sentences.	You have written two complete sentences.	You have written only one complete sentences.
Communication	Most of your sentences are clear.	Some of your sentences are clear.	Your sentences are not very clear.
Accuracy	You make few mistakes in grammar and vocabulary.	You make some mistakes in grammar and vocabulary.	You make many mistakes in grammar and vocabulary.

Escribir C

> **¡AVANZA!** **Goal:** Write about you and your school.

Step 1

Respond to the following survey by writing how you feel when certain things happen at school.

Cuando...	¿Cómo estás?
pasas un rato con amigos	
estás en la clase de inglés	
estás en la clase de matemáticas	
estás en el gimnasio	
estás en la cafetería	

Step 2

Use four answers from the survey above to describe how you feel at school.

_____

_____

_____

_____

Step 3

Evaluate your writing using the information in the table below.

Writing Criteria	Excellent	Good	Needs Work
Content	You have included four sentences to describe how you feel.	You have included three sentences to describe how you feel.	You include two or fewer sentences to describe how you feel.
Communication	Most of your response is clear.	Some of your response is clear.	Your message is not very clear.
Accuracy	You make few mistakes in grammar and vocabulary.	You make some mistakes in grammar and vocabulary.	You make many mistakes in grammar and vocabulary.

Cultura A

> ¡AVANZA! **Goal:** Review cultural information about Mexico.

1 **Mexican culture** Read the following statements and answer *true* or *false*.

T F **1.** Frida Kahlo was influenced by indigenous culture.

T F **2.** The Andrés Barbero Museum of Ethnography is in Mexico.

T F **3.** San Andrés is the capital of Mexico.

T F **4.** Tortillas and enchiladas are typical Mexican dishes.

2 **In Mexico and the Dominican Republic** Choose the correct word to complete the following sentences.

1. The Piedra del Sol was a (calendar / clock) that the Aztecs created.

2. (Forestry / Tourism) is an important industry in the Dominican Republic.

3. Two of the languages spoken in Mexico are Spanish and (Portuguese / Maya).

4. Mexico's currency is called the (peso / dollar).

5. The National Museum of (Mexico / Anthropology) contains artifacts from indigenous cultures of Mexico.

3 **Art** Write a brief paragraph describing Frida Kahlo. What kind of art did she create?

_____

_____

_____

_____

_____

_____

_____

_____

Cultura B

UNIDAD 2
Lección 2

Cultura B

> ¡AVANZA! **Goal:** Review cultural information about Mexico.

1 **Mexico** Complete the following sentences with one of the multiple choice phrases.

1. The languages spoken in Mexico are _____

   a. Spanish, chibcha, and other indigenous languages

   b. Spanish, maya, and other indigenous languages

   c. Spanish, taíno, and other indigenous languages

2. Frida Kahlo was a Mexican artist; she painted many _____

   a. self-portraits

   b. murals

   c. landscapes

3. Frida Kahlo was influenced by _____ culture in her style of painting and style of dress.

   a. Caribbean

   b. European

   c. indigenous

2 **Sites in Mexico** Where in Mexico are the following places?

Place to Visit	Where Are They Located?
The Museo Nacional de Antropología	
Jardín Principal	
The pyramid of Kukulcán	

3 **In the Anthropology Museum** The **Piedra del Sol** is stored in the National Museum of Anthropology. Describe the **Piedra del Sol.** Which culture is it from and what was it used for? What does it look like? Also, describe the museum. What are some of the rooms found there? What other items might you expect to find in the museum?

_____

_____

_____

_____

_____

_____

_____

_____

Cultura C

> ¡AVANZA! **Goal:** Review cultural information about Mexico.

1 **In Mexico** Complete the following sentences with the correct word or phrase.

1. This museum has artifacts from various indigenous cultures in Mexico.

   _____

2. The currency of Mexico _____

3. A calendar created by the Aztecs _____

4. One of the languages, other than Spanish, spoken in Mexico _____

5. The capital of Mexico _____

2 **Art and Artifacts** Answer the following questions about Mexico.

1. How was Frida Kahlo influenced by indigenous culture?

   _____

2. What type of painting did Frida Kahlo often create?

   _____

3. How much does the Piedra del Sol weigh?

   _____

3 **Museums** Think of a museum you have visited or that you know about, and compare it to the National Museum of Anthropology. Write a paragraph that describes what kinds of objects are kept there. Where are they from? Who made them?

_____

_____

_____

_____

_____

Comparación cultural: Horarios y clases

Lectura y escritura

After reading the paragraphs about how Rafael, Andrea, and Juan Carlos spend a typical day at school, write a paragraph about your daily schedule. Use the information on the clocks to write sentences, and then write a paragraph that describes your daily schedule.

Step 1

Complete the two clocks by listing your classes and after-school activities. Use arrows to point to the correct times.

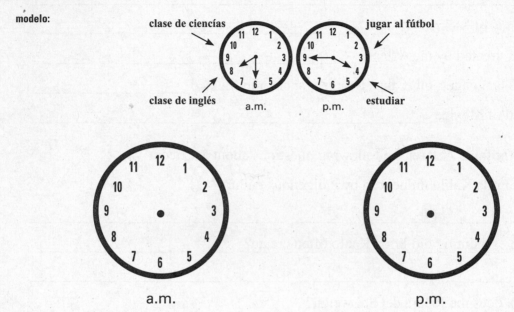

modelo:

clase de ciencías

clase de inglés

a.m.

jugar al fútbol

estudiar

p.m.

a.m.

p.m.

Step 2

Now take the details from the two clocks and write a sentence for each of the activities you labeled on the clocks.

_____
_____
_____
_____
_____
_____
_____

Comparación cultural: Horarios y clases
Level 1, pp. 132-133

Lectura y escritura (continued)

Step 3

Now write your paragraph using the sentences you wrote as a guide. Include an introductory sentence and use: **tener, tener que, ir,** and **ir a** to write about your daily schedule.

_____

_____

_____

_____

_____

_____

_____

Checklist

Be sure that…

☐ all the details about your daily schedule from your clocks are included in the paragraph;

☐ you use details to describe, as clearly as possible, all your after school activities;

☐ you include new vocabulary words and **tener, tener que, ir** and **ir a**.

Rubric

Evaluate your writing using the rubric below.

Writing criteria	Excellent	Good	Needs Work
Content	Your paragraph includes many details about your daily schedule.	Your paragraph includes some details about your daily schedule.	Your paragraph includes few details about your daily schedule.
Communication	Most of your paragraph is organized and easy to follow.	Parts of your paragraph are organized and easy to follow.	Your paragraph is disorganized and hard to follow.
Accuracy	Your paragraph has few mistakes in grammar and vocabulary.	Your paragraph has some mistakes in grammar and vocabulary.	Your paragraph has many mistakes in grammar and vocabulary.

Comparación cultural: Horarios y clases

Level 1, pp. 132-133

Compara con tu mundo

Now write a comparison about your daily schedule and that of one of the three students from page 133. Organize your comparison by listing morning and afternoon activities, and classes.

Step 1

Use the table to organize your comparison by times. Write details for each activity in your daily schedule and that of the student you chose.

MI HORARIO a.m.	EL HORARIO DE _____ a.m.
8:00	8:00
9:00	9:00
10:00	10:00
11:00	11:00
12:00	12:00
MI HORARIO p.m.	EL HORARIO DE _____ p.m.
1:00	1:00
2:00	2:00
3:00	3:00
4:00	4:00
5:00	5:00

Step 2

Now use the details from the table to write a comparison. Include an introductory sentence and write about each part of the schedules. Use **tener, tener que, ir, ir a** to describe your daily schedule and that of the student you chose.

_____

_____

_____

_____

_____

_____

_____

_____

Vocabulario A

¡AVANZA! **Goal:** Talk about foods and beverages.

1 Natalia likes to eat a healthy breakfast. Write an "X" next to each breakfast food from those listed below.

1. ____ el cereal

2. ____ los huevos

3. ____ la banana

4. ____ la hamburguesa

5. ____ la manzana

6. ____ el jugo de naranja

7. ____ la pizza

8. ____ el sándwich de jamón y queso

9. ____ los refrescos

10. ____ la sopa

2 Carlos is making lunch. Complete the following sentences with a word or expression from the box.

| leche | compartir | tengo hambre | nutritivas |

1. A Alfredo le gustan las comidas _____ .

2. A nosotros nos gusta beber _____ .

3. Es la hora del almuerzo. Yo _____ . Necesito comer.

4. Ella no tiene almuerzo. Tengo que _____ mi sándwich con una amiga.

3 What do you like to eat for dinner? Answer the following questions in complete sentences.

1. ¿Te gusta comer sopa en la cena?

_____

2. ¿Te gusta beber jugo de naranja?

_____

3. ¿Qué frutas te gusta comer?

_____

Vocabulario B

¡AVANZA! **Goal:** Talk about foods and beverages.

---

1 We all like to eat good, nutritious foods. From the choices below, choose the one that best completes each sentence.

1. Es importante comer comidas (horribles / nutritivas).

2. ¿Quién quiere beber un (jugo / pan)?

3. Todos los días Verónica tiene que (compartir / vender) su sándwich porque es muy grande.

4. Antes de ir a la escuela, Juan prepara cereal para (la cena / el desayuno).

5. El (yogur / refresco) es nutritivo.

2 Gustavo and Carla discuss their eating habits. Complete their conversation.

tengo ganas de	tengo sed	leche	jugo
cereal	nutritivas	horrible	

Gustavo: A mí me gusta comer **1.** _____ en el desayuno.

Carla: A mí me gusta comer huevos en el desayuno. También me gusta beber

2. _____ . Es rica.

Gustavo: A mí no me gusta la leche. **3.** Es _____ . Cuando

4. _____ me gusta más beber **5.** _____

de naranja.

Carla: Todos los días como uvas porque son **6.** _____ .

Gustavo: Ahora **7.** _____ comer una hamburguesa. Siempre tengo

hambre a las doce.

3 ¿Qué te gusta comer? Answer the following questions in complete sentences.

1. ¿Qué te gusta comer en el desayuno?

_____

2. ¿Te gusta más comer el desayuno o el almuerzo? ¿Por qué?

_____

Vocabulario C

¡AVANZA! **Goal:** Talk about foods and beverages.

---

1 Asking questions is a good way to get to know people. Complete the following questions using words from the box.

1. ¿ _____ te gusta más: una hamburguesa o un sándwich? Me gusta más un sándwich.

2. ¿ _____ bebes jugo de naranja y no bebes un refresco? Porque es más nutritivo.

3. ¿ _____ venden comidas nutritivas? Venden comidas nutritivas en la cafetería.

4. ¿ A _____ les gustan los huevos? A mis amigos les gustan.

dónde
quiénes
cuál
por qué

2 It's important to eat healthy foods. Choose a word from the vocabulary to complete each sentence:

1. En la cafetería de mi escuela _____ muchas comidas y bebidas.

2. No nos gusta beber _____ con el desayuno; nos gusta más beber leche.

3. Yo bebo jugo de naranja porque _____ .

4. ¿ _____ es más nutritivo: una banana o pan?

3 Look at the following drawing and write three sentences about it. Where is it? What meal is it? What foods are there?

_____

_____

_____

UNIDAD 3 • Vocabulario C
Lección 1

Gramática A *Gustar* with Nouns

Level 1, pp. 145–149

¡AVANZA! **Goal:** Ask questions and talk about which foods you like and don't like.

1 Everyone likes something different. Underline the verb that completes each sentence.

1. A Victoria (le gusta/ le gustan) la comida que prepara la mamá.

2. A nosotros (nos gustan / nos gusta) las papas fritas.

3. A Elena y a Sonia no (les gusta / les gustan) la sopa.

4. A ti no (te gusta / te gustan) el café.

5. A mí (me gusta / me gustan) las uvas.

2 What do the following people like? Write the correct form of the verb **gustar** in each sentence.

1. A mí _____ la cena que prepara Sebastián.

2. A Patricia _____ las hamburguesas, las papas fritas y los refrescos.

3. A nosotras _____ la comida nutritiva.

4. A ustedes _____ las manzanas y las uvas.

5. ¿A ti _____ mucho los huevos?

3 In complete sentences, answer the following questions.

modelo: A mí me gusta (me gustan)...

1. ¿Qué comidas te gustan más?

_____

2. ¿Qué comidas no te gustan?

_____

UNIDAD 3 • Gramática A
Lección 1

Unidad 3, Lección 1
Gramática A

102

¡Avancemos! 1
Cuaderno: Práctica por niveles

Gramática B *Gustar* with Nouns

> **¡AVANZA!** **Goal:** Ask questions and talk about which foods you like and don't like.

1 What do they like? Ask these people what they like using the words from the box.

los huevos	el café	el jugo de naranja
el yogur	la leche	las uvas

modelo: Ernesto: *¿Te gusta el yogur?* _____

1. Lucía y Augusto: _____

2. Señora Menchero: _____

3. Gregorio y Luz: _____

2 These students like cafeteria food. Complete the following paragraph with the appropriate form of the verb **gustar**.

A mis amigos **1.** _____ mucho la comida de la

cafetería. A Esmeralda **2.** _____ las papas fritas y los

refrescos. A Rodrigo **3.** _____ más la fruta.

A mí **4.** _____ los sándwiches y la leche. Pero a

todos nosotros **5.** _____ mucho el yogur. Y a ti, ¿qué

6. _____ ?

3 Answer the following questions about food. Use complete sentences.

1. ¿Qué te gusta en el almuerzo?

_____

_____

2. ¿Te gustan las comidas nutritivas? ¿Cuáles te gustan más?

_____

_____

UNIDAD 3
Lección 1

UNIDAD 3 • Gramática B

Gramática C *Gustar* with Nouns

> **¡AVANZA!** **Goal:** Ask questions and talk about which foods you like and don't like.

1 We all like to eat different things. Complete each sentence with a form of **gustar**.

1. A Valeria _____ las frutas.

2. A Juanjo y a Bruno no _____ el café.

3. A Teresa y a mí _____ el yogur en el desayuno.

4. A nosotros _____ las comidas nutritivas.

5. A ti _____ los huevos en la cena.

2 What do these people like? Follow the model and write complete sentences.

modelo: Hernán / la fruta **A Hernán le gusta la fruta.**

1. Sandra / los refrescos

_____

2. Carla y Octavio / los sándwiches

_____

3. tú / el yogur en la cena

_____

4. yo / más la leche

_____

3 Write two complete sentences about two different friends of yours and what they like to eat for lunch in the school cafeteria. Then write one more sentence about what you like.

_____

_____

_____

Gramática A *Present Tense of -er and -ir Verbs* Level 1, pp. 150-152

> **¡AVANZA!** **Goal:** Use the present tense to tell what people do.

1 Match each subject on the left with its appropriate ending on the right.

1. _____ Yo...
2. _____ Luis y Gustavo...
3. _____ Tú...
4. _____ Carla...
5. _____ Natalia y yo...

a. aprendemos mucho en las clases.
b. compartes el almuerzo con amigos.
c. bebe jugo de naranja.
d. como huevos en el desayuno.
e. leen un libro.

2 Complete each sentence with the correct form of the appropriate verb. Each verb will be used only once.

1. Tú siempre _____ agua después de correr.
2. Yo siempre _____ la tarea después de las clases.
3. La cafetería _____ unas hamburguesas muy ricas.
4. ¿Usted _____ correos electrónicos a sus amigos?
5. ¿ _____ un sándwich, tú y yo? Es muy grande para una persona.

| hacer |
| beber |
| escribir |
| compartir |
| vender |

3 What are these people doing? Use elements from each box to write three complete sentences.

nosotras	aprender	el almuerzo
usted	compartir	una carta
yo	escribir	el español

1. _____
2. _____
3. _____

Gramática B *Present Tense of -er and -ir Verbs*

| ¡AVANZA! | **Goal:** Use the present tense to tell what people do. |

1 Everyone does something different. Underline the correct form of the verb.

1. Anastasia (corre / corres) todas las mañanas.

2. Yo (comes / como) un sándwich en la cafetería.

3. Mis amigos (hacemos / hacen) mucha tarea.

4. Penélope y yo (leen / leemos) un libro en la biblioteca.

5. ¿(Bebes / Beben) tú leche en el desayuno?

2 Complete each sentence with the correct form of one of the following verbs: **beber, compartir, escribir,** or **vender**.

1. Nosotras _____ frutas muy ricas.

2. Roberto y Mario son amigos y siempre _____ el almuerzo.

3. Jacinto y yo _____ correos electrónicos todos los días.

4. ¿Por qué el señor López no _____ café?

3 Look at the drawings below and write what these people eat and drink for breakfast every day. Follow the model.

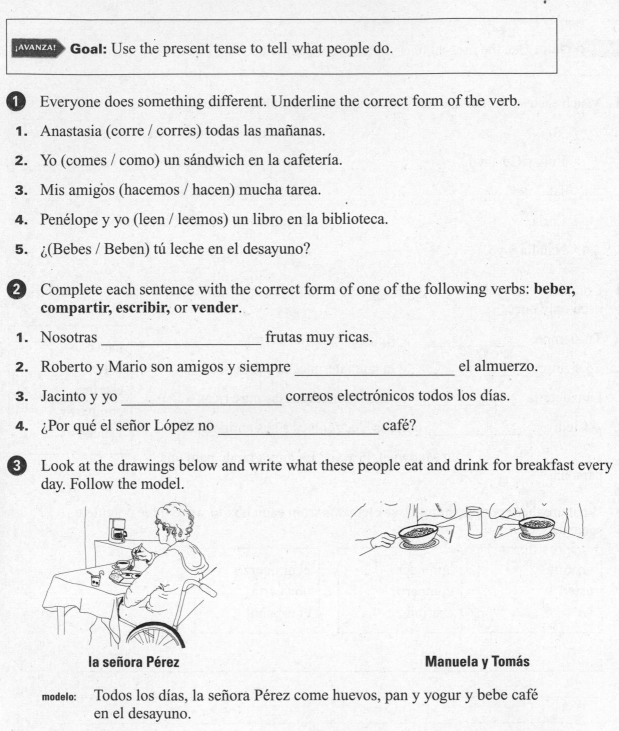

la señora Pérez

Manuela y Tomás

modelo: Todos los días, la señora Pérez come huevos, pan y yogur y bebe café en el desayuno.

1. _____

_____

Gramática C *Present Tense of -er and -ir Verbs*

> ¡AVANZA! **Goal:** Use the present tense to tell what people do.

1 Complete each sentence with the correct form of the appropriate verb.

hacer	beber	comer
leer	compartir	

1. Todas las mañanas, la señora Mendoza _____ un café.

2. Mis amigas Lucía y Andrea _____ en la cafetería.

3. A las ocho de la noche, yo _____ la tarea para la clase de español.

4. ¿Cuál de estos libros _____ usted esta tarde?

5. Eduardo y yo _____ todo.

2 Write sentences to describe what these people are doing.

1. Julia / beber un refresco

_____

2. María y yo / escribir en el pizarrón

_____

3. tú / aprender el español

_____

4. yo / hacer mucha tarea

_____

3 You and your friends always buy lunch at the cafeteria. Write three complete sentences about what food and drink is in the cafeteria and what you and your friends eat and drink. Do you share anything?

_____

_____

_____

_____

Integración: Hablar

There is very popular diner called "El Sándwich Divertido" near Alejandro's workplace, but it is always busy. He's very happy because he can now look at the menu online, and leave a phone message to order what he wants to have for lunch the next day, without waiting in line. Read the menu and listen to the phone message to find out what he likes to eat.

Fuente 1 Leer

Read the online menu for "El Sándwich Divertido."

El Sándwich Divertido

Menú de almuerzo

Comidas

Hamburguesa	$ 4.50
Sándwich de jamón y queso	$ 3.75
Papas fritas	$ 2.25
Sopa	$ 3.00

Bebidas

Refrescos	$ 0.75
Jugo de naranja	$ 0.60
Jugo de manzana	$ 0.70
Agua	$ 0.50

Fuente 2 Escuchar   *CD 02 track 02*

Then listen to Alejandro's voicemail message for "El Sándwich Divertido." Take notes.

_____

_____

Hablar

Based on the information given, what does Alejandro feel like having for lunch at "El Sándwich Divertido?"

modelo: Alejandro tiene ganas de... Porque no le gustan....También tiene ganas de...

Integración: Escribir

Ramón plays in a soccer league. He logs onto an educational Web site called "Fútbol para Todos" and finds out that a soccer player must follow a nutritious, healthy diet like any other athlete. Ramón believes he doesn't have the kinds of food at home in order to have a healthy breakfast the next morning. However, his mom leaves a message for him saying it's not so. Read the ad and listen to the voicemail in order to write about what Ramón eats for breakfast.

Fuente 1 Leer

Read the ad on the soccer Web site.

> ▶ Comida que tienes que comer para jugar al fútbol.
>
> **¿Te gusta jugar al fútbol?** Muy bien, tienes que preparar un desayuno bueno. Tienes que comer yogur, cereal y beber mucho jugo de naranja, ¡no café! Necesitas beber jugo de naranja porque es nutritivo. También es bueno comer frutas en el desayuno. Tienes que comer manzanas. El desayuno es una comida muy importante en el día. Tienes que comer comida nutritiva para jugar al fútbol.

Fuente 2 Escuchar   *CD 02 track 04*

Listen to the voicemail message that Ramón's mother left on his answering machine. Take notes.

_____

_____

_____

_____

Escribir

Based on the information provided, what kinds of food and drinks should Ramón have for breakfast? What kinds of food and drinks should he avoid?

modelo: Ramón tiene que comer... No...y no es bueno...

_____

_____

_____

_____

_____

_____

Escuchar A

¡AVANZA! **Goal:** Listen to find out about what some people eat.

---

1 Listen to Carla and take notes. Then, read each sentence and answer **cierto** (*true*) or **falso** (*false*).

C F **1.** Elena bebe leche.

C F **2.** A Carla le gusta el jugo de fruta.

C F **3.** Carla y Elena siempre comen hamburguesas.

C F **4.** A Elena le gustan más los refrescos.

C F **5.** El desayuno de Elena es nutritivo.

2 Listen to Natalia and take notes. Then, complete the sentences below.

1. Natalia come en _____ hoy.

2. En la cafetería _____ sopa.

3. Natalia bebe _____ .

4. A Natalia le gustan _____ de la cafetería.

5. Amalia no come con Natalia y los otros amigos porque no le gusta la comida

_____ .

Escuchar B

> ¡AVANZA! **Goal:** Listen to find out about what some people eat.

1 Listen to Andrés and take notes. Then, complete the following sentences.

1. El papá de Andrés siempre prepara _____ para la familia.

2. El papá de Andrés come _____ todos los días.

3. A Andrés y al papá les gusta beber _____ .

4. La mamá de Andrés come _____ .

5. Andrés y la mamá comparten _____ .

2 Listen to Mrs. Márquez. Then, answer the questions below in complete sentences.

1. ¿A todos les gusta la comida de la señora Márquez?

_____

2. ¿A quiénes les gusta el jugo de naranja?

_____

3. ¿Quién come frutas y cereal?

_____

4. ¿Qué comparten Andrea y la señora Márquez?

_____

Escuchar C

| ¡AVANZA! | **Goal:** Listen to find out about what some people eat. |

1 Listen to Lucía talk about her food. Take notes. Then list the foods she likes and she does not like.

Le gustan   No le gustan

1. _____   6. _____

2. _____   7. _____

3. _____   8. _____

4. _____   9. _____

5. _____   10. _____

2 Listen to Santiago and take notes. Then, in complete sentences, answer the questions about what they like.

1. ¿Qué come Ana?

_____

2. ¿Qué le gusta a Santiago?

_____

_____

3. ¿Qué comparten los dos amigos?

_____

UNIDAD 3 • Escuchar C
Lección 1

Unidad 3, Lección 1
Escuchar C

112

¡Avancemos! 1
Cuaderno: Práctica por niveles

Leer A

> **Goal:** Read about what types of food people like.

The school cafeteria conducted a survey of what students like to eat and drink. Alfonsina and her friends listed the following.

¿Qué te gusta?

Nombre	¿Qué comes?	¿Qué bebes?
Alfonsina	hamburguesas y papas fritas	refrescos
Carla	yogur y frutas	jugos de frutas
Iván	papas fritas	refrescos
Santiago	sándwiches de jamón y papas fritas	leche

¿Comprendiste?

Answer the following questions in complete sentences.

1. ¿Qué bebidas le gustan a Alfonsina?

_____

2. ¿Iván bebe bedidas nutritivas?

_____

3. ¿Quién come comida nutritiva?

_____

4. ¿Qué comida les gusta más a los estudiantes?

_____

¿Qué piensas?

1. ¿Es bueno comer papas fritas todos los días?

_____

_____

2. ¿Qué te gusta comer?

_____

UNIDAD 3
Lección 1 • Leer A

Leer B

> ¡AVANZA! **Goal:** Read about what types of food people like.

Nora is a school athlete who likes nutritious foods. She wrote this letter to the school newspaper about what she eats.

Hola. Me llamo Nora. Ahora, contesto la pregunta de muchos chicos: ¿Qué comes tú? A mí me gusta la comida nutritiva. Es buena y rica. Nunca bebo café y nunca bebo refrescos porque no son buenos. Me gustan más la leche, el yogur y los jugos de frutas. Siempre como frutas, huevos, sopa y otras comidas nutritivas. No me gustan las papas fritas y no me gusta la pizza. Sí, son ricas, pero no son nutritivas.

Nora Ayala

¿Comprendiste?

Read Nora's letter. Then complete the sentences below:

1. La pregunta de los chicos es: ¿ _____ ?

2. La comida nutritiva también _____ .

3. A Nora no le gusta beber _____ .

4. A Nora no le gusta comer _____ .

5. Las papas fritas y la pizza son ricas pero no son _____ .

¿Qué piensas?

1. ¿Qué comida nutritiva es rica?

   _____

2. ¿Te gustan comidas que no son nutritivas? ¿Cuáles?

   _____

   _____

UNIDAD 3
Lección 1

Leer B

114 Unidad 3, Lección 1
Leer B

¡Avancemos! 1
Cuaderno: Práctica por niveles

Leer C

> **¡AVANZA!** **Goal:** Read about what types of food people like.

Carmen wrote the following e-mail message to her friend, Carla.

Carla:
Tengo que comer comida más nutritiva (leche, huevos, jugo de naranja). Pero me gustan más otras comidas. Me gustan mucho las papas fritas y los refrescos. Siempre como papas fritas y bebo refrescos en el almuerzo. ¡Las papas fritas son muy ricas! Tú tienes una lista de comidas nutritivas en el cuaderno, ¿no? ¿Compartes la lista?
        -Carmen

¿Comprendiste?

Read Carmen's e-mail message. Then, read each sentence and circle **C** for **cierto** (*true*) or **F** for **falso** (*false*).

C   F   **1.** A Carmen no le gusta la comida nutritiva.

C   F   **2.** Es bueno comer papas fritas.

C   F   **3.** Carmen siempre bebe leche.

C   F   **4.** A Carmen le gusta más el jugo de naranja.

C   F   **5.** Carla tiene en el cuaderno un menú de comidas nutritivas.

¿Qué piensas?

1. En tu opinión, ¿los chicos de hoy comen comida nutritiva?

_____

_____

2. ¿Por qué necesita vender frutas la cafetería?

_____

_____

Escribir A

> **¡AVANZA!** **Goal:** Write about what you eat and drink.

Step 1

Your school cafeteria wants to know about your eating habits. Complete the following chart.

¿Qué te gusta comer?	¿Qué te gusta beber?
1.	1.
2.	2.
3.	3.

Step 2

Write two sentences about whether you like healthy food and why. Use the verbs **hacer** and **comer**.

_____

_____

Step 3

Evaluate your writing using the information in the table.

Writing Criteria	Excellent	Good	Needs Work
Content	You include two sentences about whether you like healthy food and why.	You include one sentence aobut whether you like healthy food and why.	You do not include sentences about whether you like healthy food and why.
Communication	Most of your writing is organized and easy to follow.	Some of your writing is organized and easy to follow.	Your writing is disorganized and hard to follow.
Accuracy	Your writing has few mistakes in grammar and vocabulary.	Your writing has some mistakes in grammar and vocabulary.	Your writing has many mistakes in grammar and vocabulary.

Escribir B

> ¡AVANZA! **Goal:** Write about what you eat and drink.

Step 1

What types of foods do you eat? Write your answers in the chart below.

Desayuno	Almuerzo
1.	1.
2.	2.
3.	3.
4.	4.

Step 2

Write three complete sentences about foods that you like to eat during the day, and when.

modelo: Me gusta el cereal porque es nutritivo. Como cereal y leche en el desayuno.

_____

_____

_____

Step 3

Evaluate your writing using the information in the table.

Writing Criteria	Excellent	Good	Needs Work
Content	You include three sentences about foods you like to eat and when.	You include two sentences about foods you like to eat and when.	You include one or fewer sentences about foods you like to eat and when.
Communication	Most of your paragraph is organized and easy to follow.	Parts of your paragraph are organized and easy to follow.	Your paragraph is disorganized and hard to follow.
Accuracy	You paragraph has few mistakes in grammar and vocabulary.	Your paragraph has some mistakes in grammar and vocabulary.	You paragraph has many mistakes in grammar and vocabulary.

Escribir C

> ¡AVANZA! **Goal:** Write about what you eat and drink.

Step 1

Answer the following survey about what nutritious foods and beverages also taste good.

Comidas nutritivas y ricas	Bebidas nutritivas y ricas
1.	1.
2.	2.
3.	3.
4.	4.

Step 2

Use the survey above to write five complete sentences about a nutritious meal you prepare at your house. State who likes what foods and beverages.

_____

_____

_____

_____

Step 3

Evaluate your writing using the information in the table.

Writing Criteria	Excellent	Good	Needs Work
Content	You include five sentences about a nutritious meal you prepare.	You include three to four sentences about a nutritious meal you prepare.	You include two or fewer sentences about a nutritious meal you prepare.
Communication	Most of your paragraph is organized and easy to follow.	Parts of your paragraph are organized and easy to follow.	Your paragraph is disorganized and hard to follow.
Accuracy	You paragraph has few mistakes in grammar and vocabulary.	Your paragraph has some mistakes in grammar and vocabulary.	You paragraph has many mistakes in grammar and vocabulary.

Cultura A

> ¡AVANZA! **Goal:** Review cultural information about Puerto Rico.

1 **Puerto Rico** Read the following statements about Puerto Rico and circle *true* or *false*.

T   F   **1.** The capital of Puerto Rico is San José.

T   F   **2.** Puerto Rico is an island.

T   F   **3.** The currency of Puerto Rico is the U.S. dollar.

T   F   **4.** *Pinchos* are a typical food from Puerto Rico.

2 **Puerto Rican culture** Complete the following sentences.

1. The **coquí** is a (butterfly / frog) found throughout the Parque Nacional El Yunque.

2. You can find colonial-style houses painted with bright colors in the district known as (Nuevo / Viejo) San Juan.

3. A popular site in the Parque Nacional El Yunque is the (Cascada / Calle) de la Coca.

4. (Tostones / Pupusas) are a common side dish in Puerto Rico.

5. A popular cold treat in Puerto Rico is a(n) (alcapurria / piragua).

3 **The Plaza de Colón** Describe the Plaza de Colón. Where is it located? What can people see and do there? How would you spend an afternoon at this plaza?

_____

_____

_____

_____

_____

_____

_____

UNIDAD 3
Lección 1   ·   Cultura A

Cultura B

¡AVANZA! **Goal:** Review cultural information about Puerto Rico.

1 **Puerto Rico and El Salvador** Choose the multiple choice item that best completes each statement.

1. **La piragua** is a name for a Puerto Rican ____ .

   a. river   **b.** cold dessert   **c.** dance

2. A typical Salvadorean food is the ____ .

   a. pupusa   **b.** piragua   **c.** pincho

3. The capital of Puerto Rico is ____ .

   a. San José   **b.** San Jacinto   **c.** San Juan

4. The currency of Puerto Rico is the ____ .

   a. peso   **b.** dollar   **c.** bolívar

2 **In Puerto Rico** Complete the following sentences.

1. Puerto Ricans like to eat a food known as _____ , which are skewers of chicken or pork.

2. The _____ is a tree frog that is found in Puerto Rico.

3. One of the waterfalls in the Parque Nacional El Yunque is called the Cascada de la _____ .

4. You can find a statue of Christopher Columbus in _____ .

5. _____ is the colonial quarter of Puerto Rico's capital.

3 **Puerto Rican Cuisine** Create a menu for a Puerto Rican restaurant that serves traditional cooking, or *la cocina criolla*. Include an introduction sentence that describes the influences of la cocina criolla *and brief descriptions of each dish, along with prices.*

_____

_____

_____

_____

_____

Cultura C

> **¡AVANZA!** **Goal:** Review cultural information about Puerto Rico.

1 **Activities in Puerto Rico** Write where you can do the following in Puerto Rico.

I can....	in/at
See waterfalls	
Eat *pinchos*	
See colonial-style houses	

2 **Puerto Rico** Answer the following questions about Puerto Rico.

1. What are the two official languages of Puerto Rico? _____

   _____

2. What famous waterfall is in the Parque Nacional El Yunque? _____

   _____

3. Where do Puerto Ricans like to spend time with their families? _____

   _____

4. What is **la cocina criolla?** _____

   _____

3 **Viejo San Juan** Puerto Rico has many beautiful places of interest. The island is known for its parks, colonial homes, waterfalls, and many other attractions. Write a paragraph about two places that you would most like to visit if you had the opportunity to go to Puerto Rico. Describe what you would do in each place and why you would like to visit it.

_____

_____

_____

_____

_____

_____

Vocabulario A

> ¡AVANZA! **Goal:** Talk about family.

1 Look at Andrés' family tree. Then, read each sentence and circle **C** for **cierto** *(true)* or **F** for **falso** *(false)*.

C   F   **1.** Cecilia es la prima de Andrés.

C   F   **2.** Julián es el abuelo de Andrés y Luis.

C   F   **3.** Isabel es la tía de Mariela.

C   F   **4.** Javier es el tío de Luis.

C   F   **5.** Elena es la abuela de Cecilia y Mariela.

2 Look at the family tree above. Then, fill in each blank to complete the sentences.

1. Elena es _____ de Armando.

2. Luis es _____ de Mariela.

3. Cecilia es _____ de Andrés.

4. Mariela y Luis son _____ de Andrés y Cecilia.

3 Answer the following question in a complete sentence. Write all numbers in words. Follow the model.

modelo: Hoy es el doce de enero de dos mil siete.

1. ¿Cuál es la fecha de hoy?

_____

Vocabulario B

> **¡AVANZA!** **Goal:** Talk about family.

1 Betania is talking about her family. Underline the word that best completes each sentence.

1. Mi padre es (el hijo / el hermano) de mi tía.

2. Mi tía es (la madre / la abuelo) de mi primo.

3. Mi prima es (la madrasta / la hija) de mi tía.

4. Mi abuelo es (el hermano / el padre) de mi tío.

2 Complete the following sentences with the family relationships.

1. El hermano de mi padre es mi _____ .

2. Mis abuelos tienen dos hijas. La tía de mi prima es mi _____ .

3. El padre de mi madre es mi _____ .

4. La hija del hermano de mi padre es mi _____ .

3 Answer the following questions in complete sentences. Write any numbers in words.

1. ¿Cuál es la fecha de hoy?

_____

2. ¿Tienes un gato o un perro?

_____

Vocabulario C

> **¡AVANZA!** **Goal:** Talk about family.

1 Santiago is talking about his family. Fill in the correct answers.

Me llamo Santiago. Yo soy el hijo de Gloria Soriano. Mi

_____ se llama Victoria; ella también es la hija de

Gloria Soriano. El hermano de mi madre se llama Federico López. Él

es mi _____ . Mi tío tiene tres hijos. Ellos son mis

_____ .

2 Use the chart below to answer the questions about Jorge's family.

Persona	Cumpleaños	Años
	17/10	60
	25/2	15

1. ¿Cuándo es el cumpleaños de la madre de Jorge?

_____

2. ¿Cuántos años tiene el primo de Jorge?

_____

3 ¿Cuál es la fecha de nacimiento de estas personas? Write your answers in complete sentences. Write any numbers in words and use the information in parentheses.

1. **Cristóbal Colón (August 26, 1451):** _____

_____

2. **Simón Bolívar (July 24, 1783):** _____

_____

Gramática A *Possessive adjectives*

> **¡AVANZA!** **Goal:** Use possessive adjectives to talk about family.

1 Alejandro talks about family. Underline the word that best completes each sentence.

1. Tengo tres hermanos. (Mis / Sus) hermanos se llaman Miguel, Luis y Pedro.

2. Los padres de Javier son jóvenes. (Sus / Su) madre tiene 35 años.

3. Mis hermanos y yo hablamos con los abuelos todos los domingos. (Sus / Nuestros) abuelos son muy buenos.

4. Tú vives con (tus / sus) padres.

5. A María y a Néstor les gustan los primos. (Su / Sus) prima mayor se llama Ariana.

2 Change the following possessive adjectives and their nouns from singular to plural.

modelo: mi hermano / **mis** hermano**s**

1. nuestro primo / _____

2. su tío / _____

3. mi amiga / _____

4. tu hermano mayor / _____

3 Look at the drawings. Then, write complete sentences.

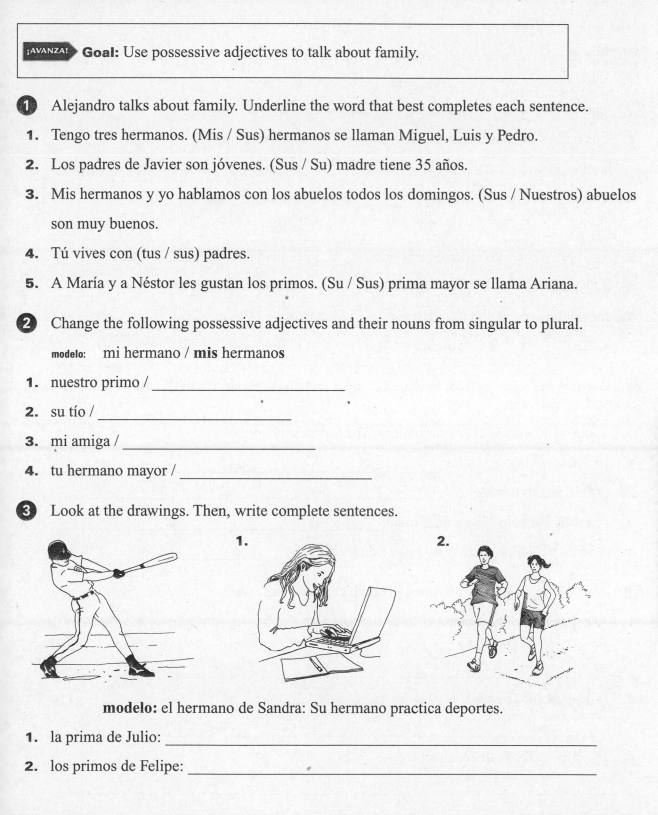

1.

2.

modelo: el hermano de Sandra: Su hermano practica deportes.

1. la prima de Julio: _____

2. los primos de Felipe: _____

¡Avancemos! 1
Cuaderno: Práctica por niveles

UNIDAD 3 · Gramática A
Lección 2

Unidad 3, Lección 2
Gramática A   **125**

Gramática B *Possessive adjectives*

┌───┐
│ ¡AVANZA! **Goal:** Use possessive adjectives to talk about family.   │
└───┘

1 Choose the word that best completes each sentence.

1. Los padres de Inés tienen tres hijos. _____ hijo mayor estudia arte.

    a. Sus   **b.** Su   **c.** Tus

2. Tú tienes una abuela muy joven. _____ dos abuelas son jóvenes.

    a. Tus   **b.** Tu   **c.** Sus

3. Mis hermanos y yo tenemos dos primos. _____ primos viven en Boston.

    a. Nuestro   **b.** Nuestras   **c.** Nuestros

4. Inés tiene una familia muy grande. _____ familia es de Miami.

    a. Tu   **b.** Sus   **c.** Su

2 Use possessive adjectives to write complete sentences about Miguel's family. Follow the model.

    modelo: tú / padres / ser / simpáticos: Tus padres son simpáticos.

1. yo / hermanos / ser / altos _____

2. usted / tías / vivir / lejos _____

3. nosotros / abuelo / llamarse / Julián _____

4. Andrés y Cecilia / hermana / tener / cinco años _____

3 Answer the following questions in complete sentences.

1. ¿Cuál es la fecha de nacimiento de tu padre?

_____

_____

2. ¿Cuántos años tienes?

_____

4. ¿Cuál es tu fecha de nacimiento?

_____

_____

Gramática C *Possessive adjectives*

| ¡AVANZA! | **Goal:** Use possessive adjectives to talk about family. |

1 Julián describes his family. Complete the paragraph using possessive adjectives.

Las hijas de mi tía son **1.** _____ primas. Una

se llama Noemí y **2.** _____ hermanas se llaman

Rosario y Débora. **3.** _____ madres son hermanas.

4. _____ abuelo es joven. Él tiene cincuenta y cinco

años y **5.** _____ cumpleaños es el veinte de junio.

2 Describe your own family members or those of a family you know by answering the following questions.

1. ¿Quién es atlético(a)?

_____

2. ¿Quién prepara la cena?

_____

3. ¿Quiénes tienen catorce años o más?

_____

4. ¿Quién tiene un cumpleaños en junio, julio o agosto?

_____

5. ¿Quién es la persona menor en la familia? ¿Cuándo es su cumpleaños?

_____

_____

3 Write three complete sentences to describe your family or a family you know. Use **mi(s)**, **su(s)** and **nuestro(s)** or **nuestra(s)**.

1. _____

2. _____

3. _____

UNIDAD 3
Lección 2 • Gramática C

Gramática A *Comparatives*

> **¡AVANZA!** **Goal:** Make comparisons.

1 Draw a line from the word pair on the left to the appropriate comparison on the right.

1. aprender / enseñar
2. una ventana / un lápiz
3. un café / una pizza
4. Rafael Tufiño / yo

a. más grande que

b. menos rico que

c. tan importante como

d. más artístico que

2 Use the comparatives **más... que, menos... que**, **tan... como** and **tanto como** to complete the following sentences.

1. Luisa es _____ joven _____ su abuela.

2. Trabajar es _____ divertido _____ pasar un rato con los amigos.

3. Soy atlético; me gusta jugar al fútbol _____ _____ correr.

4. Beber leche es _____ nutritivo _____ comer yogur.

3 Answer the following question in a complete sentence.

1. ¿Te gusta la clase de matemáticas tanto como la clase de español? ¿Por qué?

_____

_____

_____

Gramática B *Comparatives*

| ¡AVANZA! | **Goal:** Make comparisons. |

1 Read each sentence and fill in the blank with the correct answer from the choices given.

1. Roberta tiene trece años y su hermano tiene once años. Su hermano es ____ que ella.

    a. peor
    b. mayor
    c. menor

2. Roberta tiene tres hermanos mayores. Ellos tienen ____ que ella.

    a. más años
    b. menos años
    c. tantos años

3. Roberta tiene trece años. Enrique tiene veinte años y Sandra también tiene veinte años.

    Sandra es ____ de Roberta.

    a. la hermana mayor
    b. la hermana menor
    c. la madre

2 Use comparatives to complete the following sentences.

1. estudiar / aprender / tan importante como

    _____

2. la clase de matemáticas / la clase de arte / tan interesante como

    _____

3. preparar la cena / trabajar después de las clases / menos difícil que

    _____

4. hablar por teléfono / mirar la televisión / tan interesante como

    _____

3 Use a comparative expression to describe what these people like more. Follow the model.

   modelo: A mi papá le gusta practicar deportes más que trabajar.

1. ¿Qué le gusta más a tu amigo: el yogur o la leche?

    _____

2. ¿Qué le gustan más a tu amiga: los gatos o los perros?

    _____

Gramática C *Comparatives*

> ¡AVANZA! **Goal:** Make comparisons.

1 Your teacher has asked you to compare activities and things in your life. Use a comparative expression with the word in parentheses to complete each sentence.

1. Mirar la televisión es _____ montar en bicicleta. (divertido)

2. La clase de ciencias es _____ la clase de matemáticas. (fácil)

3. El yogur es _____ un refresco. (rico)

4. Un refresco es _____ el yogur. (nutritivo)

2 Re-write these statements using a different comparative expression.

1. Estudiar es más importante que practicar deportes.

_____

2. No preguntar es más inteligente que preguntar.

_____

3. El desayuno es menos nutritivo que la cena.

_____

4. Los gatos son tan malos como los perros.

_____

3 Use comparative expressions to describe what your friends like more.

1. _____

_____

2. _____

_____

3. _____

_____

UNIDAD 3 • Gramática C
Lección 2

130 **Unidad 3, Lección 2**
Gramática C

¡Avancemos! 1
Cuaderno: Práctica por niveles

Integración: Hablar

Juan is very happy. The new school year has begun and he has a Spanish teacher that is related to the recently elected president of the country. The whole school is interested in learning more about the Spanish teacher, so she writes about her family on the school Web site, and the principal talks about her over the loudspeaker on the first day of the school year. Read the Web article and listen to the announcement to find out how she is related to the president.

Fuente 1 Leer

Read the school newspaper article...

FAMILIA DEL PRESIDENTE

¡Hola! Me llamo María Cristina, soy la maestra de español. Me gusta enseñar el español en la escuela. Yo no soy la hija del presidente de nuestro país. Yo soy un año y ocho meses mayor que la hija del presidente. Pero ella y yo somos familia del presidente. El padre de ella es hijo del padre de mi padre. Sí, el presidente es hijo de mi abuelo.

Fuente 2 Escuchar *CD 02 track 12*

Listen to the principal's loudspeaker message on the first day of the school year. Take notes.

_____

_____

_____

_____

Hablar

What is the relationship between María Graciela and María Cristina? Explain.

modelo: María Graciela es... María Cristina es..., porque el presidente es...

Integración: Escribir

Today, Mr. Juan Márquez has become the oldest man in the country. Newspapers and radio shows are talking about him. Everyone wants to know more about him; how he spends his time, when he was born, who his family is, and more! Read the newspaper article and listen to the radio show to find out how old he is.

Fuente 1 Leer

Read the newspaper article about Juan Márquez, the oldest man in the country.

¡Feliz cumpleaños señor Márquez!

Su nombre es Juan Márquez. Es mayor que usted, es mayor que yo y mayor que todos en el país. Sí, ¡es de nuestro país! Su familia es muy grande y tiene hermanos, hermanas y primos. Pero todos tienen menos años que él. Hoy todos están emocionados, porque hoy es 23 de enero y es su cumpleaños. Ahora él es el hombre más viejo del país. ¡Feliz cumpleaños señor Márquez!

Fuente 2 Escuchar   CD 02 track 14

Listen to the radio talk show about señor Juan. Take notes.

_____

_____

_____

_____

Escribir

How old is Mr. Márquez? Explain your answer.

modelo: El señor Márquez tiene..., porque su fecha...Y hoy es...

_____

_____

_____

_____

_____

_____

Escuchar A

| ¡AVANZA! | **Goal:** Listen to find out about family relationships. |

1 Listen to Enrique and take notes. Then, match the names with the family relationship that each person has to Enrique.

1. Alicia y Jorge   **a.** primos

2. Norma   **b.** abuelos

3. Raúl y Julia   **c.** padres

4. Sofía   **d.** tía

5. Ernesto y Luisa   **e.** hermana

2 Listen to Sofía and take notes. Then, complete the sentences below.

1. Sofía es _____ que su hermano.

2. Sofía y su familia van a Puerto Rico en _____ .

3. A Sofía le gusta estar con _____ más que con sus amigos.

4. El primo _____ de Sofía es inteligente.

Escuchar B

¡AVANZA! **Goal:** Listen to find out about family relationships.

1 Listen to Jimena and take notes. Then, indicate which family members Jimena has and doesn't have by putting the following words in the correct column.

abuelos	padre	hermanos	tía	primos
madre	madrastra	abuelas	hermana	primas

Tiene   **No tiene…**

_____   _____

_____   _____

_____   _____

_____

_____

2 Listen to Enrique and take notes. Then, answer the following questions.

1. ¿Cómo es Blanca?

_____

2. ¿Qué le gusta hacer a Blanca?

_____

3. ¿Qué hacen los primos con los abuelos?

_____

4. ¿Cómo es la comida de su abuela?

_____

Escuchar C

¡AVANZA! **Goal:** Listen to find out about family relationships.

1 Listen to Mariano and take notes. Then explain how the following people are related to him by filling in the blank with the appropriate word.

1. Javier es su _____

2. Teresa es su _____

3. Diana es su _____

4. Carmen y Felipe son sus _____

5. Tomás es su _____

6. Anita es su _____

2 Listen to Lucía and take notes. Then answer the questions below in complete sentences.

1. ¿Por qué a Lucía le gusta pasar un rato con sus primos?

_____

2. ¿Es Lucía mayor que sus primos?

_____

3. ¿Es la hermana de Lucía mayor que sus primos?

_____

4. ¿Qué les gusta hacer a los primos de Lucía?

_____

_____

5. ¿Cómo es la hermana de Lucía?

_____

Leer A

> **¡AVANZA!** **Goal:** Read about a family reunion.

The following is an invitation to a family reunion.

Reunión de la familia Serrano
¡Atención a todos los Serrano!

Nuestra reunión anual es el 29 de julio a las 5:00 en el Club campestre.
En la reunión hay más personas que antes... ¡porque en abril y mayo hay
dos nacimientos! Como siempre, en la reunión hay mucha comida y música.
Los abuelos Serrano, Irma y Juan, van a la reunión con sus 9 hijos. Y los
9 hijos llevan a todos sus hijos. ¡Son más de 40 chicos! Este año la reunión
es muy especial porque también es el día del cumpleaños de Juan.

Tíos, primos, hermanos, abuelos... ¡todos a la reunión!

¿Comprendiste?

Read the Serrano family invitation. Then, read each sentence and circle **C** for **cierto** (*true*)
or **F** for **falso** (*false*).

C F **1.** La reunión es el veintiséis de julio.

C F **2.** La familia Serrano es más grande que antes.

C F **3.** Irma es abuela de más de cuarenta chicos.

C F **4.** Juan no tiene hijos.

C F **5.** El veintinueve de julio es el cumpleaños de Juan.

¿Qué piensas?

¿Qué te gusta hacer con tus amigos(as)?

_____

_____

Unidad 3, Lección 2
Leer A

136

¡Avancemos! 1
Cuaderno: Práctica por niveles

UNIDAD 3
Lección 2 • Leer A

Leer B

> **¡AVANZA!** **Goal:** Read about family.

Paula wrote a letter to her friend Marisol, explaining why she can't go to her birthday.

> *Marisol:*
>
> *No voy a tu cumpleaños porque tengo que estar con mis abuelos. Mis abuelos viven lejos en Puerto Rico, y llegan el día de tu cumpleaños, el primero de septiembre. Todos los años, llegan en diciembre, pero el mes de septiembre les gusta más que diciembre. Mis tíos y mis padres están muy emocionados porque llegan sus padres. También mis primos están contentos. Yo estoy tan contenta como ellos, pero también estoy triste porque no voy a tu cumpleaños. Salimos y bebemos un refresco el día después de tu cumpleaños... ¿Te gusta mi idea?*
>
> *Tu amiga,*
>
> *Paula*

¿Comprendiste?

Read Paula's letter. Then, complete the following sentences.

1. Paula no va al cumpleaños porque tiene que estar con sus _____ .

2. Los tíos y los padres de Paula están muy emocionados porque llegan _____ padres.

3. Los primos de Paula están _____ contentos _____ ella.

4. Paula también está _____ porque no va al cumpleaños.

5. A los abuelos de Paula les gusta el mes de _____ menos que el mes de septiembre.

¿Qué piensas?

¿Te gusta pasar un rato con tu familia? ¿Por qué?

_____

_____

Leer C

> | ¡AVANZA! | **Goal:** Read about family.

Rubén and Emilio are both going to Puerto Rico. They talk about their families.

> Hola Emilio: Tengo que hablar con mis padres pero no hay problema.
> A mis padres les gusta descansar más que trabajar... ¡ Y en Puerto Rico,
> ellos descansan mucho! Pero, ¿cuándo vamos a Puerto Rico? Yo tengo
> ganas de ir en marzo, cuando hace frío en Nueva York. ¿Te gusta la idea?
> Rubén
>
> ----
> >Hola Rubén: ¿Cómo estás? ¿Cómo está tu familia? Tienes que hablar con
> >ellos sobre cuándo vamos a Puerto Rico. No escribo más ahora porque
> >mi madre y yo tenemos que preparar la cena: ¡una pizza de jamón! Me
> >gusta la pizza de mi madre más que la pizza de la cafetería.
> >Emilio

¿Comprendiste?

Read the e-mails. Then answer the following questions in complete sentences.

1. ¿Qué les gusta hacer a los padres de Rubén? ¿Qué hacen en Puerto Rico?

   _____

   _____

2. ¿Por qué no escribe más ahora Emilio?

   _____

3. ¿Qué le gusta más a Emilio?

   _____

4. ¿Cuándo tiene ganas de ir Rubén a Puerto Rico?

   _____

¿Qué piensas?

1. ¿Es divertido ir a otro país con un amigo?

   _____

2. ¿Te gusta ir a otro país con amigos más que con tu familia?

   _____

Escribir A

> ¡AVANZA! **Goal:** Write about family.

Step 1

Complete this chart using information about yourself and someone important in your life. Write out all dates in words.

Nombre	Fecha de nacimiento

Step 2

Use the information from the chart above to write two sentences about your birth date and the birth date of someone important in your life.

_____

_____

_____

Step 3

Evaluate your writing using the information in the table.

Writing Criteria	Excellent	Good	Needs Work
Content	Your have included two sentences about your birth date and the birth date of someone important to you.	Your have included one sentences about your birth date and the birth date of someone important to you.	Your have not included sentences about your birth date and the birth date of someone important to you.
Communication	Most of your response is organized and easy to follow.	Parts of your response are organized and easy to follow.	Your response is disorganized and hard to follow.
Accuracy	Your response has few mistakes in grammar and vocabulary.	Your response has some mistakes in grammar and vocabulary.	Your response has many mistakes in grammar and vocabulary.

UNIDAD 3
Lección 2
•
Escribir A

Escribir B

> **¡AVANZA!** **Goal:** Write about family.

Step 1

Complete this chart. Write the dates in words.

Tu fecha de nacimiento	Fecha de nacimiento de una persona de tu familia	Fecha de nacimiento de tu amigo(a)

Step 2

Write four sentences about the dates above and why they are important to you.

_____

_____

_____

_____

Step 3

Evaluate your writing using the information in the table.

Writing Criteria	Excellent	Good	Needs Work
Content	Your paragraph describes why three dates are important to you.	Your paragraph describes why two dates are important to you.	Your paragraph describes why one date is important to you.
Communication	Most of your paragraph is organized and easy to follow.	Parts of your paragraph are organized and easy to follow.	Your paragraph is disorganized and hard to follow.
Accuracy	Your paragraph has few mistakes in grammar and vocabulary.	Your paragraph has some mistakes in grammar and vocabulary.	Your paragraph has many mistakes in grammar and vocabulary.

UNIDAD 3
Lección 2

Escribir B

Unidad 3, Lección 2
Escribir B

140

¡Avancemos! 1
Cuaderno: Práctica por niveles

Escribir C

> **¡AVANZA!** **Goal:** Write about family.

Step 1

Complete the chart below. Write in the missing months. In the middle column, write the name and birthday of the family member or friend who has a birthday that month. Also write the relationship between that person and you. In the third column, write the year of birth in words.

Mes	Cumpleaños	Año de nacimiento

Step 2

Write about the chart above in six complete sentences. Include family relationships.

_____

_____

_____

_____

Step 3

Evaluate your writing using the information in the table.

Writing Criteria	Excellent	Good	Needs Work
Content	Your paragraph includes many details and new vocabulary.	Your paragraph includes some details and new vocabulary.	Your paragraph includes little information or new vocabulary.
Communication	Most of your paragraph is clear.	Some of your paragraph is clear.	Your paragraph is not clear.
Accuracy	Your paragraph has few mistakes in grammar and vocabulary.	Your paragraph has some mistakes in grammar and vocabulary.	Your paragraph has many mistakes in grammar and vocabulary.

Cultura A

Level 1, pp. 184-185

> **¡AVANZA!** **Goal:** Review cultural information about Puerto Rico.

1 **Puerto Rico** Read the following statements about Puerto Rico and circle *true* or *false*.

T   F   **1.** The capital of Puerto Rico is San José.

T   F   **2. Sobremesa** is when families spend time together after a meal.

T   F   **3.** The currency of Puerto Rico is the U.S. dollar.

T   F   **4.** Puerto Rico is a commonwealth of the United States.

T   F   **5.** In Puerto Rico there are only two political parties.

T   F   **6.** Puerto Rican elections generally have a low voter turnout.

2 **Puerto Rico and Peru** Choose the correct word to complete the following sentences.

1. The fifteenth birthday celebration for young women in Puerto Rico is called (**fiesta** / **quinceañero**).

2. The artist who painted many portraits called *Goyita* is (Picasso / Rafael Tufiño).

3. The *Goyita* paintings are portraits of the artist's (mother / grandmother).

4. Peruvian girls often have fourteen or fifteen (dances / maids of honor) at their fifteenth birthday celebration.

3 **Quinceañeras** Describe a **quinceañera.** Compare this celebration with the *Sweet Sixteen* celebration in the United States. How are they similar or different? What are some traditional activities for each?

_____

_____

_____

_____

_____

_____

_____

Cultura B

> ¡AVANZA! **Goal:** Review cultural information about Puerto Rico.

1 **About Puerto Rico** Choose the multiple choice item that best completes each statement.

1. During the elections in Puerto Rico a _____ is elected.

    a. governor **b.** president **c.** prime minister

2. The political party that wants Puerto Rico elected as the 51st state is _____

    a. Independista Puertorriqueño **b.** **Popular Democrático** **c. Nuevo Progresista**

3. Puerto Rico is a(n) _____

    a. peninsula **b.** island **c.** bay

2 **Celebrations and art** Answer the following questions about Puerto Rico and Peru in complete sentences.

1. Who does artist Rafael Tufiño represent in his series of paintings called *Goyita?*

    _____

2. How does Peruvian artist Fernando Sayán Polo's painting *Niña campesina sonriente* reflect his country? _____

    _____

3. What is a **quinceañera?** _____

    _____

4. What are three **quinceañera** traditions? _____

    _____

3 It is very important to Puerto Ricans to vote and participate in the elections. Briefly compare elections and political parties in Puerto Rico and in the United States, and explain why it is important to vote.

_____

_____

_____

_____

_____

_____

UNIDAD 3
Lección 2 · Cultura B

Cultura C

> **¡AVANZA!** **Goal:** Review cultural information about Puerto Rico.

1 **Political parties** In the chart below, briefly describe what each political party supports.

Name of political party	In favor of...
Popular Democrático	
Independentista Puertorriqueño	
Nuevo Progresista	

2 **Puerto Rico** Answer the following questions about Puerto Rico.

1. What are young women called when they have their fifteenth birthday?

_____

2. Instead of having a fifteenth birthday celebration, which birthday do many Puerto Rican girls celebrate with a large party?

_____

3. Who painted the *Goyita* portraits and who is represented in the paintings?

_____

3 **Plan a quinceañero** Write an invitation for a **quinceañero.** In your invitation, describe what will take place at the party. What kind of food will be served and what kind of music will be played? What kinds of traditional activities will be part of the celebration? Also include important details, such as when and where it will take place.

_____

_____

_____

_____

_____

_____

_____

_____

_____

Comparación cultural: ¿Qué comemos?

Level 1, pp. 186-187

Lectura y escritura

After reading the paragraphs about how María Luisa, Silvia, and José enjoy a Sunday meal, write a paragraph about a typical Sunday meal. Use the information on your mind map to write sentences, and then write a paragraph that describes your typical Sunday meal.

Step 1

Complete the mind map describing as many details as possible about your Sunday meals.

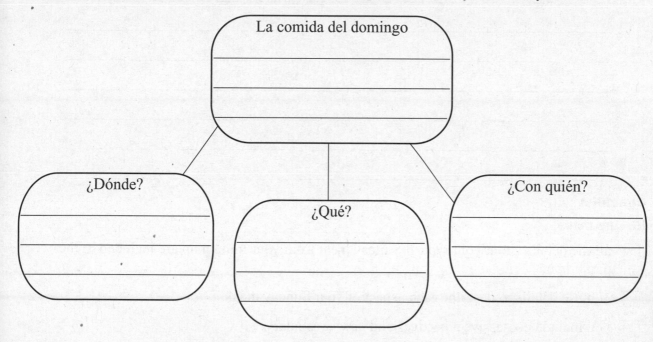

La comida del domingo

¿Dónde?

¿Qué?

¿Con quién?

Step 2

Now take the details from the mind map and write a sentence for each topic on the mind map.

_____

_____

_____

_____

_____

_____

_____

_____

_____

_____

UNIDAD 3 • Comparación
Lección 2   cultural

Comparación cultural: ¿Qué comemos?

Level 1, pp. 186-187

Lectura y escritura (continued)

Step 3

Now write your paragraph using the sentences you wrote as a guide. Include an introduction sentence and use possessive adjectives such as **mi, mis, su, sus** to write about your typical Sunday meal.

_____

_____

_____

_____

_____

_____

_____

Checklist

Be sure that…

☐ all the details about your typical Sunday meal from your mind map are included in the paragraph;

☐ you use details to describe each aspect of your Sunday meal;

☐ you include possessive adjectives and new vocabulary.

Rubric

Evaluate your writing using the rubric below.

Writing criteria	Excellent	Good	Needs Work
Content	Your paragraph includes many details about your typical Sunday meal.	Your paragraph includes some details about your typical Sunday meal.	Your paragraph includes few details about your typical Sunday meal.
Communication	Most of your paragraph is organized and easy to follow.	Parts of your paragraph are organized and easy to follow.	Your paragraph is disorganized and hard to follow.
Accuracy	Your paragraph has few mistakes in grammar and vocabulary.	Your paragraph has some mistakes in grammar and vocabulary.	Your paragraph has many mistakes in grammar and vocabulary.

UNIDAD 3 Lección 2 • Comparación cultural

Comparación cultural: ¿Qué comemos?

Level 1, pp. 186-187

Compara con tu mundo

Now write a comparison about your typical Sunday meal and that of one of the students on page 187. Organize your comparison by topics. First, compare the place where you have your Sunday meal, then the food you eat, and lastly with whom you eat.

Step 1

Use the table to organize your comparison by topics. Write details for each topic about your typical Sunday meal and that of the student you chose.

Categorías	Mi almuerzo/cena	El almuerzo/cena de _____
¿Dónde?		
¿Qué?		
¿Con quién?		

Step 2

Now use the details from the table to write a comparison. Include an introduction sentence and write about each category. Use possessive adjectives such as **mi, mis, su, sus** to describe your typical Sunday meal and that of the student you chose.

_____

_____

_____

_____

_____

_____

_____

_____

_____

UNIDAD 3 • Comparación
Lección 2 cultural

Vocabulario A

¡AVANZA! **Goal:** Talk about clothes.

1 You need to get dressed. Place an "x" next to those items that go on the upper part of your body.

____ la chaqueta   ____ los zapatos

____ los pantalones   ____ los jeans

____ la blusa   ____ la camiseta

____ el sombrero   ____ la camisa

____ los calcetines   ____ los pantalones cortos

2 There are many things in the store in a variety of colors. Choose the correct word in parentheses to complete the following sentences.

1. A mí me gustan las camisas (rojas / azul) como una manzana.

2. El vestido es tan (negro / blanco) como la leche.

3. Esa camisa es del color de una banana. Es (amarilla / negro).

4. Muchas veces los jeans son (azules / anaranjados).

5. En Estados Unidos el dólar es (verde / marrón).

3 Answer the following question in a complete sentence.

1. ¿Qué estación te gusta más?

_____

_____

2. ¿Qué ropa te gusta comprar en el verano?

_____

_____

3. ¿Qué ropa te gusta comprar en el otoño?

_____

_____

UNIDAD 4 • Vocabulario A
Lección 1

148

Unidad 4, Lección 1
Vocabulario A

¡Avancemos! 1
Cuaderno: Práctica por niveles

Vocabulario B

> ¡AVANZA! **Goal:** Talk about clothes.

1 **¿Tienes frío o tienes calor?** In the left column, write three cold weather clothing items. In the right column, write three warm weather clothing items. Use the words from the box.

Frío	Calor
_____	_____
_____	_____
_____	_____

los pantalones
  cortos
la chaqueta
la blusa
los calcetines
el vestido
el gorro

2 Norma and Laura tend to be opposites. Complete the sentences below.

1. A Norma le gusta la primavera pero a Laura le gusta _____ .

2. A Laura le gusta una camisa blanca pero a Norma le gusta más una

camisa _____ .

3. Cuando Norma tiene calor Laura _____ .

4. A Laura le gusta la ropa vieja pero a Norma le gusta la ropa _____ .

3 Answer the following questions about your life in complete sentences.

1. ¿Te gusta ir de compras?

_____

2. ¿Cuál es la tienda que más te gusta?

_____

3. ¿Qué ropa te gusta comprar?

_____

4. ¿Cuánto cuestan los pantalones?

_____

¡Avancemos! 1
Cuaderno: Práctica por niveles

Unidad 4, Lección 1
Vocabulario B **149**

UNIDAD 4 • Vocabulario B
Lección 1

Vocabulario C

¡AVANZA!	**Goal:** Talk about clothes.

1 Fill in the blank with the appropriate color word.

1. La banana es _____ .

2. Los jeans son _____ .

3. Mi tío es muy viejo. Tiene el cabello _____ .

4. A mí me gustan las manzanas _____ .

5. Cuando está muy oscuro, todo es de color _____ .

2 **¿Vamos de compras?** Write the answer to the following questions.

1. ¿Adónde te gusta ir de compras?

_____

2. ¿Con qué tipo de dinero tienes que pagar en Estados Unidos?

_____

3. ¿Con qué tipo de dinero tienes que pagar en Europa?

_____

4. ¿Por qué llevamos gorros y chaquetas en invierno?

_____

3 Write three sentences describing what clothes you like to wear from head to toe in spring. Make sure to include the colors of the items you describe and where you buy them.

_____

_____

_____

Gramática A *Stem-Changing Verbs: e→ie*

> **¡AVANZA!** **Goal:** Use stem-changing verbs to talk about shopping.

1 Underline the verb in parentheses that completes each sentence.

1. Jimena tiene suerte. Siempre compra la ropa que (prefieres / prefiere).

2. Yo no (entiendo / entiendes) qué quieres.

3. Santiago (pierden / pierde) su sombrero.

4. En el otoño Luis y Rosana (compramos / compran) la ropa de invierno.

5. La tienda de ropa (cierra / cierran) a las 8:00 p.m.

2 Complete the sentences using the verbs in parentheses.

1. Nosotros no _____ pantalones negros. (querer)

2. Paula _____ en qué cosas puede comprar para el cumpleaños de
   Juan. (pensar)

3. Alejandro y Noemí _____ bien las clases de matemáticas. (entender)

4. Irma, ¿ _____ (tú) ir a comprar una blusa roja? (querer)

5. Todas las mañanas, Jaime _____ su día contento. (empezar)

3 In a complete sentence, explain what you want to buy for a friend's birthday at your
favorite clothing store.

modelo: Yo quiero comprar unos pantalones amarillos y una camiseta azul para
el cumpleaños de Marisol.

_____

_____

_____

¡Avancemos! 1
Cuaderno: Práctica por niveles

Unidad 4, Lección 1
Gramática A **151**

UNIDAD 4 • Lección 1
Gramática A

Gramática B *Stem-Changing Verbs: e→ie*

> ¡AVANZA! **Goal:** Use stem-changing verbs to talk about shopping.

1 Lucía and her friends go shopping. Choose the verb that completes each sentence.

1. Lucía, ¿ _____ ir a comprar unos pantalones para tu cumpleaños?

    a. quieres   **b.** quiere   **c.** quiero   **d.** queremos

2. Sergio y Eduardo _____ que no necesitan un gorro en invierno.

    a. piensas   **b.** piensa   **c.** pienso   **d.** piensan

3. Ana y yo _____ las preguntas de la señora.

    a. entiendo   **b.** entiendes   **c.** entendemos   **d.** entiende

4. Cuando voy de compras con él, Juan siempre _____ el dinero.

    a. pierden   **b.** pierde   **c.** pierdes   **d.** perdemos

5. Javier y tú _____ temprano la tienda.

    a. cierro   **b.** cierras   **c.** cierra   **d.** cerráis

2 **¿Qué hacen?** Write complete sentences using the elements below.

1. entender el español / nosotras

_____

2. no querer sombreros amarillos / Ramón y Antonio

_____

3. preferir la primavera / vosotras

_____

4. ¿hacer / tú / qué / querer?

_____

3 Write two sentences describing what you wear in winter and why.

_____

_____

_____

_____

UNIDAD 4 • Gramática B
Lección 1

Unidad 4, Lección 1
Gramática B

152

¡Avancemos! 1
Cuaderno: Práctica por niveles

Gramática C *Stem-Changing Verbs: e→ie*

> **¡AVANZA!** **Goal:** Use stem-changing verbs to talk about shopping.

1 María and her friend Lucas like to shop. Complete the text below with the correct verb form.

Mi amigo Lucas y yo siempre **1.** _____ ir de compras.

Él compra ropa de invierno en verano. El señor de la tienda nunca

2. _____ por qué necesita una chaqueta en julio.

Muchas veces la tienda **3.** _____ y nosotros no

compramos nada.

| querer |
| cerrar |
| entender |

2 Complete the following sentences by conjugating the correct verb from the pair in parentheses.

1. Laura y Ana nunca _____ sus sombreros. (empezar / perder)

2. Camila y Julia _____ las camisas rojas. (cerrar / preferir)

3. En España, el invierno _____ en diciembre. (entender / empezar)

4. Nosotros no _____ a las personas que llevan pantalones cortos en

invierno. (entender / tener)

5. Pablo _____ su chaqueta cuando tiene frío. (pensar / cerrar)

3 Write three complete sentences about why you go to the mall. What do you want to buy when you go there? Use the following verbs: **querer**, **preferir** and **pensar**.

_____

_____

_____

_____

¡Avancemos! 1
Cuaderno: Práctica por niveles

Unidad 4, Lección 1
Gramática C   **153**

UNIDAD 4
Lección 1 • Gramática C

Gramática A   *Direct Object Pronouns*

Level 1, pp. 204–206

> **¡AVANZA!**   **Goal:** Use direct object pronouns to talk about clothes.

1 Everyone likes new clothes. Write the direct object pronoun for each sentence.

1. Me gusta esa blusa. Quiero comprar _____ .

2. Jorge tiene unos zapatos muy bonitos. Él _____ compra en la tienda.

3. Mi hermana prefiere un sombrero grande. No quiere perder _____ .

4. ¿Prefieres los pantalones negros? _____ compro para tu cumpleaños.

2 We all love shopping! Re-write the following sentences, replacing the direct object with the direct object pronouns.

1. Quiero la blusa verde.

_____

2. Prefieren los zapatos marrones.

_____

3. Las personas del centro comercial entienden a mis amigos y a mí.

_____

4. Queremos comprar la chaqueta.

_____

3 Write what the following people want or prefer. Replace the words in parentheses with a direct object pronoun.

modelo: (Una camisa azul) / yo / querer: **Yo la quiero**.

1. (Dos chaquetas negras) / las chicas / preferir:

_____

2. (Tres pantalones cortos) / Manuel / querer:

_____

3. (El sombrero grande) / nosotros / querer:

_____

Gramática B *Direct Object Pronouns*

¡AVANZA! **Goal:** Use direct object pronouns to talk about clothes.

---

1 Underline the correct direct object pronoun for each sentence.

1. Tengo una blusa azul. ¿(La / Lo) necesitas?

2. Tengo un sombrero blanco. ¿Vosotros (lo / te) queréis?

3. Tenemos que hablar. ¿Prefieres llamar(te / me) por teléfono?

4. Necesito una camiseta verde. La tienda (nos / la) vende.

5. Mi prima y yo tenemos muchos vestidos. Siempre (los / nos) compartimos.

2 Write a complete sentence using the elements below and replacing the words in parentheses with a direct object pronoun.

modelo: Mabel / hablar (yo) Mabel me habla.

1. Jorge y Ernesto / quieren cerrar (su tienda) temprano

_____

_____

2. Sonia y yo / nunca perder (el dinero) en la tienda

_____

3. yo / no entender (tú)

_____

4. tú / hablar del invierno en España (nosotros)

_____

3 Write complete sentences using a direct object pronoun.

modelo: ¿Necesitas una camisa para la fiesta? Sí, (No, no) la necesito para la fiesta.

1. ¿Necesitas unos calcetines para el invierno?

_____

2. ¿Necesitas las camisetas anaranjadas para la escuela?

_____

3. ¿Necesitas el vestido para la escuela?

Gramática C *Direct Object Pronouns*

> **¡AVANZA!** **Goal:** Use direct object pronouns to talk about clothes.

1 Mariela and Sebastián are shopping. Write the correct direct object pronoun.

Mariela: Hola, Sebastián. ¡Qué camisa más linda!, ¿ ____ compras?

Sebastián: Hola, Mariela. Sí, ____ compro y también los pantalones. ¿Te gustan?

Mariela: Sí, me gustan. ____ venden por cuarenta euros.

Sebastián: Yo prefiero el vestido negro.

Mariela: ¿Un vestido negro? Ya ____ tengo, pero quiero los pantalones.

Sebastián: Pero tienes que comprar ____ ahora. La tienda cierra en diez minutos. ¿Me entiendes?

Mariela: Sí, ____ entiendo. ¡Vamos!

2 **Vamos de compras**. Write the correct direct object pronoun.

1. Necesito ropa nueva. _____ compro hoy.

2. ¿Dónde están mis zapatos? Siempre _____ pierdo.

3. Tú no debes comprar el sombrero. Prefiero comprar_____ yo.

4. Las chaquetas son bonitas. _____ venden en el centro comercial.

5. Siempre _____ entiendo pero tú nunca me entiendes.

3 We all have new clothes. Write sentences using the elements below. Replace the direct objects with the correct direct object pronoun.

1. Aníbal / preferir (unas camisas de color rojo)

_____

2. Julieta y Emma / comprar (unos vestidos)

_____

3. Yo / entender (la clase de ciencias)

_____

4. Tú / tener que llamar (a nosotros) mañana

_____

_____

Unidad 4, Lección 1
Gramática C

156

¡Avancemos! 1
Cuaderno: Práctica por niveles

UNIDAD 4
Lección 1 • Gramática C

Integración: Hablar

Winter isn't over yet but many stores already have great sales on winter clothes. Carmen sees an ad in the newspaper and is somewhat interested. But then she listens to a radio commercial for the same store and decides to go right away to get a special offer.

Fuente 1 Leer

Read the newspaper ad from "Señor Invierno".

Señor Invierno

¡Es invierno! ¿Tienes toda la ropa que necesitas para no tener frío?
Tienes que ver cuántas cosas tenemos para la estación más fría del año.

¡Señor Invierno tiene de todo!

Chaquetas negras o marrones: $ 65
Calcetines de invierno, todos los colores: $ 5
Gorros muy divertidos, muchos colores: $ 12
Jeans azules o negros: $ 35

Estamos en el centro comercial «Las Estaciones».

Fuente 2 Escuchar   *CD 02 track 22*

Listen to the radio ad that Carmen listened to. Take notes.

_____

_____

_____

_____

Hablar

It is eight o'clock and Carmen is rushing to the store to take advantage of a special offer. What does she have to buy at "Señor Invierno" to get a free black blouse?

modelo: En la tienda de ropa, Carmen tiene que...

Integración: Escribir

Level 1, pp. 207–209
WB CD 2 track 23

Ramón sends an e-mail to the school principal to let him know what kind of clothing students prefer to wear during the summer. The principal is happy to know about students' concerns, so he decides to address them the next day in the morning through the school's loudspeakers.

Fuente 1 Leer

Read Ramón's e-mail to the school principal.

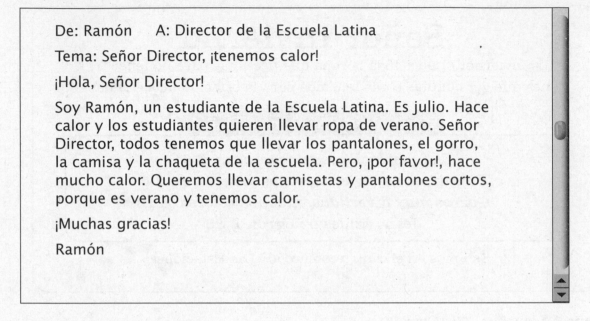

De: Ramón   A: Director de la Escuela Latina

Tema: Señor Director, ¡tenemos calor!

¡Hola, Señor Director!

Soy Ramón, un estudiante de la Escuela Latina. Es julio. Hace calor y los estudiantes quieren llevar ropa de verano. Señor Director, todos tenemos que llevar los pantalones, el gorro, la camisa y la chaqueta de la escuela. Pero, ¡por favor!, hace mucho calor. Queremos llevar camisetas y pantalones cortos, porque es verano y tenemos calor.

¡Muchas gracias!

Ramón

Fuente 2 Escuchar   *CD 02 track 24*

Listen to the principal talking to students. Take notes.

_____

_____

_____

_____

Escribir

What items do students have to wear now for the summer at Escuela Latina? Explain why.

modelo: Los estudiantes tienen que...Pero no tienen que...

_____

_____

_____

_____

_____

Escuchar A

> **¡AVANZA!** **Goal:** Listen to people talk about clothes.

1 Listen to the conversation between Fernanda and her mother, Carmen. Take notes. Then underline the word that completes each sentence below.

1. Los sombreros cuestan (quince euros / quince dólares).

2. Cuando empieza el verano, los chicos necesitan sombreros (grandes / nuevos).

3. El sombrero de Fernanda es (blanco / negro).

4. Carmen quiere un sombrero (rojo / blanco).

5. Fernanda prefiere comprar un sombrero (rojo / amarillo).

6. La tienda cierra (tarde / los martes).

2 Now listen to Bárbara. Then, complete the following sentences with the words in the box.

comprarla	ropa	chaquetas	la cierran

1. Bárbara tiene que llegar en cinco minutos a la tienda, porque _____ temprano.

2. Bárbara necesita _____ nueva de invierno.

3. Bárbara quiere comprar _____ , gorros y zapatos.

4. Bárbara quiere ropa de invierno. Ella prefiere _____ en otoño.

Escuchar B

| ¡AVANZA! | **Goal:** Listen to people talk about clothes. |

1 Listen to Agustina. Then, draw a line from the people on the left to what they do.

1. Alejandra, Beatriz y Agustina

2. Alejandra

3. Las amigas de Beatriz

4. Agustina

5. Beatriz

a. compra la ropa de invierno en otoño.

b. no entienden a Beatriz.

c. compra la ropa de invierno en invierno.

d. quieren comprar todo en la tienda.

e. va siempre al centro comercial.

2 Listen to Carina. Then, complete the sentences below:

1. _____ de la amiga de Carina quiere ir de compras.

2. Su amiga _____ que su hermano es un buen amigo.

3. Carina no quiere ir de compras en _____ porque tiene frío.

4. Carina prefiere _____ con ellos mañana.

Escuchar C

> **¡AVANZA!** **Goal:** Listen to people talk about clothes.

1 Listen to Emilio. Then, read each sentence and fill in the blanks with the correct season.

1. La familia de Emilio prefiere el _____ .

2. En _____ hacen menos cosas.

3. En _____ , montan en bicicleta y pasean.

4. La ropa de _____ es fea.

5. Los colores de _____ no son feos.

2 Listen to Alicia and take notes. Then answer the following questions with complete sentences:

1. ¿Qué hace Alicia?

_____

2. ¿Por qué trabajan mucho?

_____

3. ¿Qué venden cuando empieza una estación?

_____

4. ¿Por qué venden muchos sombreros ahora?

_____

5. ¿Cómo prefieren los sombreros los chicos?

_____

Leer A

> **¡AVANZA!** **Goal:** Read about the seasons.

Hola, soy Julieta. Tengo quince años y vivo en España. Llevo una chaqueta y un gorro porque tengo mucho frío. Ahora es invierno y en invierno nunca tengo calor. A mí me gusta más el verano. Hago más actividades en verano y la ropa de verano es muy bonita. Prefiero llevar vestidos de verano y pantalones cortos.

¿Quieres escribirme? ¡Quiero ser tu amiga!

Besos,

Julieta

¿Comprendiste?

Read Julieta's letter. Then, read each sentence and answer **cierto** *(true)* or **falso** *(false)*.

C F **1.** Julieta prefiere el verano.

C F **2.** Julieta tiene un gorro porque le gusta.

C F **3.** En invierno, Julieta no tiene calor.

C F **4.** Las chaquetas son para el verano.

C F **5.** La ropa de verano es más bonita.

¿Qué piensas?

¿Prefieres la ropa de invierno, o la ropa de verano? ¿Por qué?

_____

_____

_____

_____

Leer B

> ▶ ¡AVANZA! **Goal:** Read about the seasons.

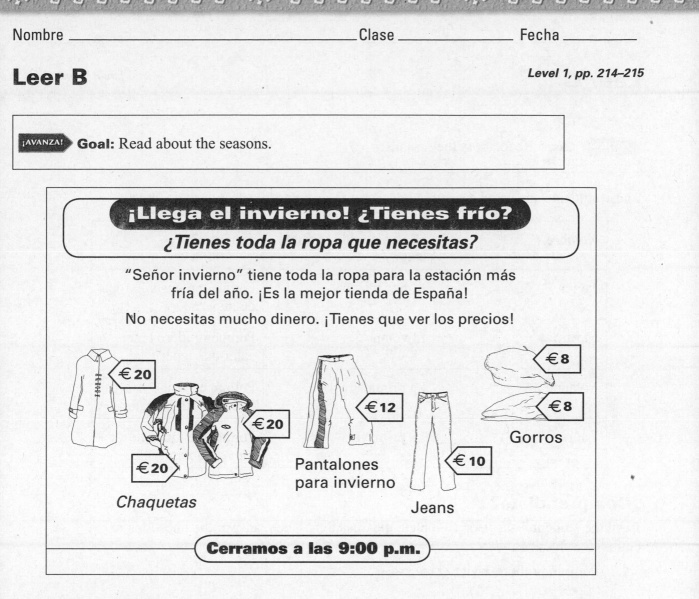

¡Llega el invierno! ¿Tienes frío?

¿Tienes toda la ropa que necesitas?

"Señor invierno" tiene toda la ropa para la estación más fría del año. ¡Es la mejor tienda de España!

No necesitas mucho dinero. ¡Tienes que ver los precios!

€ 20

€ 20

€ 20

Chaquetas

€ 12

Pantalones para invierno

€ 10

Jeans

€ 8

€ 8

Gorros

Cerramos a las 9:00 p.m.

¿Comprendiste?

Read the store's ad. Then, answer the following questions in complete sentences:

1. ¿Qué ropa venden en la tienda?

_____

2. ¿Cuánto cuestan las chaquetas?

_____

3. ¿Por qué la tienda no tiene pantalones cortos?

_____

¿Qué piensas?

¿Prefieres ir de compras con un amigo? ¿Por qué?

_____

_____

Leer C

> ¡AVANZA! **Goal:** Read about the seasons.

These students answered a survey about what their favorite season is and why.

Nombre	¿Qué estación te gusta más?	¿Por qué?
Javier	El invierno	Porque me gusta la ropa de invierno.
Martín	El verano	Porque prefiero tener calor que tener frío.
Yolanda	La primavera	Porque no tengo frío y no hace mucho calor.
Laura	La primavera	Porque me gusta llevar mi vestido amarillo.

¿Comprendiste?

Read the students' answers. Complete the questions. Then, answer the questions in complete sentences.

1. ¿Por qué prefiere Javier el invierno?

_____

2. ¿A Martín le gusta tener frío?

_____

3. ¿Qué piensan Laura y Yolanda?

_____

4. ¿Cuándo lleva Laura su vestido amarillo?

_____

¿Qué piensas?

¿Qué estación te gusta más? ¿Por qué?

_____

_____

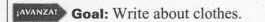

Escribir A

┌───┐
│ **¡AVANZA!** **Goal:** Write about clothes.   │
└───┘

Step 1

Look at the drawings. Then make a list of which items you prefer to wear in the winter.

1.   2.   3.   4.

_____

_____

_____

Step 2

Use the list above to write two sentences about the kinds of clothes you like to wear during the summer and during the winter.

_____

_____

_____

Step 3

Evaluate your writing using the information in the table below.

Writing Criteria	Excellent	Good	Needs Work
Content	You included two sentences to tell about the kinds of clothes you like to wear.	You included two sentences to tell about the kinds of clothes you like to wear.	You included one sentence to tell about the kinds of clothes you like to wear.
Communication	Most of your response is clear.	Some of your response is clear.	Your message is not very clear.
Accuracy	You make few mistakes in grammar and vocabulary.	You make some mistakes in grammar and vocabulary.	You make many mistakes in grammar and vocabulary.

¡Avancemos! 1
Cuaderno: Práctica por niveles

Unidad 4, Lección 1
Escribir A   **165**

UNIDAD 4
Lección 1 • Escribir A

Nombre _____ Clase _____ Fecha _____

Escribir B

> ¡AVANZA! **Goal:** Write about clothes.

Step 1

Write a list of which clothes above you and your friends prefer wearing.

En invierno, yo

_____

_____

En verano, mis amigos

_____

_____

Step 2

In four complete sentences, say what season it is and describe what you are wearing today.

_____

_____

Step 3

Evaluate your writing using the information in the table below.

Writing Criteria	Excellent	Good	Needs Work
Content	You have included four sentences about the clothes you are wearing.	You have included two to three sentences about the clothes you are wearing.	You have included one or fewer sentences about the clothes you are wearing.
Communication	Most of your sentences are clear.	Some of your sentences are clear.	Your sentences are not very clear.
Accuracy	Your sentences have few mistakes in grammar and vocabulary.	Your sentences have some mistakes in grammar and vocabulary.	Your sentences have many mistakes in grammar and vocabulary.

UNIDAD 4
Lección 1

Escribir B

Unidad 4, Lección 1
Escribir B

166

¡Avancemos! 1
Cuaderno: Práctica por niveles

Escribir C

> **¡AVANZA!** **Goal:** Write about clothes.

Step 1

¿Qué ropa quieres comprar? Make a list of four items of clothing you want to buy.

_____

_____

Step 2

Write complete sentences about the four items above and about how much you think each item you want to buy costs.

_____

_____

_____

_____

Step 3

Evaluate your writing using the information in the table below.

Writing Criteria	Excellent	Good	Needs Work
Content	You have included five sentences to talk about the clothes you want to buy.	You have included three to four sentences to talk about the clothes you want to buy.	You have You have included two sentences to talk about the clothes you want to buy.
Communication	Most of your response is clear.	Some of your response is clear.	Your message is not very clear.
Accuracy	Your response has few mistakes in grammar and vocabulary.	Your response has some mistakes in grammar and vocabulary.	Your response has many mistakes in grammar and vocabulary.

¡Avancemos! 1
Cuaderno: Práctica por niveles

UNIDAD 4
Lección 1 • Escribir C

Unidad 4, Lección 1
Escribir C **167**

Cultura A

> **¡AVANZA!** **Goal:** Review cultural information about Spain.

1 **Spanish culture** Read the following sentences about Spain and answer *true* or *false*.

T   F   **1.** Spain is a country in Europe.

T   F   **2.** The capital of Spain is Morelos.

T   F   **3.** Most people in Spain shop at large shopping malls.

T   F   **4.** **Paella** is a typical dish of Spain.

T   F   **5.** Miguel Cervantes de Saavedra was a famous Spanish writer.

2 **About Spain** Complete the following sentences with one of the multiple-choice words or phrases.

1. The currency used in Spain is the ____

   a. euro   **b.** dollar   **c.** peso

2. In Spain, many young people dress for **sevillanas** during the **Feria de** ____

   a. **Junio**   **b.** **Abril**   **c.** **Mayo**

3. Surrealist art is often inspired by ____

   a. history   **b.** dreams   **c.** nature

3 **Compare climates** Fill out the chart to compare the months of February and July in Chile, Spain, and in your state. Then, briefly describe the climate in these places and explain how they are similar and different.

	February	July
Spain		
Chile		
My state		

_____

_____

_____

_____

_____

Cultura B

> **¡AVANZA!** **Goal:** Review cultural information about Spain.

1 **In Spain** Complete the following sentences about Spanish culture.

1. The climate in Spain in July is often _____ .

2. The capital of Spain is _____ .

3. One of the favorite sports of Spaniards is _____ .

4. A famous Spanish artist who painted Don Quijote and Sancho Panza was

   _____ .

5. Aside from tortilla española and paella, _____ is another typical

   Spanish food.

6. The traditional costume of Seville is called **el traje de** _____ .

2 **Artists and writers** Draw lines to match the following artists or writers with their works.

Don Quijote novel   Salvador Dalí

«Invierno tardío» poem   Miguel Cervantes de Saavedra

La Persistencia de la   Antonio Colinas
Memoria painting

3 **Surrealism** Describe what surrealist art is like using the painting *La persistencia de la memoria* on page 203 of your book as an example. Do you like this style of art? Why or why not?

_____

_____

_____

_____

_____

_____

_____

_____

_____

¡Avancemos! 1
Cuaderno: Práctica por niveles

Unidad 4, Lección 1
Cultura B **169**

UNIDAD 4
Lección 1 • Cultura B

Cultura C

Level 1, pp. 214–215

> ¡AVANZA! **Goal:** Review cultural information about Spain.

1 **Spain** Complete the following sentences about Spain.

1. Don Quijote and Sancho Panza are characters in a novel by _____ .

2. The official languages of Spain are _____ , _____ , _____ and _____ .

3. *La persistencia de memoria* is a famous painting by _____ .

4. The capital of Spain is _____ .

5. Paella is a typical _____ of Spain.

6. Girls from Seville wear **el traje de sevillana** during the _____ celebration.

2 **Spanish culture** Answer the following questions with complete sentences.

1. What is the climate like in Spain in the month of July? _____

_____

2. In the games against Barcelona FC, which chant do the Real Madrid fans sing?

_____

_____

3. What are some characteristics of surrealist art?

_____

_____

3 **Spanish poetry** Describe the imagery in Antonio Colinas' poem *Invierno tardío* on page 211. What is the message of this poem?

_____

_____

_____

_____

Unidad 4, Lección 1
Cultura C

170

¡Avancemos! 1
Cuaderno: Práctica por niveles

UNIDAD 4
Lección 1

Cultura C

Vocabulario A

¡AVANZA! **Goal:** Describe food, places and events in town.

1 You're going out with friends. Place the related words from the box in the columns.

el cine   **el restaurante**

1. _____   4. _____

2. _____   5. _____

3. _____   6. _____

la película
el camarero
la ventanilla
las entradas
el plato principal

2 This is what people are eating in a restaurant. Write the name of the food you see.

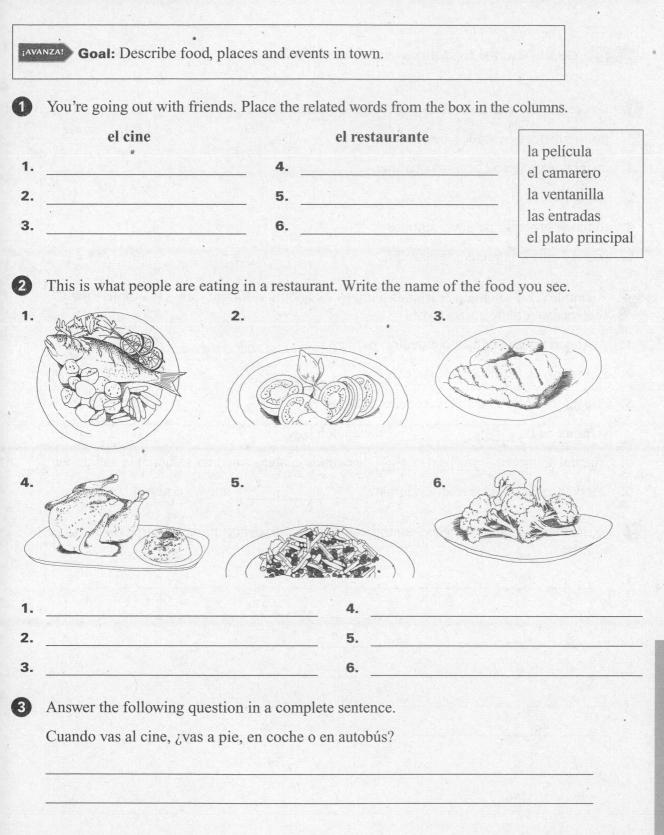

1. _____   4. _____

2. _____   5. _____

3. _____   6. _____

3 Answer the following question in a complete sentence.

Cuando vas al cine, ¿vas a pie, en coche o en autobús?

_____

_____

Vocabulario B

> ┃AVANZA!┃ **Goal:** Describe food, places and events in town.

1 Underline the word that does not belong in each series.

1. pollo / bistec / pescado / ensalada

2. cuenta / camarero / propina / parque

3. teatro / cine / frijoles / concierto

4. tomate / brócoli / patatas / autobús

5. pastel / cine / entradas / ventanilla

2 Alejandro and Manuel are friends but they like doing different things. Complete the sentences with the correct word.

1. A Alejandro no le gusta ir al teatro; prefiere ir al _____ a ver películas.

2. El brócoli es verdura y el bistec es _____ .

3. Alejandro no va al centro en coche. Siempre va a _____ , pero Manuel

siempre va en _____ o en autobús.

4. Manuel siempre _____ la comida cuando van a un restaurante a almorzar.

5. Alejandro piensa que ir al restaurante _____ mucho dinero.

3 Write two complete sentences stating the means of transportation your friends use to get to school.

1. _____

_____

_____

2. _____

_____

_____

UNIDAD 4 • Vocabulario B
Lección 2

Unidad 4, Lección 2
Vocabulario B

172

¡Avancemos! 1
Cuaderno: Práctica por niveles

Vocabulario C

Level 1, pp. 218–222
WB CD 2 tracks 35–36

> **¡AVANZA!** **Goal:** Describe food, places and events in town.

1 Úrsula and Andrés go out every weekend. Circle the word that completes the following sentences.

1. A Úrsula le gusta ver una película en el (cine / parque / café).

2. A Andrés le gusta ir a un (autobús / coche / concierto) para escuchar música rock.

3. Úrsula y Andrés compran (pollo / entradas / frijoles) para el cine.

4. Úrsula y Andrés van a comer a un (teatro / ventanilla / restaurante).

2 Answer the questions with complete sentences, using the words from the vocabulary.

1. ¿Adónde vas a comer cuando tienes hambre?

_____

2. ¿Qué necesitas del camarero para poder pagar?

_____

3. ¿Qué tienes que leer para pedir la comida?

_____

4. ¿Qué postre preparan para un cumpleaños?

_____

5. ¿Qué recibe el camarero cuando hace un buen trabajo?

_____

3 Write four sentences about what you do when you go to a restaurant. Remember to mention how you go, what you do and what you order.

_____

_____

_____

_____

Gramática A *Stem-Changing Verbs: o → ue*

Level 1, pp. 223–227

> 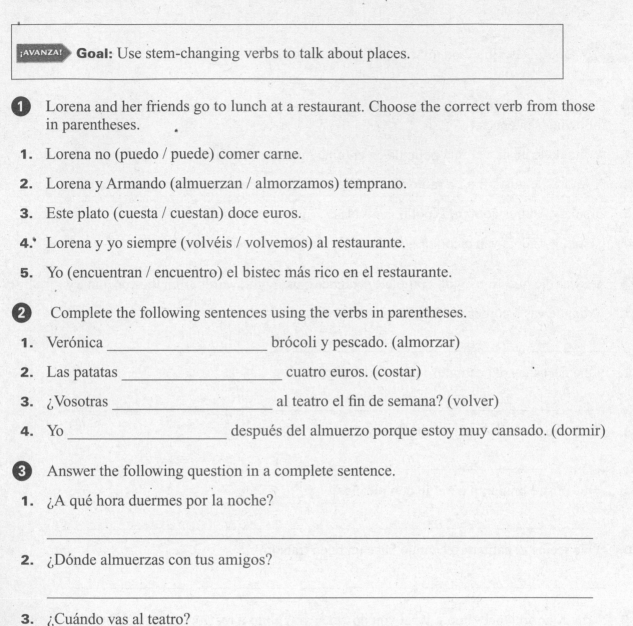 **¡AVANZA!** **Goal:** Use stem-changing verbs to talk about places.

1 Lorena and her friends go to lunch at a restaurant. Choose the correct verb from those in parentheses.

1. Lorena no (puedo / puede) comer carne.

2. Lorena y Armando (almuerzan / almorzamos) temprano.

3. Este plato (cuesta / cuestan) doce euros.

4. Lorena y yo siempre (volvéis / volvemos) al restaurante.

5. Yo (encuentran / encuentro) el bistec más rico en el restaurante.

2 Complete the following sentences using the verbs in parentheses.

1. Verónica _____ brócoli y pescado. (almorzar)

2. Las patatas _____ cuatro euros. (costar)

3. ¿Vosotras _____ al teatro el fin de semana? (volver)

4. Yo _____ después del almuerzo porque estoy muy cansado. (dormir)

3 Answer the following question in a complete sentence.

1. ¿A qué hora duermes por la noche?

_____

2. ¿Dónde almuerzas con tus amigos?

_____

3. ¿Cuándo vas al teatro?

_____

UNIDAD 4 • Gramática A
Lección 2

174

Unidad 4, Lección 2
Gramática A

¡Avancemos! 1
Cuaderno: Práctica por niveles

Gramática B *Stem-Changing Verbs: o → ue*

Level 1, pp. 223–227

> **¡AVANZA!** **Goal:** Use stem-changing verbs to talk about places.

1 Julián and his friends have fun around town. Choose the correct verb to complete each sentence.

1. Julián _____ muy contento del concierto.

   a. vuelves   **b.** vuelve   **c.** vuelvo   **d.** volvemos

2. Claudia y Tomás _____ en el restaurante de la calle Madrid.

   a. almorzamos   **b.** almorzáis   **c.** almuerzan   **d.** almuerza

3. Pedro, Lucas y yo _____ ir al café a las 3:00 p.m.

   a. puede   **b.** pueden   **c.** puedes   **d.** podemos

4. Las entradas del cine _____ cinco euros.

   a. cuesta   **b.** cuestas   **c.** cuesto   **d.** cuestan

5. ¿Tú _____ a Laura en el parque?

   a. encuentras   **b.** encuentran   **c.** encuentra   **d.** encontráis

2 Use the information from the table to write three sentences about what these people do.

Luis	volver	a la 1:30 p.m.
Raúl y Graciela	almorzar	la calle del cine
Cecilia y yo	encontrar	el restaurante

1. _____

2. _____

3. _____

3 Write a complete sentence to describe what you can have for lunch at your favorite restaurant.

_____

_____

_____

Gramática C *Stem-Changing Verbs: o → ue*

> ¡AVANZA! **Goal:** Use stem-changing verbs to talk about places.

1 Armando always has lunch at the restaurant on calle Infanta. Complete the sentences below using the verbs in parentheses:

1. Armando _____ carne o pollo. (almorzar)

2. Armando y Noemí _____ ir a pie al restaurante. (poder)

3. Armando y yo _____ a casa en autobús. (volver)

4. Nosotros _____ un restaurante para almorzar. (encontrar)

5. El almuerzo _____ quince euros. (costar)

2 Your friends go to many places. Write sentences about your friends using the verbs provided.

1. (almuerzan)

   _____

2. (dormís)

   _____

3. (encuentro)

   _____

4. (podemos)

   _____

5. (vuelves)

   _____

3 Write three sentences about your weekend. Use the verbs **poder**, **dormir** and **almorzar**.

   _____

   _____

   _____

   _____

Gramática A *Stem-Changing Verbs: e → i*

> ¡AVANZA! **Goal:** Use stem-changing verbs to talk about what you do.

1 **¡Vamos a almorzar!** Underline the correct verb to complete the dialogue between Jimena and Lucas.

1. Jimena: ¿Tú (pide / pides) el menú?

2. Lucas: Lo tengo aquí. Yo (piden / pido) bistec como siempre.

3. Jimena: ¿El camarero (sirve / sirven) nuestra mesa?

4. Lucas: No, los camareros (sirven / servimos) la otra mesa.

5. Jimena: ¿Nosotros ya (pedís / pedimos) la comida?

2 Everybody loves going to the restaurant on **calle Córdoba**! Complete the sentences with the correct form of the verbs given.

1. Cecilia _____ unas patatas. (pedir)

2. Javier y yo _____ pollo. (pedir)

3. ¿Qué _____ tú? (pedir)

4. El camarero _____ muchos platos durante el día. (servir)

5. Los camareros del restaurante _____ muy bien la comida. (servir)

3 Answer the following questions about yourself in a complete sentence:

1. ¿Qué pides muchas veces como plato principal?

_____

2. ¿Qué piden tus amigos como plato principal?

_____

3. ¿Dónde almuerzas?

_____

¡Avancemos! 1
Cuaderno: Práctica por niveles

Unidad 4, Lección 2
Gramática A **177**

UNIDAD 4 • Gramática A
Lección 2

Gramática B *Stem-Changing Verbs: e → i*

Level 1, pp. 228–230

> **¡AVANZA!** **Goal:** Use stem-changing verbs to talk about what you do.

1 Today is Juan's birthday. Choose the verb that completes each sentence.

1. Juan ____ pollo y arroz.

   a. pido   **b.** pides   **c.** piden   **d.** pide

2. ¿Tú ____ bistec y verduras?

   a. pides   **b.** piden   **c.** pedimos   **d.** pido

3. Los camareros ____ nuestra comida.

   a. sirvo   **b.** sirve   **c.** sirven   **d.** servimos

2 Juan and Norma go out to eat. Tell what they order by using the words in parentheses and then tell what the waiter serves them by using the words in the box.

tomate	pastel	brócoli	bistec

modelo: Norma (carne): Norma pide carne y el camarero sirve un bistec.

1. Juan (verduras) _____

2. Norma y Juan (ensalada) _____

_____

3. Norma (postre) _____

3 Answer the following questions in a complete sentence.

1. ¿Qué pides siempre para almorzar?

_____

2. ¿Qué pides cuando no hay carne?

_____

3. ¿Qué piden tus padres para almorzar?

_____

UNIDAD 4 • Gramática B
Lección 2

Unidad 4, Lección 2
Gramática B

178

¡Avancemos! 1
Cuaderno: Práctica por niveles

Gramática C   Stem-Changing Verbs: e → i

> **¡AVANZA!**   **Goal:** Use stem-changing verbs to talk about what you do.

1 One group of friends always goes out to eat on the weekend. Complete the dialog using the verbs **pedir** and **servir**.

Roberto: Yo pido un bistec con patatas. ¿Qué _____ tú?

Natalia: Yo _____ pollo con verduras.

Roberto: El camarero _____ un pollo muy rico.

Natalia: ¡Roberto! Hoy ellos no _____ bistec. ¿Pides otra cosa?

Roberto: Bueno, nosotros _____ pollo.

2 Some friends are at a restaurant for lunch. However, the waiter mixes up their orders. Write what each person orders and what the waiter serves in complete sentences.

modelo: bistec (Raúl) / pollo: Raúl pide bistec pero el camarero sirve pollo.

1. pescado (Irma y Raúl) / ensalada:

_____

2. brócoli (Irma y yo) / tomate:

_____

3. arroz (Raúl y tú) / patatas:

_____

4. pescado (Yo)/ verduras:

_____

3 You are having friends over for lunch. Write three sentences about what you serve each person.

1. _____

2. _____

3. _____

Integración: Hablar

Level 1, pp. 231–233
WB CD 2 track 31

Gabriela, who lives in Madrid, loves to go to the movies. She is looking for movie ads in the city's online newspaper. An ad for the movie *¿Dónde está mi hijo?* catches her eye, but she wants to know more about it, so she listens to the movie review on a radio show. Unfortunately, they end up giving away the entire plot.

Fuente 1 Leer

Read the movie ad in an online newspaper.

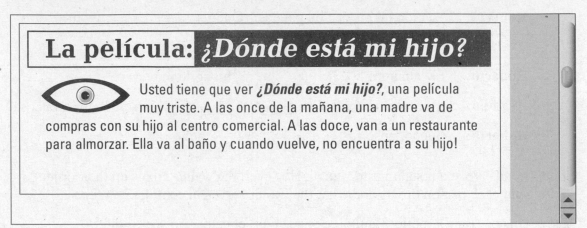

La película: *¿Dónde está mi hijo?*

Usted tiene que ver *¿Dónde está mi hijo?*, una película muy triste. A las once de la mañana, una madre va de compras con su hijo al centro comercial. A las doce, van a un restaurante para almorzar. Ella va al baño y cuando vuelve, no encuentra a su hijo!

Fuente 2 Escuchar   *CD 02 track 32*

Listen to a review of the movie on a radio program. Take notes.

_____

_____

_____

_____

Hablar

What is the sequence of events in the movie *¿Dónde está mi hijo?* Remember to include information from both the newspaper ad and the review in the radio show.

modelo: En la película, una madre va...Pero quince años...

Integración: Escribir

Restaurante de la Abuela has an ad in a newspaper. They claim that their food tastes like traditional homemade Spanish food. Ramiro reads the ad and decides to leave a message for his friend Liliana. He wants to meet her for lunch at the restaurant. Ramiro knows what Liliana likes to eat, so he lets her know his suggestions.

Fuente 1 Leer

Read the ad for "Restaurante de la Abuela"...

Restaurante de la Abuela
RESTAURANTE PARA TODA LA FAMILIA

♡

¿Puedes pensar en el mejor lugar para comer? La comida del Restaurante de la Abuela es como la comida que comes en casa.

Aquí encuentras el menú más rico de toda la ciudad: platos principales de carne, pollo y pescado; verduras, como brócoli y patatas; arroz español; ensaladas de tomate muy ricas. Cuando vienes una vez, ¡vuelves siempre!

Estamos en la Calle Valladolid, número trescientos.

Fuente 2 Escuchar   *CD 02 track 34*

Listen to Ramiro's voicemail to Liliana. Take notes.

_____

_____

_____

_____

Escribir

Explain what Liliana can eat at the restaurant.

modelo: Liliana no come..., pero en el Restaurante de la Abuela...

_____

_____

_____

_____

_____

_____

Escuchar A

> **¡AVANZA!** **Goal:** Listen to people talking about doing things around town.

1 Listen to Norberto. Then, read each statement and answer **cierto** *(true)* or **falso** *(false)*.

C　F　**1.** Norberto compra las entradas.

C　F　**2.** Las entradas cuestan diez euros.

C　F　**3.** Mariela compra su entrada.

C　F　**4.** Norberto llega dos horas antes al cine.

C　F　**5.** Norberto va a estar en la puerta del cine a las dos.

2 Listen to Mariela. Then answer the following questions:

1. ¿A qué hora tiene que estar Mariela en el cine? _____

_____

2. ¿Por qué Mariela no va a pie al cine? _____

_____

3. ¿Cuándo llega el autobús? _____

_____

Unidad 4, Lección 2
Escuchar A

182

¡Avancemos! 1
Cuaderno: Práctica por niveles

UNIDAD 4 • Escuchar A
Lección 2

Escuchar B

¡AVANZA! **Goal:** Listen to people talking about doing things around town.

1 Listen to Carmen and take notes. Then, draw a line from each person to his or her order.

1. Julio   **a.** pescado y verduras

2. Andrés   **b.** ensalada

3. Norma   **c.** bistec y patatas

4. Carmen   **d.** postre

5. Todos   **e.** pollo y arroz

2 Listen to the waiter and take notes. Then answer the following questions in complete sentences.

1. ¿Qué día van más personas al restaurante?

   _____

   _____

2. ¿Por qué vuelven las personas?

   _____

   _____

3. ¿Qué encuentra el camarero en la mesa con la cuenta?

   _____

   _____

Escuchar C

> **¡AVANZA!** **Goal:** Listen to people talking about doing things around town.

1 Listen to Francisco and take notes. Then, complete the sentences below:

1. Francisco y sus amigos tienen hoy _____ de música.

2. Van al _____ para el concierto.

3. El concierto empieza a _____ .

4. _____ cuesta dos euros.

5. No piden mucho _____ por las entradas.

2 Listen to Olga and Nicolás. Then answer the questions below in complete sentences:

1. ¿Nicolás puede ir al teatro a las dos?

_____

_____

2. ¿Qué hay en el teatro? ¿A qué hora?

_____

_____

3. ¿Por qué Olga quiere ir al centro con Nicolás a las dos?

_____

_____

4. ¿Por qué Nicolás vuelve temprano?

_____

_____

5. ¿Cuánto cuesta la entrada del concierto?

_____

_____

Leer A

> ¡AVANZA! **Goal:** Read about food and places.

Manuel and Antonia go to the movies every Thursday. They see the following sign on the door.

Cine Gran Ilusión

Hoy presentamos la película "¡Adiós a mi gran amor!"

La entrada cuesta cinco euros y puedes comprarla en la ventanilla de 10:00 a.m. a 1:00 p.m.

Horario de película

2:00 p.m.

4:00 p.m.

6:00 p.m.

8:00 p.m.

El restaurante Estrellas, dentro del cine, es muy bueno.

¿Comprendiste?

Read the movie theater's sign and then complete the following sentences:

1. Manuel y Antonia pagan _____ por sus entradas de cine.

2. Manuel y Antonia pueden comer en _____ del cine.

3. Manuel y Antonia compran las entradas en _____ .

4. "¡Adiós a mi gran amor!" es el nombre de _____ .

¿Qué piensas?

¿A qué hora puedes ir al cine de tu ciudad?

_____

_____

_____

_____

Leer B

> **¡AVANZA!** **Goal:** Read about food and places.

Julia wants to eat lunch. She reads the following menu.

Ⓜ e n ú

Plato principal

Bistec con patatas............quince euros

Pollo con arroz..................once euros

Pescado con brócoli.........diez euros

Plato del día

Verduras.......................................nueve euros

Carne con ensalada de tomate.....doce euros

¿Comprendiste?

Read the menu. Then, answer the following questions in complete sentences:

1. Julia lleva diez euros, ¿qué platos puede pedir?

_____

2. ¿Por qué?

_____

3. ¿Qué platos de carne sirven en el restaurante?

_____

4. ¿Qué sirven de postre?

_____

¿Qué piensas?

¿Qué te gusta pedir en tu restaurante favorito? ¿Por qué?

_____

_____

_____

UNIDAD 4 Lección 2 Leer B

Unidad 4, Lección 2
Leer B

186

¡Avancemos! 1
Cuaderno: Práctica por niveles

Leer C

> **¡AVANZA!** **Goal:** Read about food and places.

María writes a letter to a friend in another city. Read María's letter and answer the questions.

> *Hola Norma:*
>
> *Quiero invitarte a mi casa. Mis amigos y yo salimos mucho. Todos los sábados, vamos a un concierto de música rock y los domingos vamos al cine. Todos los jueves almorzamos en un restaurante pequeño pero muy bueno. Los viernes vamos al teatro. Los lunes vamos al parque por las tardes. De allí, vamos a un café en el centro comercial y hablamos.*
>
> *¿Puedes venir?*
>
> *Besos,*
>
> *María.*

¿Comprendiste?

Read Maria's letter. Then, write the things that Maria and her friends do on the following days:

1. lunes: _____
2. jueves: _____
3. viernes: _____
4. sábados: _____
5. domingos: _____

¿Qué piensas?

1. ¿Haces las actividades que hacen María y sus amigos?

_____

_____

2. ¿Te gusta almorzar con tus amigos? ¿Qué comen? ¿Dónde?

_____

_____

Escribir A

¡AVANZA! **Goal:** Write about foods and places.

Step 1

Make a list of four things you and your friends like doing. You can use words from the box.

| cine | teatro | restaurante | concierto | parque |

_____

_____

_____

_____

Step 2

Write two complete sentences to say where you and your friends like to go and what you do there. Use your list.

1. _____

_____

2. _____

_____

Step 3

Evaluate your writing using the information in the table below.

Writing Criteria	Excellent	Good	Needs Work
Content	Your sentences include many details and new vocabulary.	Your sentences include some details and new vocabulary.	Your sentences include little information or new vocabulary.
Communication	Most of your sentences are clear.	Some of your sentences are clear.	Your sentences are not very clear.
Accuracy	Your sentences have few mistakes in grammar and vocabulary.	Your sentences have some mistakes in grammar and vocabulary.	Your sentences have many mistakes in grammar and vocabulary.

UNIDAD 4 • Escribir A
Lección 2

188
Escribir A

Unidad 4, Lección 2
Escribir A

¡Avancemos! 1
Cuaderno: Práctica por niveles

Escribir B

> **¡AVANZA!** **Goal:** Write about foods and places.

Step 1

Rearrange the letters of the following words and you will find a new word using the circled letters.

1. recaroma: ____ ____ ____ ____ ____ ____ ____

2. tecbis: ____ ____ ____ ____ ____ ____

3. laendasa: ____ ____ ____ ____ ____ ____ ____ ____

4. teresrantau: ____ ____ ____ ____ ____ ____ ____ ____ ____ ____ ____

   Hidden word: _____

Step 2

Use the words from **Step 1** to write three complete sentences about what you and your family do at a restaurant.

1. _____

   _____

2. _____

   _____

3. _____

   _____

Step 3

Evaluate your writing using the information in the table below.

Writing Criteria	Excellent	Good	Needs Work
Content	Your sentences include many details and new vocabulary.	Your sentences include some details and new vocabulary.	Your sentences include little information or new vocabulary.
Communication	Most of your sentences are clear.	Some of your sentences are clear.	Your sentences are not very clear.
Accuracy	Your sentences have few mistakes in grammar and vocabulary.	Your sentences have some mistakes in grammar and vocabulary.	Your sentences have many mistakes in grammar and vocabulary.

¡Avancemos! 1
Cuaderno: Práctica por niveles

Unidad 4, Lección 2
Escribir B **189**

UNIDAD 4
Lección 2 • Escribir B

Escribir C

¡AVANZA!	**Goal:** Write about foods and places.

Step 1

¿Qué te gusta pedir en un restaurante? Write four complete sentences about two things you like ordering at a restaurant and two things you don't like ordering.

1. _____

2. _____

3. _____

4. _____

Step 2

Write an e-mail to your friend, describing what you always order at your favorite restaurant.

_____

_____

_____

_____

_____

_____

_____

_____

_____

Step 3

Evaluate your writing using the information in the table below.

Writing Criteria	Excellent	Good	Needs Work
Content	Your email includes many details and new vocabulary.	Your email includes some details and new vocabulary.	Your email includes little information or new vocabulary.
Communication	Most of your email is clear.	Some of your email is clear.	Your email is not very clear.
Accuracy	Your email has few mistakes in grammar and vocabulary.	Your email has some mistakes in grammar and vocabulary.	Your email has many mistakes in grammar and vocabulary.

Cultura A

> ¡AVANZA! **Goal:** Review cultural information about Spain.

1 **Spain and Guatemala** Complete the following sentences with one of the multiple choice words or phrases.

1. El Rastro is a famous _____ in Madrid.

    a. restaurant   **b.** park   **c.** flea market

2. At the market in Chichicastenango, Guatemala, you can buy handicrafts from the _____ culture.

    a. Maya-Quiché   **b.** Taino   **c.** Aztec

3. Three typical Spanish foods are _____

    a. **chile con carne,**   **b.** **gazpacho, paella,**   **c.** **pasteles, arroz con**
       burritos, and fajitas   **and tortilla**   **gandules, and pernil**

2 **Sites in Spain and Chile** There are many interesting places in Spain and Chile. Match the places with the corresponding description.

La Casa del Campo   mall in Santiago, Chile

El Corte Inglés   plaza in Madrid with a stamp market on Sundays

La Plaza de Armas   plaza in Santiago with concerts on Sundays

La Plaza Mayor   Spanish department store

Alto Las Condes   park in Madrid with a zoo and swimming pool

3 *Las meninas* Both Diego Velázquez and Salvador Dalí created paintings titled *Las meninas*. Describe and compare both paintings on page 230, and tell how they are similar and different.

_____

_____

_____

_____

_____

_____

Cultura B

> **¡AVANZA!** **Goal:** Review cultural information about Spain.

1 **Spain** Read the following sentences about Spain and circle *true* or *false*.

T   F   **1.** The princesses of the Spanish royal family are called **infantas.**

T   F   **2.** One of the oldest flea markets in Madrid is El Rastro.

T   F   **3.** The official painter of King Felipe IV of Spain was Salvador Dalí.

T   F   **4.** In Spain, the only language spoken is Spanish.

T   F   **5.** El Corte Inglés is a Spanish department store.

2 **Things to do in Spain and Chile** In Madrid, Spain, and Santiago, Chile, there are many places to visit. Tell what you can do in the following places.

Places	Things to do
La Casa del Campo	
El Rastro	
La Plaza Mayor	
Plaza de Armas	
El Cerro San Cristóbal	

3 **Visiting Madrid** In Madrid, there are many places to take a walk or visit on the weekend. Would you like to visit some? Write a short paragraph about which places in Madrid you would like to visit and why.

_____

_____

_____

_____

_____

_____

_____

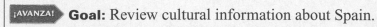

Nombre _____ Clase _____ Fecha _____

Cultura C

> **¡AVANZA!** **Goal:** Review cultural information about Spain.

1 **Spain** Choose the correct word to complete the following sentences.

1. (Diego Velázquez / Pablo Picasso) was the official painter of King Felipe IV of Spain.

2. (Pinchos / gazpacho) is/are a typical food in Spain.

3. In the Plaza (Mayor / Menor) of Madrid there is a stamp market on Sundays.

4. The (princesses / queens) of the Spanish royal family are called **infantas**.

2 **Spanish culture** Answer these questions using complete sentences.

1. Who are some of the people in the painting *Las Meninas* by the Spanish painter Diego Velázquez?

_____

_____

2. What can people buy when they visit El Rastro in Madrid?

_____

_____

3. Which languages are spoken in Spain?

_____

_____

3 **At the market** Describe both El Rastro and the Chichicastenango markets. What would you buy in each place? Which market would you prefer to visit and why?

_____

_____

_____

_____

_____

_____

_____

_____

¡Avancemos! 1
Cuaderno: Práctica por niveles

Unidad 4, Lección 2
Cultura C   **193**

UNIDAD 4
Lección 2   •   Cultura C

Level 1, pp. 240–241

Comparación cultural: ¿Adónde vamos el sábado?

Lectura y escritura

After reading the paragraphs about what Anita, Rodrigo, and Armando do for fun on Saturdays, write a paragraph about what you like to do on Saturdays. Use the information on your activity chart to write sentences, and then write a paragraph that describes what you do for fun on Saturdays.

Step 1

Complete the activity chart describing as many details as possible about the activities you do for fun on Saturdays.

Categoría	Detalles
lugares	
ropa	
actividades	

Step 2

Now take the details from the activity chart and write a sentence for each topic on the chart.

_____

_____

_____

_____

_____

_____

_____

_____

_____

UNIDAD 4 • Comparación
Lección 2   cultural

194

Unidad 4
Comparación cultural: ¿Adónde vamos el sábado?

¡Avancemos! 1
Cuaderno: Práctica por niveles

Level 1, pp. 240–241

Comparación cultural: ¿Adónde vamos el sábado?
Lectura y escritura (continued)

Step 3

Now write your paragraph using the sentences you wrote as a guide. Include an introduction sentence and use the verbs **ir a** + **infinitive** and **querer** + **infinitive** to write about what you do for fun on Saturdays.

_____

_____

_____

_____

_____

_____

_____

Checklist

Be sure that…

☐ all the details about your Saturday activities from your chart are included in the paragraph;

☐ you use details to describe what you do for fun on Saturdays.

☐ you include new vocabulary words and the verbs **ir a** + **infinitive** and **querer** + **infinitive.**

Rubric

Evaluate your writing using the rubric below.

Writing criteria	Excellent	Good	Needs Work
Content	Your paragraph includes many details about what you do for fun on Saturdays.	Your paragraph includes some details about what you do for fun on Saturdays.	Your paragraph includes few details about what you do for fun on Saturdays.
Communication	Most of your paragraph is organized and easy to follow.	Parts of your paragraph are organized and easy to follow.	Your paragraph is disorganized and hard to follow.
Accuracy	Your paragraph has few mistakes in grammar and vocabulary.	Your paragraph has some mistakes in grammar and vocabulary.	Your paragraph has many mistakes in grammar and vocabulary.

UNIDAD 4 • Comparación
Lección 2   cultural

Comparación cultural: ¿Adónde vamos el sábado?
Compara con tu mundo

Now write a comparison about what you do for fun on Saturdays and that of one of the three students from page 241. Organize your comparison by topics. First, compare the places you go, then the clothes you wear, and lastly your favorite activities.

Step 1

Use the table to organize your comparison by topics. Write details for each topic about what you do for fun on Saturdays and that of the student you chose.

Categoría	Mi descripción	La descripción de _____
lugares		
ropa		
actividades		

Step 2

Now use the details from the table to write a comparison. Include an introduction sentence and write about each topic. Use the verbs **ir a** + **infinitive, querer** + **infinitive** to describe the sequence of your Saturday activities and those of the student you chose.

_____

_____

_____

_____

_____

_____

_____

_____

Vocabulario A

| ¡AVANZA! | **Goal:** Describe a house and household items. |

1 Lucas' house is very big. Draw a line from the places in the house to the activities done in each.

1. el cuarto   mirar la televisión

2. la escalera   preparar la comida

3. la sala   comer con la familia

4. el comedor   dormir

5. la cocina   subir y bajar

2 There's always a lot to do at home. Complete the following sentences with a word from the box.

| discos compactos | lector DVD | videojuegos |
| sillón | cortinas | |

1. En la sala, mi hermano y yo jugamos _____ .

2. A mi familia le gusta la música; por eso tenemos muchos _____ .

3. En mi cuarto veo películas con mi _____ .

4. Delante de las ventanas, mi mamá usa _____ blancas.

5. Mi padre descansa en un _____ en la sala.

3 Answer the following questions in complete sentences.

1. ¿Tienes un tocadiscos compactos en tu cuarto?

_____

_____

2. ¿Tienes un lector DVD en la sala de tu casa?

_____

_____

Vocabulario B

> ¡AVANZA! **Goal:** Describe a house and household items.

1 Luis invites his friends to his house. Circle the word that completes each sentence.

1. Luis tiene un (radio / patio) en su cuarto.

2. El padre de Luis usa (el sillón / las cortinas) para descansar.

3. La hermana de Luis compró un (jardín / espejo).

4. La madre de Luis tiene unas (alfombras / cortinas) en el suelo.

5. Luis y sus amigos escuchan unos (discos compactos / muebles).

6. La casa de Luis tiene dos (pisos / suelos).

2 Pedro is doing some things in his house. Complete the following sentences:

modelo: Pedro baja del primer piso a la planta baja del apartamento.

1. Pedro prepara el desayuno en _____ .

2. Pedro duerme en una cama en _____ .

3. Pedro come con su familia en _____ .

4. Pedro sube _____ .

5. Pedro tiene ropa en _____ de su cuarto.

6. Pedro juega al fútbol en _____ .

3 In three complete sentences describe the furniture you have in your living room.

_____

_____

_____

_____

_____

_____

Vocabulario C

Level 1, pp. 248-252

> ¡AVANZA! **Goal:** Describe a house and household items.

1 Look at the words in the vocabulary box and write them in the appropriate column. Items in the word bank may be used more than once.

las cortinas	el televisor	la cama
el armario	el comedor	el sofá
el espejo	la cómoda	la lámpara

el comedor	el cuarto	la sala

2 Ana has a big house. In complete sentences, describe what she does in each of the places below.

modelo: Escalera: **Ana sube la escalera para ir a su cuarto.**

1. comedor: _____

2. sala: _____

3. cocina: _____

4. cuarto: _____

5. jardín: _____

3 In two complete sentences, describe what you do in your room.

1. _____

2. _____

Gramática A *Ser and estar*

> ⯈ **¡AVANZA!** **Goal:** Describe people and locations using ser or estar.

1 Julieta's friends all have different personal traits. Complete the sentences below using the verb in parenthesis.

1. María _____ inteligente. (ser)

2. Julio y Marcos _____ en Ecuador. (estar)

3. Norma y yo _____ cansadas. (estar)

4. Tú _____ un estudiante de español. (ser)

5. Hoy _____ el tres de agosto. (ser)

2 There's a lot to say about the students below. Complete the following sentences using the words from the word box.

están	estás	soy	son
somos	estoy	están	está

1. Yo _____ de Ecuador.

2. Rafael _____ contento.

3. Nosotros _____ estudiantes.

4. María y tú _____ bien.

5. Ellos _____ mis maestros.

6. Señora y Señor Perdomo, ¿ustedes _____ en casa hoy?

7. ¡Hola, María Fernanda! ¿Cómo _____ tú?

8. ¡Hola, Mario! Yo _____ bien.

3 Describe yourself and your friends by answering the following questions with a complete sentence.

1. ¿Cómo estás?

_____

2. ¿Cómo son tus amigos o tus amigas?

_____

Gramática B *Ser and estar*

Level 1, pp. 253-257

¡AVANZA! **Goal:** Describe people and locations using **ser** or **estar**.

1 Write four complete sentences about the following students' characteristics. Use the information in the table.

Laura	ser	inteligente(s)
Silvia y Andrés	estar	ocupado(a)(s)
Camila y yo	ser	de Ecuador
Ramiro	estar	cansad(o)(a)

1. _____

2. _____

3. _____

4. _____

2 Nicolás is introducing his friends. Complete the sentences with either **ser** or **estar**.

1. Javier _____ maestro.

2. Armando y Luisa _____ en la escuela.

3. Miguel y yo _____ enojados.

4. Tú _____ un buen amigo.

5. Norberto y tú _____ emocionados.

3 Using two complete sentences, describe two of your friends and say where he or she is from.

_____

_____

_____

_____

_____

Gramática C *Ser and estar*

> ¡AVANZA! **Goal:** Describe people and locations using **ser** or **estar**.

1 Carina and her friends each have their own characteristics. Get to know them by completing the following sentences with the correct verb form of **ser** or **estar**.

1. Ernesto y Matías _____ buenas personas.

2. Isabel _____ bien.

3. Miriam y yo _____ maestras.

4. ¿Tú _____ contento?

5. Marta _____ mi amiga.

6. El _____ feliz.

7. Ellos _____ de México.

8. Ustedes _____ cansados.

2 Using the cues below, write complete sentences to say where the following people are or what they are like.

1. Elisa / su cuarto.

   _____

2. María y Diego / inteligentes.

   _____

3. Pedro y yo / buenos amigos.

   _____

4. Gabriela y tú / cansados de caminar.

   _____

3 Write three complete sentences about what you are like, where you are from, and how you are feeling.

_____

_____

_____

_____

Gramática A *Ordinal Numbers*

> **¡AVANZA!** **Goal:** Use ordinal numbers to talk about the floors of a building and to indicate the order of things.

1 Match the ordinal numbers in the left column to the appropriate numerals in the right column.

a. tercero   **5**

b. quinto   **4**

c. primero   **6**

d. sexto   **2**

e. cuarto   **3**

f. segundo   **1**

2 The following friends are standing in line, one behind the other, to go into the movies. They are in the following order: Julia, Aníbal, Santiago, Pedro, and Lucía. Complete the sentences below, stating where each is in line.

1. Lucía es la _____ persona.

2. Aníbal es la _____ persona.

3. Pedro es la _____ persona.

4. Santiago es la _____ persona.

5. Julia es la _____ persona.

3 Answer the following question in a complete sentence.

1. ¿Qué es la primera cosa que haces cuando llegas a la escuela?

_____

_____

2. ¿Qué es la segunda cosa que haces en la mañana?

_____

_____

3. ¿Qué es la primera cosa que haces cuando llegas de la escuela?

_____

_____

Gramática B *Ordinal Numbers*

¡AVANZA! **Goal:** Use ordinal numbers to talk about the floors of a building and to indicate the order of things.

1 Look at the numbers next to each drawing that indicate the floor on which you can find each item. Use ordinal number to complete the sentences.

1. Hay sillones en _____ piso.

2. Hay alfombras en _____ piso.

3. Hay radios en _____ piso.

4. Hay lámparas en _____ piso.

5. Hay televisores en _____ piso.

2 Pablo, Marcos, Letty, Mirna, and Julio are waiting in line at the bookstore. They are standing in line in the same order they have been mentioned.

1. Mirna es _____ en la fila.

2. Marcos es _____ en la fila.

3. Pablo es _____ en la fila.

4. Julio es _____ en la fila.

5. Letty es _____ en la fila.

3 Answer the following questions in complete sentences.

1. ¿Qué es la primera cosa que ves cuando vuelves a tu casa?

_____

_____

2. ¿Cuál es tu tercera clase los lunes?

_____

_____

Gramática C   Ordinal Numbers

¡AVANZA! **Goal:** Use ordinal numbers to talk about the floors of a building and to indicate the order of things.

1 The following runners are in a race. Look at their time and tell in which place each runner got to the finish line. Sigue el modelo.

modelo: Katy Méndez   2:00   **cuarto lugar**

1. Juana López   3:10   _____
2. Manuel Antonio   1:57   _____
3. Pablo Santos   2:05   _____
4. José Colón   3:01   _____
5. Julio Ortíz   1:58   _____
6. María Gonzalez   2:45   _____
7. Roberto Martínez 2:38   _____
8. Rosa Castillo   1:59   _____
9. Melvin Bravo   2:01   _____

2 There are five people in line, in the following order: María, Diana, Carlos, Paola, y Verónica. Complete the text with ordinal numbers.

Hay cuatro personas detrás de la **1.** _____

persona. Diana está detrás de María y delante de Carlos. Diana es la

2. _____ persona en la fila. Verónica está

detrás de Carlos y Paola. Verónica es la

3. _____ persona en la fila. Carlos está entre

Diana y Paola. Carlos es la **4.** _____ persona

en la fila. Paola está delante de Verónica. Verónica es la

5. _____ persona de la fila.

3 Write a complete sentence stating what your first, second, and third classes are on Fridays.

_____

_____

Integración: Hablar

Débora has a new apartment and needs to buy things for it. Also, she has to buy clothes for the housewarming party. She hears a radio commercial for a nearby mall where they have everything she wants to buy. So, she decides to go shopping there.

Fuente 1 Leer

Read the information in the mall directory.

CENTRO COMERCIAL ALTAVISTA

PRIMER PISO: ROPA DE MUJERES

SEGUNDO PISO: ROPA DE HOMBRES

TERCER PISO: ROPA DE NIÑOS

CUARTO PISO: MUEBLES

QUINTO PISO: COSAS PARA LA SALA

SEXTO PISO: CINES Y COSAS DIVERTIDAS

Fuente 2 Escuchar   *CD 03 track 02*

Listen to the radio ad that Débora listened to before going to the mall. Take notes.

_____

_____

_____

_____

Hablar

What items can Débora buy for her new place and for the party? Explain where she can find these items.

modelo: Débora puede comprar... en el... piso. Después, puede comprar...en...

Integración: Escribir

Vilma is very happy because her parents bought a new house. She really likes the house, so she writes and e-mail to her best friend, Patricia, about the distribution of rooms, colors, and size of her new place. Then Vilma goes to a big department store with her family to buy things for the new place.

Fuente 1 Leer

Read Vilma's e-mail to Patricia...

¡Hola Patricia!

¡Tengo una casa nueva! Es la casa ideal. Tiene una cocina muy grande y tres cuartos. También hay un comedor donde comemos la cena cada noche. Está al lado de la cocina y detrás de la sala. Delante de la casa hay un jardín muy bonito y detrás de la casa hay un patio más grande que el jardín. Esta casa es más grande que la otra y necesitamos más muebles.

Besos,

Vilma

Fuente 2 Escuchar   *CD 03 track 04*

Listen to Manuel, the clerk at the deparment store, calling the stockroom on the second floor. Take notes.

_____
_____
_____
_____

Escribir

Vilma's family bought a lot of things to furnish their new house. How can they distribute them inside the house?

Modelo: Los sillones están en...y la...

_____
_____
_____
_____
_____
_____

Escuchar A

Level 1, pp. 268-269
WB CD 03 tracks 05-06

> ¡AVANZA! **Goal:** Listen to hear about household items.

1 Listen to Cristian. Then, look at the list and draw a line through the articles that his parents do not buy.

cómoda

cortinas

televisor

sillón

espejo

alfombra

lector DVD

radio

2 Listen to Olga Uribe talk about her home. Then choose the correct answer to each question.

1. ¿Por qué necesitan Olga y su esposo una casa más grande? _____

   a. Porque sus hijos vuelven de otra ciudad.

   b. Porque no les gusta la casa que tienen.

2. ¿Qué quieren comprar para sus hijos? _____

   a. Quieren comprar un sillón, un tocadiscos compactos y un lector DVD.

   b. Quieren comprar camas nuevas, cortinas, radios y alfombras.

3. ¿Dónde están los hijos de Olga? _____

   a. Están en su cuarto.

   b. Están en otra ciudad.

Escuchar B

| ¡AVANZA! | **Goal:** Listen to hear about household items. |

1 Listen to Carmen and take notes. Then, place an "X" next to the things she has in her room.

1. ____ escalera

2. ____ cortinas

3. ____ espejo

4. ____ cama

5. ____ cómoda

6. ____ discos compactos

7. ____ radio

8. ____ armario

9. ____ lector DVD

10. ____ sillón

2 Listen to Lorena and Norberto. Then, answer the questions in complete sentences.

1. ¿Qué discos de su músico preferido tiene Lorena?

_____

_____

2. ¿Qué quiere Lorena?

_____

_____

3. ¿Quién tiene el disco que no tiene Lorena?

_____

_____

Escuchar C

> **¡AVANZA!** **Goal:** Listen about household items.

1 Listen to the conversation between Claudia and Ana. Take notes. Then complete the table below with what each one does. (Notice that Ana speaks first.)

ser un buen amigo	comprar un radio	comprar discos compactos
comprar un espejo	comprar un apartamento	comprar una alfombra
ir al centro comercial	almorzar con su hermano	

¿Quién?	¿Qué hace?
Claudia	
Ana	
El hermano de Ana	
Ana y Claudia	

2 Listen to Martín and take notes. Then complete the sentences.

1. Primero, Martín tiene que _____

_____

2. Segundo, Martín tiene que _____

_____

3. Tercero, Martín tiene que _____

_____

4. Cuarto, Martín tiene que _____

_____

Leer A

> **¡AVANZA!** **Goal:** Read about households.

Juan has a new apartment. There are four different families that live in the building.
The girl on the first floor gives him a list of the families that live there.

La Familia Ordóñez vive en la planta baja.
La Familia Gutiérrez vive en el piso uno.
La Familia Pérez vive en el piso dos.
Juan vive en el piso tres.
La Familia Martínez vive en el piso cuatro.
La Familia Gómez vive en el piso cinco.

¿Comprendiste?

Read the list of families. Then, complete the sentences below using ordinal numbers.

1. La familia Pérez vive en el _____ piso.

2. La familia Gómez está en el _____ piso.

3. La familia Gutiérrez está en el _____ piso.

4. Juan vive en el _____ piso.

5. La familia Martínez vive en el _____ piso.

¿Qué piensas?

¿Piensas que es mejor vivir en el primer piso o en el quinto piso? ¿Por qué?

_____

_____

_____

_____

_____

_____

Leer B

> **¡AVANZA!** **Goal:** Read about households.

Señora Díaz has a new house and goes to the mall to buy furniture and appliances. She writes a note about what she buys and at what time. The problem is that she does not write the items in order.

> La señora Díaz compró los discos compactos a las 9:45 a.m. Pero, quince minutos antes, compró un espejo. Dos horas después de comprar los discos compactos, compró las cortinas. A las 10:15 a.m. compró un lector DVD, y luego a las 12:10 p.m. compró una cómoda. A las 4:00 p.m. compró un sillón.

¿Comprendiste?

Read Señora Díaz' notes. Complete the chart with the ordinal number indicating the order in which she bought the following items.

Cosas	Orden
discos compactos	
sillón	
cómoda	
cortinas	
espejo	
lector DVD	

¿Qué piensas?

¿Adónde vas de compras? ¿Cuántos pisos hay allí?

_____
_____
_____
_____
_____
_____
_____

Leer C

▶ **¡AVANZA!** **Goal:** Read about households.

Roberto writes a letter to his sister to tell her about his new apartment and the people who live in the building.

Julia:

Tengo muchos amigos aqui. Encima de mi apartamento vive Inés, una maestra de ciencias. Encima de Inés, y debajo de Walter, vive Hugo, un estudiante de otra ciudad. Encima del apartamento de Walter está el apartamento de Lorena. Son cinco pisos. Debajo de mi apartamento, en la planta baja, está el apartamento de Ernesto. Alli escuchamos música todos los viernes.

Besos,

Roberto

¿Comprendiste?

Read Roberto's letter. Then complete the table below with the name of the person who lives on each floor.

Piso	Nombre
planta baja	
primer piso	
segundo piso	
tercer piso	
cuarto piso	
quinto piso	

¿Qué piensas?

¿Piensas que es divertido vivir en un apartamento con muchos pisos? ¿Por qué?

_____

_____

_____

_____

Escribir A

Level 1, pp. 268-269

> **¡AVANZA!** **Goal:** Write about your house and household items.

Step 1

Make a list of six places in your house.

1. _____   4. _____

2. _____   5. _____

3. _____   6. _____

Step 2

Classify your list in the table. Choose three places from your list, and write the items you would put in them.

1.	1.	1.
2.	2.	2.
3.	3.	3.

Step 3

Write three sentences to state each of the three rooms you chose and what they contain. Use the information from the chart.

_____

_____

Step 4

Evaluate your writing using the information in the table.

Writing Criteria	Excellent	Good	Needs Work
Content	You described three rooms.	You described two rooms.	You described one room.
Communication	Most of your response is clear.	Some of your response is clear.	Your message is not very clear.
Accuracy	You make few mistakes in grammar and vocabulary.	You make some mistakes in grammar and vocabulary.	You make many mistakes in grammar and vocabulary.

Escribir B

> ¡AVANZA! **Goal:** Write about your house and household items.

Step 1

Complete the following table with an alphabetical list of furniture and household items in your house:

Muebles	Otras cosas para la casa
Primero:	Primero:
Segundo:	Segundo:
Tercero:	Tercero:
Cuarto:	Cuarto:

Step 2

Write a paragraph using the four items from the chart. Use **ser** and **estar**.

_____

_____

_____

Step 3

Evaluate your writing using the information in the table.

Writing Criteria	Excellent	Good	Needs Work
Content	You have used the four items from the chart.	You have used some items from the chart.	You have not used any items from the chart.
Communication	Most of your response is clear.	Some of your response is clear.	Your message is not very clear.
Accuracy	You make few mistakes in grammar and vocabulary.	You make some mistakes in grammar and vocabulary.	You make many mistakes in grammar and vocabulary.

Escribir C

Level 1, pp. 268-269

> ¡AVANZA! **Goal:** Write about your house and household items.

Write a list of the favorite items you have at home in the order that you like them.

Step 1

Complete the table with facts about your favorite things using complete sentences. Use **ser** and **estar**.

Objeto	Ser	Estar

Step 2

Write a paragraph using the information from the chart. Write about your favorite objects and in the order that you like them.

_____

_____

_____

_____

Step 3

Evaluate your writing using the information in the table.

Writing Criteria	Excellent	Good	Needs Work
Content	You have used all items from the chart.	You have used some items from the chart.	You have not used items from the chart.
Communication	Most of your response is clear.	Some of your response is clear.	Your message is not very clear.
Accuracy	You make few mistakes in grammar and vocabulary.	You make some mistakes in grammar and vocabulary.	You make many mistakes in grammar and vocabulary.

Cultura A

> ¡AVANZA! **Goal:** Review cultural information about Ecuador.

1 **Ecuadorian culture** Complete the following sentences with one of the multiple choice words or phrases.

1. The capital of Ecuador is _____

   a. Guayaquil   **b.** Quito   **c.** Otavalo

2. Quechua is one of the _____ of Ecuador.

   a. typical foods   **b.** volcanoes   **c.** languages

3. Camilo Egas was the Ecuadoran artist who painted _____

   a. *Las coristas*   **b.** *Las porristas*   **c.** *Las floristas*

2 **Ecuador and Argentina** Choose the correct word to complete the following sentences.

1. Otavalo is a (town / mountain) north of Quito.

2. Cotopaxi, the active volcano, is the (shortest / tallest) in the world.

3. Ushuaia, Argentina is the (southernmost / smallest) city in the world.

4. The Andean mountain chain is in (Central / South) America.

5. Since 2000, the Ecuadorian currency has been the (dollar / peso).

3 **Geography of Ecuador** Explain what is unique about Ecuador's geographical location. What is the Mitad del Mundo monument? Would you like to visit it? Why or why not?

_____

_____

_____

_____

_____

_____

_____

Cultura B

Level 1, pp. 268-269

> **¡AVANZA!** **Goal:** Review cultural information about Ecuador.

1 **Ecuador** Read the following sentences about Ecuador and answer *true* or *false*.

T   F   **1.** The Copa Mundial is a baseball tournament.

T   F   **2. Canguil** is a typical Ecuadorian dish.

T   F   **3.** The town of Otavalo is south of Quito.

T   F   **4.** In Quito and Guayaquil, the major league soccer teams play on the weekends.

T   F   **5.** The two main languages of Ecuador are Spanish and Quechua.

2 **In Ecuador** Read the following sentences about Ecuador and write the correct words from the box.

Quito	quechua	Egas
Andes	Otavalo	

1. Capital of Ecuador: _____

2. Last name of the painter of *Las floristas:* _____

3. A language other than Spanish spoken in Ecuador: _____ .

4. Mountain range in South America: _____

5. Market town in Ecuador, north of Quito: _____

3 **Ecuadorian art** You work at an art museum that is having an exhibit featuring Ecuadorian art. Describe the paintings on p. 245 and p. 255. Tell who painted each and how the painting reflects Ecuadorian culture. Also, give your impressions of each painting.

_____

_____

_____

_____

_____

Cultura C

¡AVANZA! **Goal:** Review cultural information about Ecuador.

1 **Ecuadorian culture** Complete the following sentences about Ecuador by filling in the correct word.

1. Julio Jaramillo was a famous Ecuadorian _____ .

2. _____ is the capital of Ecuador.

3. In Ecuador, they speak Spanish and many indigenous languages such as _____ .

4. Cotopaxi is a _____ found in Ecuador.

5. Ecuador is located in _____ America.

2 **Ecuadorian culture** Answer these questions about Ecuador with complete sentences.

1. What has been the currency of Ecuador since 2000? _____

_____

2. Who was Camilo Egas and what kind of work did he create? _____

_____

3. Which is the tallest active volcano in the world? _____

_____

3 **Trip to Ecuador** In Ecuador, there are many beautiful places to visit. If you won a trip for two days to Ecuador, which places would you visit? Write a paragraph about which parts of Ecuador you would like to visit and why.

_____

_____

_____

_____

Vocabulario A

¡AVANZA! ▶ **Goal:** Talk about chores and responsibilities.

1 We've got to do chores! Place an "x" next to those activities that are household chores.

1. _____ cantar

6. _____ decorar

2. _____ barrer

7. _____ planchar

3. _____ bailar

8. _____ barrer

4. _____ limpiar

9. _____ comer

5. _____ lavar

10. _____ celebrar

2 Miriam's dad talks to her about what she has to do around the house today. Complete their conversation using the words from the box.

lavar	la basura	la mesa	las camas	pasar

Padre: ¡Miriam!, tenemos que hacer _____ del cuarto de Luis.

Miriam: Sí, papá, también tenemos que _____ la aspiradora.

Padre: Además, tenemos que _____ los platos.

Miriam: Yo prefiero poner _____ .

Padre: Yo saco _____ .

3 Answer the following questions in a complete sentence.

1. ¿Qué cosas haces para limpiar tu cuarto?

_____

2. ¿Te gusta bailar en las fiestas?

_____

3. ¿Con quién celebras tu cumpleaños?

_____

Vocabulario B

| ¡AVANZA! | **Goal:** Talk about chores and responsibilities. |

1 Inés wants to clean the house. Underline the word that best completes each sentence.

1. Ellas tienen que hacer muchos (secretos / quehaceres) en casa.

2. Inés tiene que pasar (la aspiradora / la ropa).

3. Inés y su mamá tienen que hacer (la basura / la cama).

4. El hermano de Inés tiene que cortar (el césped / el suelo).

5. La mamá de Inés tiene que cocinar (la comida / la mesa).

6. Inés tiene que lavar (los regalos / los platos).

2 Luisa's mom asks her to do some chores around the house. Complete the sentences with the appropriate verb.

1. Tienes que _____ al gato.

2. Debes _____ en la cocina; el suelo está sucio.

3. Tienes que _____ de tu hermano y la ropa de tu hermana también.

4. Hay que _____ antes de las 6:00 p.m.

5. Debes _____ del comedor para la cena.

3 Write three complete sentences to describe what you do to clean up around the house and when you do it.

1. _____

2. _____

3. _____

Vocabulario C

> **¡AVANZA!** **Goal:** Talk about chores and responsibilities.

1 A clean house is nicer! Draw a line from the verbs to the nouns to complete the list of chores.

1.	hacer	**a.**	el césped
2.	barrer	**b.**	la basura
3.	pasar	**c.**	el suelo
4.	lavar	**d.**	la ropa
5.	cortar	**e.**	la cama
6.	planchar	**f.**	la aspiradora
7.	poner	**g.**	la mesa
8.	sacar	**h.**	los platos

2 There's a party at Norma's house today. There's still a lot to do to get ready. Complete the following text.

Hoy damos una fiesta en casa para **1.** _____

el cumpleaños de mi hermana. No debes decir nada porque

es una **2.** _____ . Tengo que

3. _____ el regalo pero necesito buscar papel

de regalo. Tenemos globos y otras **4.** _____ .

Los **5.** _____ van a llegar a las cinco y todavía

necesito hacer los quehaceres. ¡Todo está perfecto!

3 Write a description of the chores you do at home. Include at least three chores.

_____

_____

_____

_____

_____

Gramática A *Irregular Verbs*

Level 1, pp. 277-281

¡AVANZA! **Goal:** Use **dar**, **decir**, **poner**, **salir**, **traer**, and **venir** to talk about preparations for a party.

---

1 There's a party at Carla's house today. Circle the verb that completes each sentence.

1. Hoy, su familia (dan / da) una fiesta por el cumpleaños de Luis.

2. Sus amigos le (traen / traigo) muchos regalos.

3. Por la noche, todos (sales / salimos) a cenar.

4. También Carla (venís / viene) a la fiesta.

5. Yo (pone / pongo) una bonita decoración en el jardín.

6. Nosotros (digo / decimos): «¡Feliz cumpleaños, Luis!»

2 Use the elements below to write a complete sentence describing a surprise party.

1. Yo / dar una fiesta. _____

2. Jaime y yo / traer regalos. _____

3. Marcos / decir a qué hora es la fiesta. _____

4. Carmen y Marcos / poner la mesa. _____

5. Ella / pasar la aspiradora. _____

3 Answer the following question in a complete sentence.

1. ¿Das fiestas en casa?

_____

_____

2. ¿Quién viene a tus fiestas?

_____

_____

3. ¿Qué traes a la fiesta de cumpleaños de tu amigo(a)?

_____

_____

Gramática B *Irregular Verbs*

Level 1, pp. 277-281

 Goal: Use **dar**, **decir**, **poner**, **salir**, **traer**, and **venir** to talk about preparations for a party.

1 Lucas's party is tomorrow. Complete the text below, by choosing and correctly conjugating the correct verb in the box.

traer	dar	salir	decir	venir

Lucas y su familia **1.** _____ una fiesta esta tarde. Yo

2. _____ de muy lejos para esta fiesta. Mi hermana y yo

3. _____ muchos regalos para Lucas y su familia. Ellos

4. _____ que nosotros somos parte de la familia. Mi

hermana y yo **5.** _____ en el autobús de esta tarde.

2 Irma always wants to do what Manuel and Sofía do. Complete the dialogue with the correct form of **venir, traer, dar,** or **poner.**

Manuel: Sofía y yo **1.** _____ fiestas los viernes.

Irma: Yo también **2.** _____ fiestas los viernes.

Sofía: Manuel y yo **3.** _____ globos en la sala.

Irma: Yo también **4.** _____ globos en la sala.

Manuel: Nosotros **5.** _____ los discos compactos de rock.

Irma: Yo también **6.** _____ los discos compactos de rock.

Sofía: **7.** Nosotros _____ que vamos a bailar.

Irma: **8.** Yo también _____ que vamos a bailar.

3 Write three sentences using the verbs **traer, poner,** and **salir** to describe what you do when you go to a party.

_____

_____

_____

Gramática C *Irregular Verbs*

> **¡AVANZA!** **Goal:** Use **dar**, **decir**, **poner**, **salir**, **traer**, and **venir** to talk about preparations for a party.

1 Ángel and Ana are invited to a party at my house. Complete each sentences with the appropriate form of the verb.

1. Ángel _____ a las 3:00 p.m. (venir)

2. Yo nunca _____ un secreto. (decir)

3. Ángel y Ana _____ un postre muy rico. (traer)

4. Ana me ayuda y _____ la mesa. (poner)

5. ¿Tú también _____ a mi fiesta? (venir)

2 Today is Juan's birthday. Use the correct form of the verb in parentheses to complete the sentences.

1. Para la fiesta, yo (poner) _____ .

2. Mi amiga Lucía y yo (dar) _____ .

3. Jaime y tú (salir) _____ .

4. Andrea y Nicolás (traer) _____ .

5. También otros amigos de Juan (venir) _____ a la fiesta.

3 Write a four sentence paragraph describing what you do when you go to a birthday party. Use at least four of the following verbs: **dar, poner, venir, traer, salir, decir**.

_____

_____

_____

_____

_____

Gramática A Affirmative *tú* Commands and *Acabar de* + infinitive

¡AVANZA! **Goal:** Tell people what to do and say what people just did.

1 You're being asked to do some chores. Underline the sentences that are commands.

1. Ayudas en la cocina.
2. Lava los platos.
3. Pasa la aspiradora.
4. Cortas el césped.
5. Haz la cama.

6. Pon la mesa.
7. Planchan la ropa.
8. Limpiamos la sala.
9. Di el secreto.
10. Cocino todos los días.

2 All these kids do what their mothers ask. Write the mother's command. Follow the model.

modelo: Ana (barrer el suelo).
Madre: Ana, ¡barre el suelo!

1. Luis (preparar el desayuno).

   Madre: Luis, ¡ _____ el desayuno!

2. Claudia (servir la cena).

   Madre: Claudia, ¡ _____ la cena!

3. Laura (barrer el patio).

   Madre: Laura, ¡ _____ el patio!

4. Ernesto (sacar la basura).

   Madre: Ernesto, ¡ _____ la basura!

3 Answer the following questions in a complete sentences:

1. ¿Qué acabas de hacer?

   _____

2. ¿Con quién acabas de hablar?

   _____

3. ¿Adónde acabas de ir?

   _____

Gramática B   Affirmative **tú** Commands and *Acabar de* + infinitive

Level 1, pp. 282-284

| ¡AVANZA! | **Goal:** Tell people what to do and say what people just did. |

1 Your friend is having a party at home today and asks for your help. Complete the sentences by choosing the correct affirmative **tú** command.

1. _____ los regalos con papel de regalo.

   a. Envuelven   **b.** Envuelves   **c.** Envuelve   **d.** Envuelvo

2. _____ a buscar a Norma que viene en autobús.

   a. Sales   **b.** Sal   **c.** Sale   **d.** Salen

3. _____ esos globos en el patio.

   a. Pon   **b.** Pone   **c.** Ponen   **d.** Pones

4. _____ la primera persona en llegar.

   a. Soy   **b.** Son   **c.** Es   **d.** Sé

2 You and a few friends have just finished cleaning up after a party. Write a sentence with the elements below. Follow the model.

modelo: ¡Saca la basura! (Carmela y yo)
   Carmela y yo acabamos de sacar la basura.

1. ¡Limpia la cocina! (Andrés y Luis)

   _____

2. ¡Barre el suelo de la cocina! (yo)

   _____

3. ¡Pasa la aspiradora! (Luis)

   _____

4. ¡Lava los platos! (tú)

   _____

3 Your friend is helping you clean your house. Write two sentences telling him or her what to do using two affirmative **tú** commands.

   _____

   _____

   _____

Gramática C Affirmative **tú** Commands and *Acabar de* + infinitive

Level 1, pp. 282-284

> **¡AVANZA!** **Goal:** Tell people what to do and say what people just did.

1 Your friend is telling you what to do to help get ready for his party. Complete the sentences with the correct affirmative **tú** command.

1. _____ los globos en la sala. (poner)

2. _____ a la cocina para cocinar. (venir)

3. _____ el suelo en el comedor. (barrer.)

4. _____ los platos sucios. (lavar)

5. _____ a la tienda a comprar decoraciones. (ir)

6. _____ la puerta por favor. (abrir)

2 You ask a friend to help you with your party. Complete the dialog with your requests. Use direct object pronouns.

modelo: **Tu amigo(a):** Tenemos que buscar más globos.
Tú: Búscalos.

1. **Tu amigo(a):** Tenemos que servir el pastel.

    Tú: _____

2. **Tu amigo(a):** Tenemos que poner más globos.

    Tú: _____

3. **Tu amigo(a):** Tenemos que preparar el jugo.

    Tú: _____

3 Write a three-sentence message to your friend explaining what chores you've just done. Then use affirmative **tú** commands to tell him or her what to do to help you get ready for your party.

_____

_____

_____

_____

Integración: Hablar

Level 1, pp. 285-287
WB CD 03 track 11

UNIDAD 5
Lección 2

Integración:
Hablar

It's Mónica's birthday and her friends Rebeca and Cristina have plans to celebrate. Cristina is in charge of sending invitations, while Rebeca prepares her house for everybody to come.

Fuente 1 Leer

Read the invitation for the surprise party.

*Te invitamos a la fiesta
de sorpresa para Mónica.*

Fecha: 4 de febrero
Lugar: la casa de Rebeca
Hora: a las cinco de la tarde
¡*Puedes venir antes y traer
tus discos compactos!*

—*Cristina y Rebeca*

Fuente 2 Escuchar   *CD 03 track 12*

Listen to the message left by Rebeca on Cristina's voicemail. Take notes.

_____

_____

_____

_____

Hablar

Cristina is planning to arrive early to the surprise party.

modelo: La fiesta es......Si Rebeca llega a las..., tiene que...

_____

_____

_____

Integración: Escribir

Level 1, pp. 285-287
CD 03 track 13

The movie *El secreto* advertised and reviewed. Many things happen during the movie, and the sequence of events is supposed to be very entertaining.

Fuente 1 Leer

Read the movie review in a magazine.

El secreto

Esta noche, mírala por televisión.

Busca tu mejor sillón y ponlo delante del televisor. A las ocho de la noche empieza El secreto, película interesante. Una chica trabaja mucho en una casa. Ella barre el suelo, lava los platos, hace las camas y prepara la cena todos los días. Pero hay más, ¡mucho más!.

Fuente 2 Escuchar *CD 03 track 14*

Listen to a review in a radio program about the movie. Take notes.

_____

_____

_____

_____

Escribir

What is the sequence of events in the movie *El secreto*?

modelo: La chica trabaja... Después, ella...

_____

_____

_____

_____

_____

_____

_____

_____

Escuchar A

┌───┐
│ **¡AVANZA!** **Goal:** Listen to what these people have to do. │
└───┘

1 Listen to Jimena and Mabel. Then, read each statement and answer **Cierto** (*True*) or **Falso** (*False*).

C   F   **1.** Jimena todavía prepara la comida.

C   F   **2.** Mabel todavía limpia la sala.

C   F   **3.** Mabel barre y también pasa la aspiradora.

C   F   **4.** Eduardo tiene que poner la mesa.

C   F   **5.** Eduardo no está en casa.

2 Listen to Norma. Then, answer the following questions in complete sentences.

1. ¿Qué van a hacer los hermanos de Norma?

_____

_____

2. ¿Qué hacen los hermanos de Norma en su casa?

_____

_____

3. ¿Qué celebran hoy?

_____

_____

Escuchar B

> ¡AVANZA! **Goal:** Listen to what these people have to do.

1 Listen to Mariana and take notes. Then, draw a line from the actions in the right column to the person who does it on the left. One person can do more than one thing.

a. Mariana

b. Luis

c. Cecilia

1. limpiar la sala

2. limpiar su cuarto

3. dar de comer al perro

4. preparar la comida

5. cortar el césped

6. lavar los platos

7. sacar la basura

8. planchar la ropa

2 Listen to Luis and Cecilia. Then, answer the following questions in complete sentences.

1. ¿Qué le dice Cecilia a Luis?

_____

2. ¿Por qué Cecilia no quiere ir a buscarla?

_____

3. ¿Por qué no la trae Luis?

_____

4. ¿Quién va a ayudar a Luis con su cuarto?

_____

_____

Escuchar C

> ¡AVANZA! **Goal:** Listen to what these people have to do.

1 Listen to Teresa and her father and take notes. Then, complete the following sentences.

1. Teresa acaba de _____

2. El padre acaba de _____

3. Ahora, Teresa va a _____

4. Ahora, el hermano de Teresa debe _____

5. El hermano de Teresa está en _____

2 Listen to Osvaldo and take notes. Then, in complete sentences, describe what he says about the following things.

1. Los quehaceres de la casa:

_____

_____

_____

2. Cosas que hacen sus amigos:

_____

_____

_____

Leer A

Leer A

UNIDAD 5
Lección 2

> ¡AVANZA! **Goal:** Read about household chores.

Irma's mom is leaving the city. She leaves a note to tell Irma what she has to do at home.

> Irma:
>
> ¿Puedes ayudar con los quehaceres de la casa?
>
> Hay que preparar el desayuno. Luego, por favor lava los platos. Antes de ir a la escuela, haz la cama, y limpia tu cuarto. Barre la cocina dos veces, en la mañana y en la noche. El domingo hay que cortar el césped del jardín. Luego ¡puedes descansar!
>
> Gracias,
>
> Mamá

¿Comprendiste?

Read the note from Irma's mom. Write the things that Irma has to do in the kitchen. Then write what she must do in her room. Finally, what does she need to do outside?

1. _____

2. _____

3. _____

¿Qué piensas?

¿Piensas que es bueno ayudar con los quehaceres de la casa? ¿Por qué?

_____

_____

Leer B

> **¡AVANZA!** **Goal:** Read about household chores.

Guillermo's father buys a magazine about homes. The following is a letter in that magazine.

> ¡Hola! Tú eres una persona muy ocupada y quieres tu casa siempre limpia.
>
> Aquí hay unas ideas para tenerla así. Primero tu familia debe ayudar. Debes compartir los quehaceres. Tus hijos deben limpiar su cuarto. Ellos necesitan hacer sus camas y limpiar sus cuartos. Pasa la aspiradora en las alfombras una vez por semana. Saca la basura todos los días. Los zapatos necesitan estar limpios antes de entrar a la casa.

¿Comprendiste?

Read the advice from the magazine. Then, complete the sentences.

1. La familia debe _____

2. Los hijos _____

3. Para las alfombras, la familia _____

4. Antes de entrar a la casa, los zapatos _____

¿Qué piensas?

¿Piensas que es importante para una familia compartir los quehaceres? ¿Por qué?

_____

_____

_____

Level 1, pp. 292-293

¡AVANZA! **Goal:** Read about household chores.

Graciela is having a big party at her house. All of her friends receive the following e-mail.

> ¡Hola!
>
> El sábado voy a dar una fiesta en mi casa. Es mi cumpleaños y quiero estar con todos mis amigos.
>
> Ven a mi fiesta el sábado a las cinco. Trae tus discos compactos para compartir la música que te gusta con todos.
>
> Hoy pongo unas decoraciones muy bonitas en el patio. Mi papá acaba de cortar el césped y toda la familia ayuda a preparar la fiesta.
>
> ¡Ah! Trae mi regalo y envuélvelo con un bonito papel de regalo. (ja ja ja)
>
> Besos,
>
> Graciela

¿Comprendiste?

Read Graciela's e-mail and then answer the following questions.

1. ¿Por qué invita Graciela a sus amigos a su cumpleaños?

_____

2. ¿Por qué quiere Graciela los discos compactos de todos?

_____

3. ¿A qué hora es la fiesta?

_____

4. ¿Cómo quiere Graciela sus regalos?

_____

¿Qué piensas?

¿Piensas que es importante invitar a tus amigos a tu cumpleaños? ¿Por qué?

_____

_____

Escribir A

| ¡AVANZA! | **Goal:** Write about chores and responsibilities. |

Step 1

Make a list of the six chores you do most at home.

1. _____ 4. _____

2. _____ 5. _____

3. _____ 6. _____

Classify your list in the chart.

Me Gusta	No Me Gusta
1.	1.
2.	2.
3.	3.

Step 2

Write two sentences stating which chores you enjoy doing and three different chores you don't enjoy doing.

_____

_____

_____

_____

Step 4

Evaluate your writing using the information in the table.

Writing Criteria	Excellent	Good	Needs Work
Content	You have stated which chores you enjoy doing and which you don't.	You have stated some chores you enjoy doing and some you don't.	You have stated few chores you enjoy and don't enjoy doing.
Communication	Most of your response is clear.	Some of your response is clear.	Your message is not very clear.
Accuracy	You make few mistakes in grammar and vocabulary.	You make some mistakes in grammar and vocabulary.	You make many mistakes in grammar and vocabulary.

Escribir B

¡AVANZA! **Goal:** Write about chores and responsibilities.

Step 1

Make a chart with five chores.

Quehaceres
1.
2.
3.
4.
5.

Step 2

In a paragraph, say which chores you enjoy the least and which you enjoy the most. Use three ordinal numbers.

_____

_____

_____

Step 3

Evaluate your writing using the information in the table.

Writing Criteria	Excellent	Good	Needs Work
Content	You included five chores and three ordinal numbers.	You included some chores and ordinal numbers.	You included few chores and ordinal numbers.
Communication	Most of your response is clear.	Some of your response is clear.	Your message is not very clear.
Accuracy	You make few mistakes in grammar and vocabulary.	You make some mistakes in grammar and vocabulary.	You make many mistakes in grammar and vocabulary.

Escribir C

> **¡AVANZA!** **Goal:** Write about chores and responsibilities.

Step 1

Write a list of six chores your friend has to do to clean his or her house. Use ordinal numbers.

1. _____

2. _____

3. _____

4. _____

5. _____

6. _____

Step 2

Write a paragraph telling your friend what chores to do. Use command forms of the verbs and the ordinal numbers.

_____

_____

_____

Step 3

Evaluate your writing using the information in the table.

Writing Criteria	Excellent	Good	Needs Work
Content	You have included six chores and the correct command form.	You have included four to five chores and the correct command form four or five times.	You have included three or fewer chores and the correct command form less than three times.
Communication	Most of your response is clear.	Some of your response is clear.	Your message is not very clear.
Accuracy	You make few mistakes in grammar and vocabulary.	You make some mistakes in grammar and vocabulary.	You make many mistakes in grammar and vocabulary.

> ¡AVANZA!   **Goal:** Review cultural information about Ecuador.

1   **Ecuador and Panama** Complete the following sentences with one of the multiple-choice words or phrases.

1. The languages spoken in Ecuador are _____

   a. Spanish, Mayan and other indigenous languages   **b.** Spanish, Nahuatl and other indigenous languages   **c.** Spanish, Quechua and other indigenous languages

2. Ecuadorians celebrate the Festival of San Juan in the month of _____

   a. May   **b.** June   **c.** July

3. El tamborito is a traditional _____ from Panama.

   a. dance   **b.** handicraft   **c.** food

2   **Activities and places** In Ecuador there are many interesting things to see and do. Draw lines to match each word from the left column with its explanation on the right.

Otavalo   popular dance of Ecuador

Serenatas Quiteñas   tallest active volcano in the world

Sanjuanito   city known for its textiles

Fiestas de Quito   musical tributes to the city

El Cotopaxi   is celebrated every 6th of December

3   **Fiestas de Quito** The Fiestas de Quito are very joyful and there are many activities. Write about the kinds of activities that are a part of the Fiestas de Quito. What would be your favorite activity and why?

_____

_____

_____

_____

_____

Cultura B

Level 1, pp. 292-293

¡AVANZA! **Goal:** Review cultural information about Ecuador.

1 **Ecuador** Read the following sentences about Ecuador and answer *true* or *false*.

T F **1.** The languages spoken in Ecuador are Spanish, Quechua, and other indigenous languages.

T F **2.** The city of Quito was founded on December 6.

T F **3.** Ecuador is located in South America.

T F **4.** The Otavalos of Ecuador are famous for their food.

T F **5.** The **Sanjuanito** is an Ecuadorian dance with a sad rhythm.

2 **Ecuadorian culture** Complete the following sentences with the words from the box.

Otavalos	Reina	San Juan	**fritada**

1. The festival of _____ is celebrated in the month of June.

2. The _____ is a popular food in Ecuador.

3. The textile designs of the _____ may have geometric figures.

4. The _____ de Quito pageant is celebrated during the Fiestas de Quito.

3 **Serenatas** Music is very important in all Spanish-speaking countries. During the Fiestas de Quito, many people sing **serenatas quiteñas**. Write a full sentence to explain what the **serenatas** are. Then write a short **serenata** (one verse) of your own.

_____

_____

_____

_____

_____

_____

_____

Cultura C

> **¡AVANZA!** **Goal:** Review cultural information about Ecuador.

1 **Ecuador** Choose the correct word to complete the following sentences.

1. Aside from Spanish, (Quechua / Maya) is spoken in Ecuador.

2. The (Tamborito / Sanjuanito) is an Ecuadorian dance with a joyful rhythm.

3. The Otavalos of Ecuador are famous for their (food / textiles).

4. The celebration of the Fiestas de Quito last for (one week / one month).

2 **Geography and events** Answer these questions about Ecuador in complete sentences.

1. What is the tallest active volcano in the world and where is it? _____

_____

2. What is the name of the vast mountain chain in South America? _____

_____

3. What popular activities are held every year during the Fiestas de Quito? _____

_____

_____

3 **Otavalo** Describe the textiles created by the Otavalos. Where do they sell them? Compare the Otavalan textiles with other textiles or handicrafts you have seen in the United States that represent various cultures. Look at the photograph on page 284 of your book to help with your comparison.

_____

_____

_____

_____

_____

_____

_____

_____

Comparación cultural: ¡Así celebramos!

Level 1, pp. 294-295

Lectura y escritura

After reading the paragraphs about how María Elena, Carla and Daniel enjoy parties and celebrations, write a paragraph about a party or celebration of your own. Use the information on your chart to write sentences, and then write a paragraph that describes your party or celebration.

Step 1

Complete the chart describing as many details as possible about your celebration.

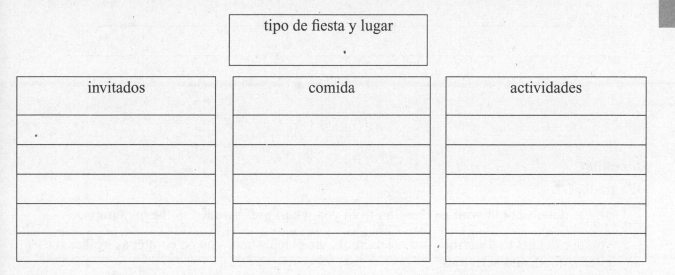

tipo de fiesta y lugar

invitados	comida	actividades

Step 2

Now take the details from the chart and write a sentence for each topic on the chart.

_____

_____

_____

_____

_____

_____

_____

_____

_____

_____

Comparación cultural: ¡Así celebramos!

Lectura y escritura (continued)

Step 3

Now write your paragraph using the sentences you wrote as a guide. Include an introductory sentence and use the verbs **celebrar, venir, traer,** and **poner** to write about your celebration.

_____

_____

_____

_____

_____

_____

Checklist

Be sure that…

☐ all the details about your celebration from your chart are included in the paragraph;

☐ you use details to describe your celebration, the place where you celebrate, as well as the guests, food, and activities;

☐ you include new vocabulary words and the verbs **celebrar, venir, traer,** and **poner.**

Rubric

Evaluate your writing using the rubric below.

Writing criteria	Excellent	Good	Needs Work
Content	Your description includes many details about your celebration.	Your description includes some details about your celebration.	Your description includes few details about your celebration.
Communication	Most of your description is organized and easy to follow.	Parts of your description are organized and easy to follow.	Your description is disorganized and hard to follow.
Accuracy	Your description has few mistakes in grammar and vocabulary.	Your description has some mistakes in grammar and vocabulary.	Your description has many mistakes in grammar and vocabulary.

UNIDAD 5
Lección 2 • Comparación cultural

Comparación cultural: ¡Así celebramos!

Compara con tu mundo

Now write a comparison about your celebration and that of one of the students from page 295. Organize your comparison by topics. First, compare the type of celebration, then the place where you celebrate and the guests, and lastly the food and activities.

Step 1

Use the table to organize your comparisons by topics. Write details for each topic about your celebration and that of the student you chose.

Categoría	Mi Fiesta	La Fiesta de _____
tipo de fiesta		
lugar		
invitados		
invitados		
comida		
actividades		

Step 2

Now use the details from the table to write a comparison. Include an introduction sentence and write about each topic. Use the verbs **celebrar, venir, traer, poner** to describe your celebration and that of the student you chose.

_____

_____

_____

_____

_____

_____

_____

Vocabulario A

> **¡AVANZA!** **Goal:** Talk about sports.

1 María loves playing baseball and tennis. In each column, place an x next to all the words associated with each sport.

El béisbol	El tenis
_____ el guante	_____ la raqueta
_____ el bate	_____ la piscina
_____ los aficionados	_____ la cancha
_____ el casco	_____ la pelota

2 These students are very sports-minded. Look at the drawings below. Then, complete the sentences with the sport they are playing.

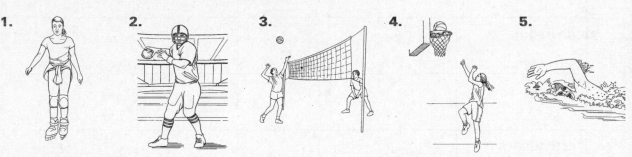

1.   2.   3.   4.   5.

1. A Norma le gusta _____ .

2. Pablo juega al _____ en el estadio.

3. Lucas y Lucía juegan al _____ en la cancha.

4. Alejandra juega al _____ en la cancha.

5. Todos los días, Arturo practica _____ en la piscina.

3 Write complete sentences to tell you what you need to play the following sports.

Modelo: el tenis: **Necesito una raqueta y una pelota.**

1. el fútbol americano: _____

2. patinar en línea: _____

3. el básquetbol: _____

Vocabulario B

> ¡AVANZA! **Goal:** Talk about sports.

1 What do you need for each sport? Draw a line from the word in the left column to its related word on the right.

1. el tenis   **a.** la piscina

2. la natación   **b.** el campo

3. el béisbol   **c.** los patines en línea

4. el fútbol americano   **d.** la raqueta

5. patinar en línea   **e.** el bate

2 Watching or playing sports can be really fun! Complete the following sentences with an expression from the word bank.

las reglas	los campeones	los partidos	un poco peligroso

1. A Juan le gusta ir a los estadios para ver _____ de fútbol americano.

2. Los jugadores que ganan son _____ .

3. Patinar en línea es _____ si no llevas un casco.

4. Leemos el libro sobre el béisbol para comprender _____ .

3 In a complete sentence, answer each question about your connection to sports.

1. ¿Cuál es tu deporte favorito?

_____

2. ¿Cuál es tu equipo favorito?

_____

3. ¿Tu equipo favorito gana siempre?

_____

Vocabulario C

> |AVANZA!| **Goal:** Talk about sports.

1 The baseball game is today. Use the words in the box to complete the dialog between two students.

los partidos	aficionado	nadar
las piscinas	un guante	campo

Jorge: ¡Hola, Pablo! ¿Eres **1.** _____ al béisbol?

Pablo: ¡Hola, Jorge! Sí, me gusta mucho ver **2.** _____ en el estadio.

Jorge: ¿Y tú practicas béisbol? ¿Tienes **3.** _____ ?

Pablo: Sí, y tengo un bate también. Todos los días voy al **4.** _____

a jugar al béisbol.

Jorge: ¡Qué bueno! Yo juego béisbol de vez en cuando, pero prefiero

5. _____ . Me gusta la natación.

Pablo: ¡Es un buen deporte! A mí también me gusta mucho nadar en

6. _____ .

2 Define the following sports-related terms in your own words.

modelo: un(a) atleta: **Es una persona que practica deportes.**

1. los ganadores:

_____

2. los aficionados:

_____

3. la cancha de tenis:

_____

3 Write three sentences that describe what you use to play your favorite sport. Use complete sentences.

_____

_____

Gramática A *The present tense of* **Jugar**

> **¡AVANZA!** **Goal:** Use the verb **jugar** to talk about sports.

1 Juan and his friends play many sports. Underline the correct form of the verb.

1. Ernesto (juega / jugamos) al voleibol.

2. Luis y Jimena (juega / juegan) al básquetbol.

3. Miriam y yo (jugamos / juegas) al tenis.

4. Yo (juega / juego) al béisbol.

5. Tú (juegas / juega) al fútbol americano.

2 Ana and her friends play sports, too. Complete the following sentences with the correct form of the verb **jugar**.

1. Julio y María, ¿ustedes _____ en un equipo de fútbol americano?

2. Señor Martín, ¿usted _____ al béisbol?

3. Lucas y Marta _____ al voleibol.

4. Alejandra _____ al tenis todos los sábados.

5. Javier y yo _____ como campeones.

3 Use each element in the table at least once to create sentences using the necessary form of **jugar**.

ustedes	al béisbol	en un equipo
María	al voleibol	los sábados
usted	al tenis	en la cancha de la escuela

modelo: Ustedes juegan al tenis los sábados.

1. _____

2. _____

3. _____

Gramática B *The present tense of Jugar*

¡AVANZA! **Goal:** Use the verb **jugar** to talk about sports.

1 There are many sports to play. Complete the sentences with the correct form of **jugar**.

1. Los jugadores de tenis _____ en las canchas al lado de la escuela.

    a. juegas   **b.** juega   **c.** juego   **d.** juegan

2. ¿Tú _____ al béisbol en el verano?

    a. juegan   **b.** jugamos   **c.** juegas   **d.** juega

3. Yo no _____ al fútbol americano.

    a. jugamos   **b.** juego   **c.** juegan   **d.** tratamos

2 Describe when the people below play their sports. Complete the sentences using the correct form of **jugar**.

modelo: El equipo de la escuela / mañana / un partido
             El equipo de la escuela juega un partido mañana.

1. Jaime y yo / siempre / al fútbol americano

_____

2. Carolina y Guillermo / al tenis / temprano

_____

3. Nora / al béisbol / casi todos los días

_____

3 Answer the following questions about the sports that you play.

modelo: ¿ Tú juegas al béisbol? **Sí, (No, no) juego al béisbol.**

1. ¿Tus amigos juegan al béisbol?

_____

2. ¿Tu familia y tú juegan al tenis?

_____

3. ¿Tú juegas al voleibol?

_____

Gramática C   *The present tense of Jugar*

> **¡AVANZA!**   **Goal:** Use the verb **jugar** to talk about sports.

1 Lucas is talking to a friend about sports. Complete the dialog with the correct form of **jugar**.

Lucas: Hola; Marcos. Mis amigos y yo **1.**_____ al fútbol americano todos los sábados. ¿Tú también **2.**_____?

Marcos: No, yo no **3.** _____ al fútbol americano. Me gusta más jugar al béisbol en el equipo de la escuela. Pedro también **4.** _____ con el equipo.

Lucas: ¿Sí? Pedro, Miguel y Antonio **5.** _____ con nosotros los sábados. ¿Ustedes **6.** _____ bien?

Marcos: Yo no **7.**_____ muy bien pero es divertido estar con ellos y aprender el deporte. Y ustedes, ¿**8.** _____ bien?

2 Where do these athletes play? Complete the following sentences with an appropriate phrase that includes the correct form of **jugar**.

modelo   Los equipos de fútbol americano <u>juegan en el campo o el estadio.</u>

1. Un jugador de fútbol _____

2. Un campeón de básquetbol _____

3. Los campeones de tenis _____

3 Write a description of a sport that you or your friends like to play. Include information about where and when you play the sport and what equipment you need.

_____

_____

_____

_____

_____

Gramática A   The present tense of *Saber* and *Conocer*   Level 1, pp. 312-314

> ¡AVANZA! **Goal:** Use the verbs **saber** and **conocer** to talk about sports.

1 Some of Marta's friends know a lot about sports. Complete the sentences below following the model.

a. Los amigos de Marta saben   **b.** Los amigos de Marta conocen

   modelo: __b__ a muchos jugadores.

1. ____ de béisbol y tenis.

2. ____ que el equipo siempre gana.

3. ____ muchos estadios.

4. ____ patinar en línea.

2 Find out what these people know about sports. Underline the verb that completes each sentence below.

1. Camila (conoce / sabe) al campeón de tenis.

2. Los jugadores (conocen / saben) dónde está el campo.

3. Nosotros (conocemos / sabemos) a los atletas de la escuela.

4. Yo (conozco / sé) que la natación no es muy peligrosa.

5. ¿Tú (conoces / sabes) quiénes son los campeones?

3 What or whom do the following people know? Complete the sentences with the correct form of either **saber** or **conocer.**

1. Yo _____ unas historias muy divertidas de deportes.

2. Mi abuelo _____ a un jugador de béisbol dominicano.

3. ¿Ustedes _____ muchos países donde juegan al béisbol?

4. Nosotros _____ patinar muy bien.

5. Yo _____ a su hermana Mirella.

6. ¿Tú _____ a qué hora juega el equipo de fútbol americano?

Gramática B *The present tense of* **Saber** *and* **Conocer**

> **¡AVANZA!** **Goal:** Use the verbs **saber** and **conocer** to talk about sports.

1 Today's game is very important. Complete the following sentences by choosing the correct verb in parentheses.

1. Los aficionados no (saben / conocen) cómo llegar al estadio nuevo.

2. Los aficionados no (saben / conocen) el estadio nuevo.

3. Los jugadores (saben / conocen) bien a los atletas del otro equipo.

4. La atleta (sabe / conoce) patinar en línea.

5. Nosotros (sabemos / conocemos) a todos los jugadores.

2 Two teams are playing today. Complete the sentences using the correct form of **saber** or **conocer**.

1. Los jugadores no _____ con quienes juegan.

2. Los atletas no _____ a los jugadores del otro equipo.

3. El equipo _____ que el partido es a las tres.

4. El equipo _____ bien la cancha.

5. Nosotros no _____ quién gana.

3 Answer the following questions in complete sentences.

1. ¿Conoces tú Los Ángeles?

_____

2. ¿Tú sabes patinar?

_____

_____

3. ¿Sabes quiénes son los campeones de béisbol?

_____

_____

4. ¿Tu amigo(a) quiere conocer a los campeones de fútbol americano?

_____

_____

Gramática C   The present tense of *Saber* and *Conocer*

> **¡AVANZA!**   **Goal:** Use the verbs **saber** and **conocer** to talk about sports.

1 Ernesto and Sofía talk about a football game. Complete the conversation with the correct forms of **saber** or **conocer**.

Ernesto: Hola, Sofía. ¿ _____ tú que hoy tu equipo juega un partido de fútbol americano?

Sofía: Sí. Yo _____ que vamos a ganar. ¿Sabes por qué?

Ernesto: No, no _____ . ¿Por qué?

Sofía: Porque Guillermo juega con nosotros.

Ernesto: No lo _____ , ¿quién es?

Sofía: Es el campeón de fútbol americano. Él _____ jugar bien.

Ernesto: ¿Tu hermano _____ a los jugadores del otro equipo?

Sofía: Sí, él _____ a todos los jugadores.

2 Which sports or athletes are you familiar with? Answer the following questions.

1. ¿Conoces a un jugador de fútbol americano?

_____

2. ¿Sabes las reglas del voleibol?

_____

3. ¿Saben patinar tú y tus amigos?

_____

4. ¿Conoces a un(a) aficionado(a) al béisbol?

_____

5. ¿Sabes cuánto cuestan unos patines en línea nuevos?

_____

3 Write about an athlete that you know. Use **saber** and **conocer**.

_____

Integración: Hablar

Alejandro has just moved to a new city and wants to practice all the sports he likes. He sees an Athletic club's Web page and decides to call and leave a message to express his interest in their sports facilities.

Fuente 1 Leer

Read Club Arco iris's Web site's main page...

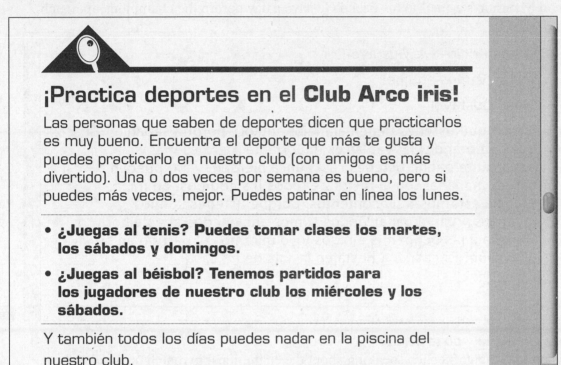

¡Practica deportes en el Club Arco iris!

Las personas que saben de deportes dicen que practicarlos es muy bueno. Encuentra el deporte que más te gusta y puedes practicarlo en nuestro club (con amigos es más divertido). Una o dos veces por semana es bueno, pero si puedes más veces, mejor. Puedes patinar en línea los lunes.

- **¿Juegas al tenis? Puedes tomar clases los martes, los sábados y domingos.**

- **¿Juegas al béisbol? Tenemos partidos para los jugadores de nuestro club los miércoles y los sábados.**

Y también todos los días puedes nadar en la piscina del nuestro club.

Fuente 2 Escuchar   *CD 03 track 22*

Listen to Alejandro's telephone message to Club Arco iris. Take notes.

_____

_____

_____

Hablar

What days can Alejandro practice the sports he likes at Club Arco iris?

modelo: Los lunes, Alejandro puede... Él también puede...

Integración: Escribir

Level 1, pp. 315–316
WB CD 03 track 23

Mauricio's friend, Gustavo, plays for the state's volleyball team. He sends an e-mail to a friend to express his views about the team, one day before the final championship match. On the day of the match, he changes his mind about having to be the winner, when he listens to Gustavo's coach talking about sportsmanship.

Fuente 1 Leer

Read Mauricio's e-mail to his friend Gustavo a day before the championship match...

De: Mauricio   A: Gustavo

Tema: ¡Vamos equipo!

¡Hola, Gustavo!

Pienso que ustedes tienen el mejor equipo, porque saben que comprender las reglas es importante, pero es más importante ganar. Ustedes casi nunca pierden, y ¡no pueden perder mañana! Son el mejor de todos los equipos. En mi escuela estamos muy contentos, porque ustedes son los favoritos y van a ganar. Todos somos aficionados al voleibol. Mañana a las ocho, mis amigos y yo miramos el partido en la televisión. Es casi una fiesta en la sala de mi casa.

Mauricio

Fuente 2 Escuchar   *CD 03 track 24*

Listen to Gustavo's coach speaking about the championship match on a radio show. Take notes.

_____

_____

_____

Escribir

Mauricio listened to Gustavo's coach on the radio, and then changed his mind about winning and losing. Why did he change his mind from one day to the other?

modelo: Un día antes, Mauricio piensa que...Pero después, comprende que...

_____

_____

_____

_____

_____

Escuchar A

> ¡AVANZA! **Goal:** Listen to discussions about sports.

1 Listen to Ernesto. Place an "x" next to the things he says he needs for his favorite sport.

1. ____ una piscina

2. ____ un libro de reglas

3. ____ una pelota de béisbol

4. ____ un guante de béisbol

5. ____ una raqueta

6. ____ unos patines en línea

7. ____ un bate

8. ____ un casco nuevo

2 Listen to Ángel. Then, complete the sentences by filling in the correct word.

1. Al hijo de Ángel le gustan muchos _____ .

2. El deporte que le gusta más es _____ .

3. El hijo de Ángel necesita cosas para _____ al béisbol.

4. Ángel quiere comprar _____ nuevo.

Escuchar B

> ¡AVANZA! **Goal:** Listen to discussions about sports.

1 Listen to Julio. Complete the table with the sport that each student plays.

Lucas y Susana	
Marcos	
Andrea	
Ana	
Miguel y Jimena	

2 Listen to the conversation between Ana and Jorge. Take notes. Then, answer the questions below in complete sentences:

1. ¿Adónde quiere ir Ana?

_____

2. ¿Quién juega?

_____

3. ¿Quién es un aficionado?

_____

4. ¿Mira Ana muchos partidos en la televisión?

_____

Escuchar C

> **¡AVANZA!** **Goal:** Listen to discussions about sports.

1 Listen to Lucas and take notes. Then, write what day(s) he does the following activities.

1. jugar al básquetbol _____

2. patinar en línea _____

3. jugar al voleibol _____

4. jugar al tenis _____

5. jugar al fútbol americano _____

6. jugar al béisbol _____

2 Listen to the conversation between Débora and her mother. Take notes. Then, answer the following questions:

1. ¿Por qué no está el hermano de Débora?

_____

2. ¿Qué encuentra la mamá de Débora?

_____

3. ¿Quiénes patinan en línea?

_____

4. ¿Quién sabe dónde Nicolás patina?

_____

5. ¿Por qué Jorge no patina en línea?

_____

Leer A

> ¡AVANZA! **Goal:** Read about sports.

The following is a flyer hanging in the hall and the cafeteria of the school.

> ### Partido de béisbol
>
> ¡Atención, aficionados!
>
> Nuestro equipo sabe jugar bien y ahora lo van a
> hacer en su nuevo estadio.
> Ven a conocer el Estadio Martínez de Punta Cana.
>
> ¿Sabes cuándo?: Hoy, el 2 de Mayo
> ¿Sabes dónde?: El Estadio Martínez
>
> Globos para los chicos
> Pelotas con los nombres de los jugadores para todos
>
> ¡Ven con toda la famila a celebrar con nuestro equipo!

¿Comprendiste?

Read the note about the game. Then, read each sentence below and answer **Cierto** (*True*) or **Falso** (*False*).

C   F   **1.** El partido es hoy.

C   F   **2.** El equipo juega mal.

C   F   **3.** El equipo juega en una cancha vieja.

C   F   **4.** El Estadio Martínez es un estadio de béisbol.

C   F   **5.** Los chicos reciben globos porque es un cumpleaños.

¿Qué piensas?

Read the note about the game. Answer the following question in a complete sentence.

1. ¿Conoces un estadio donde tú vives? ¿Cuál?

_____

2. ¿Hay un equipo de béisbol en tu escuela? ¿Dónde juegan?

_____

Leer B

> ¡AVANZA! **Goal:** Read about sports.

Laura writes a letter to her friends about her friend Ana.

> *Hola chicos:*
>
> *Tengo que salir temprano hoy. ¿Saben que esta tarde Ana juega un partido de béisbol? Ella está muy nerviosa porque no conoce a las jugadoras del otro equipo y no sabe cómo juegan. A ella no le gusta perder. Siempre digo que también debe saber que no tiene que ganar siempre. A veces ganas y a veces pierdes. Pero ella no entiende. Siempre quiere ser campeona.*
>
> *¿Vienen hoy al partido? Deben venir. Ana y el equipo necesitan tener muchos aficionados allí. Quiero verlos a ustedes en el partido.*
>
> *Hasta luego,*
>
> *Laura*

¿Comprendiste?

Read Laura's letter. Then, place an "x" next to the things that are true.

1. ____ Ana juega un partido de béisbol.

2. ____ Laura juega un partido de béisbol.

3. ____ Ana nunca pierde.

4. ____ Laura quiere ver a sus amigos.

5. ____ A Ana no le gusta perder.

6. ____ A Laura no le gusta perder.

7. ____ Ana está nerviosa.

8. ____ Laura está nerviosa.

¿Qué piensas?

Read Laura's letter. Answer the following questions in complete sentences.

1. ¿Es importante saber perder? ¿Por qué?

   _____

   _____

2. ¿Es importante ir a los partidos de tus amigos? ¿Por qué?

   _____

   _____

Leer C

> ¡AVANZA! **Goal:** Read about sports.

A brief article about the school's championship basketball team appears in the school newspaper.

¡GANAMOS OTRA VEZ!

Nuestro equipo es el campeón de básquetbol una vez más. Si conoces a los jugadores, sabes que ellos son serios y saben jugar muy bien. Los chicos del equipo también saben que es importante sacar buenas notas en clase. Ellos son trabajadores en la escuela y en la cancha. También, todos los jugadores saben que sus aficionados siempre van a venir a los partidos.

Con nuestro equipo, ¡siempre ganamos!

¿Comprendiste?

Read the article in the school newspaper. Then, read each sentence below and answer **Cierto** (*True*) or **Falso** (*False*).

C F **1.** Los jugadores saben que las buenas notas son importantes.

C F **2.** Los jugadores no saben el deporte bien.

C F **3.** Los jugadores son serios.

C F **4.** Ellos saben que sus aficionados nunca van a los partidos.

C F **5.** El equipo nunca gana.

¿Qué piensas?

Read the article in the school newspaper. Then, answer the first question in a complete sentence and give an example explaining your reason in a second sentence.

1. ¿Piensas que es difícil practicar un deporte y sacar buenas notas en la escuela? ¿Por qué?

_____

_____

2. ¿Conoces a un(a) atleta que es un(a) buena estudiante?

_____

_____

Escribir A

¡AVANZA! **Goal:** Write about sports.

Step 1

List 5 sports that are played on a court or in a field.

en una cancha	en un campo
1.	4.
2.	5.
3.	

Step 2

Answer the following questions in complete sentences.

1. ¿Qué sabes de béisbol?

_____

_____

2. ¿Qué jugador de béisbol conoces?

_____

_____

Step 3

Evaluate your writing using the information in the table below.

Writing Criteria	Excellent	Good	Needs Work
Content	You have responded to the questions completely.	You have responded to the questions partially.	You have not responded to the questions.
Communication	Most of your response is clear.	Some of your response is clear.	Your message is not very clear.
Accuracy	You make few mistakes in grammar and vocabulary.	You make some mistakes in grammar and vocabulary.	You make many mistakes in grammar and vocabulary.

Escribir B

> **¡AVANZA!** **Goal:** Write about sports.

Step 1

Complete the first column with three sports that you play all the time and the second column with three sports that you do not know how to play.

Deportes que juegas	Deportes que no sabes jugar
_____	_____
_____	_____
_____	_____

Step 2

Write three sentences saying which sports you know how to play and one thing that you know you need for each. Then, write a sentence saying which sports you do not know how to play.

modelo: Yo juego al béisbol y sé que necesito un bate. Yo no sé jugar al voleibol.

_____

_____

_____

_____

_____

Step 3

Evaluate your writing using the information in the table below.

Writing Criteria	Excellent	Good	Needs Work
Content	You include all of the information.	You include some of the information.	You include little information.
Communication	Most of your message is organized and easy to follow.	Parts of your message are organized and easy to follow.	Your message is disorganized and hard to follow.
Accuracy	You make few mistakes in grammar and vocabulary.	You make some mistakes in grammar and vocabulary.	You make many mistakes in grammar and vocabulary.

Escribir C

> **¡AVANZA!** **Goal:** Write about sports.

Step 1

Complete the following table about a few sports.

Deportes que conoces	Lugares donde los juegan	Cosas que usamos para jugarlos

Step 2

In six complete sentences, write an article about one of your school's athletic events for the school newspaper. Use the verbs **jugar, saber,** and **conocer.**

_____

_____

_____

_____

_____

Step 3

Evaluate your writing using the information in the table below.

Writing Criteria	Excellent	Good	Needs Work
Content	You include all of the verbs in your article.	You include some of the verbs in your article.	You do not include any of the verbs in your article.
Communication	Most of your message is organized and easy to follow.	Parts of your message are organized and easy to follow.	Your message is disorganized and hard to follow.
Accuracy	You make few mistakes in grammar and vocabulary.	You make some mistakes in grammar and vocabulary.	You make many mistakes in grammar and vocabulary.

Cultura A

> ¡AVANZA! **Goal:** Review cultural information about the Dominican Republic.

① **The Dominican Republic** Read the following sentences and answer *true* or *false*.

T   F   **1.** Professional baseball in the Dominican Republic is played from March through July.

T   F   **2.** The currency of the Dominican Republic is the Dominican peso.

T   F   **3.** The national sport of the Dominican Republic is soccer.

T   F   **4.** The capital of the Dominican Republic is Santo Domingo.

T   F   **5.** The Dominican Republic is part of an island.

② **Famous Dominicans** Draw lines to match the names of some famous Dominicans with their professions.

Oscar de la Renta   writer

Pedro Martínez   singer

Juan Luis Guerra   designer

Julia Álvarez   baseball player

③ **Serie del Caribe** Describe the **Serie del Caribe.** What sport is played and who participates? When does it take place? Is it similar to any other sporting events you know of? Explain.

_____

_____

_____

_____

_____

_____

Cultura B

| ¡AVANZA! | **Goal:** Review cultural information about the Dominican Republic. |

1 **Dominican Culture** Complete the sentences about the Dominican Republic.

1. The Dominican Republic shares the island of Hispaniola with _____ .

2. Many tourists enjoy going to the _____ of the Caribbean Sea in the Dominican Republic.

3. The _____ in Santo Domingo is a memorial dedicated to the heroes of the Dominican Republic's fight for freedom from Haiti.

4. The capital of the Dominican Republic is _____ .

5. **Cazabe** is a typical _____ of the Dominican Republic.

2 **People and professions** Write down the professions of the following famous Dominicans.

Famous Dominicans	Their Professions
Julia Álvarez	_____
Oscar de la Renta	_____
Juan Luis Guerra	_____
Pedro Martínez	_____

3 **The national sport** Describe the national sport of the Dominican Republic. What is it and when is it played? In your description, talk about a special Dominican sporting event.

_____

_____

_____

_____

_____

_____

Cultura C

> **¡AVANZA!** **Goal:** Review cultural information about the Dominican Republic.

1 **The Dominican Republic** Complete the following sentences with the missing words.

1. The Dominican Republic has a _____ climate.

2. The Dominican baseball fans can go to see professional baseball games from October until the month of _____ .

3. The _____ of the Dominican Republic are popular with tourists.

4. Santo Domingo is the _____ of the Dominican Republic.

2 **Dominican Culture** Answer these questions with complete sentences.

1. What are some typical foods of the Dominican Republic?_____

_____

2. What is the **Altar de la Patria** located in Santo Domingo? _____

_____

_____

3 **Serie del Caribe** Compare the **Serie del Caribe** to another sporting event you have seen or know about. Include information about what sport is involved and when it is played. Also mention where the event is held or which countries participate, along with any famous players who have competed in the event.

_____

_____

_____

_____

_____

_____

_____

_____

Vocabulario A

¡AVANZA! **Goal:** Talk about parts of the body.

---

1 Match each part of the body below with the activity associated with it.

_____	**1.** ojos	**a.** hablar
_____	**2.** orejas	**b.** escribir
_____	**3.** boca	**c.** mirar
_____	**4.** piernas	**d.** caminar
_____	**5.** manos	**e.** escuchar

2 Javier and his friends are at the beach. Complete the following sentences using the words in the box.

pesas	enferma	salud	bloqueador de sol	estómago

1. Es peligroso tomar el sol si no usas _____ .

2. Susana está _____ y no puede ir a la playa.

3. A Susana le duele el _____ porque bebe muchos refrescos.

4. Pedro levanta _____ en la playa.

5. Caminar en la playa es una buena actividad para la _____ .

3 Answer the following questions in complete sentences.

1. ¿Te duelen las piernas cuando caminas mucho?

_____

2. ¿Descansas mucho cuando estás enfermo(a)?

_____

3. Cuando nadas, ¿usas más las piernas o los brazos?

_____

Vocabulario B

> ¡AVANZA! **Goal:** Talk about parts of the body.

1 Alicia and her friends go to the beach. Complete each sentence with the correct word in parentheses.

1. Los chicos nadan en _____ . (las pesas / el mar / la salud)

2. Alicia usa bloqueador de sol en la _____ . (ojo / playa / piel)

3. Los amigos de Alicia hacen _____ . (esquí acuático / una cabeza / un corazón)

2 Inés and Carlos are also at the beach. Complete their conversation with the words from the box.

la piel	el sol	fuerte
bloqueador de sol	enfermo	

Inés: ¡Qué buen día! Tomamos **1.** _____ toda la mañana.

Carlos: ¿Usas **2.** _____ ? En la playa, tienes que usarlo.

Inés: Sí, lo uso. Pero me duele un poco **3.** _____ .

El sol está muy **4.** _____ .

Carlos: Es verdad. Yo no tengo sombrero y ya estoy un poco

5. _____ .

3 The following people are sick. Write complete sentences to describe what hurts.

1.

2.

3.

_____

_____

_____

Vocabulario C

> ¡AVANZA! **Goal:** Talk about parts of the body.

1 Place each word from the box in the appropriate category.

herido	sano	la boca	el esquí acuático
enfermo	las orejas	dolor	el mar
los ojos	el sol	el bloqueador de sol	la nariz

	La salud	La playa	La cabeza
1			
2			
3			
4			

2 We all get sick sometimes. Complete the following sentences with the reasons why. Follow the model:

modelo: Me duelen las piernas cuando **camino mucho**.

1. Me duelen los brazos cuando _____

2. Me duele la mano cuando _____

3. Me duele el estómago cuando _____

4. Me duele la piel cuando _____

3 Write three complete sentences to describe what you do at the beach. Describe the beginning of your day, the things you do at the beach, and the end of your day.

_____

_____

_____

_____

Gramática A *Preterite of –ar Verbs*

> **¡AVANZA!** **Goal:** Use the preterite of –ar verbs to talk about a day at the beach.

1 Andrea and her friends spent the day at the beach. Underline the correct form of the verb in the following sentences.

1. Andrea (invitó / invité) a sus amigos a la playa.

2. Los amigos de Andrea (nadaste / nadaron) todo el día.

3. Andrea y yo (hablaron / hablamos) de los chicos en la clase.

4. Andrea y tú (llevaron / llevó) unos sombreros muy grandes.

5. ¿Tú (ayudó / ayudaste) a Andrea a bucear?

6. Andrea (comenzaste / comenzó) a levantar pesas.

2 The following students had fun at the beach. Complete the sentences using the preterite of the verbs in parentheses.

1. Lucas y yo _____ por la playa. (caminar)

2. En la noche, yo _____ en la playa. (cantar)

3. A Antonio le duelen las piernas. Él _____ mucho con Inés. (caminar)

4. ¿Ustedes _____ bloqueador de sol? (llevar)

5. Antonio _____ un sombrero. (usar)

6. Inés está cansada. Ella _____ mucho en la tarde. (bucear)

3 Answer the following questions about what you did yesterday in complete sentences.

1. ¿Levantaste pesas?

_____

2. ¿Caminaron tú y tus amigos a la escuela?

_____

3. ¿Qué estudiaste?

_____

Gramática B *Preterite of –ar Verbs*

> **¡AVANZA!** **Goal:** Use the preterite of –ar verbs to talk about a day at the beach.

1 Alejandro and his friends went to the beach. The people who went are listed in one column and the things they did are listed in the other. Put them together to create sentences. Follow the model.

Jimena	llevamos los refrescos.
Jimena y Jorge	levanté pesas en la playa y me duelen los brazos.
Jorge y yo	hablaron de las tareas de la escuela.
Tú	escuchó su música favorita.
Yo	preparaste la comida.

modelo: Jimena escuchó su música favorita.

1. _____
2. _____
3. _____
4. _____

2 Write three sentences to describe what happened at the beach. Use the information given.

1. Yo/ llevar la guitarra de Juan _____

2. Ana y yo/ nadar en el mar _____

3. Guillermo y Carina/ mirar el sol en la tarde _____

_____

4. Ustedes/ tocar la guitarra en la playa _____

3 Complete the following sentences about what you and the people you know did yesterday. Follow the model.

modelo: (mirar) Mi amigo(a) <u>Mi amigo José miró la televisión ayer.</u>

1. (celebrar) Yo _____

2. (llevar) Mis amigos _____

3. (enseñar) Mi maestro(a) _____

Gramática C *Preterite of –ar Verbs*

> ¡AVANZA! **Goal:** Use the preterite of **–ar** verbs to talk about a day at the beach.

1 Julia spent the day at the beach with her friends. Complete the following sentences with the correct form of the verbs from the box.

hablar	cantar	bucear	caminar	llevar

Ayer, nosotros pasamos un rato en la playa. Primero, Juan, Armando

y yo **1.** _____ por la playa. Hoy me duelen las

piernas. Después, los chicos **2.** _____ en el mar.

Ana y Manuel **3.** _____ del equipo de béisbol de la

escuela y del partido. Lucía **4.** _____ su guitarra y

nosotros **5.** _____ por horas al lado del mar.

2 Write about the last time you went to the beach or pool with your friends. Use the preterite of the following verbs.

1. pasar _____

2. usar _____

3. hablar _____

4. comprar: _____

5. nadar: _____

3 Write an e-mail message to a classmate. Say what you did yesterday.

_____

_____

_____

_____

_____

_____

Gramática A Stem-Changing Verbs: –car, –gar

> **¡AVANZA!** **Goal:** Use –**car** and –**gar** verbs to talk about the past.

1 Yesterday Enrique and Ana Sofía went to the beach. Complete Ana Sofía's sentences with **yo**, **Enrique** or **nosotros**.

1. _____ pasamos el día en la playa.

   _____ llegó primero.

2. _____ llegué cinco minutos después.

   _____ busqué un lugar cerca del mar.

3. _____ almorzó pizza después de nadar.

   _____ saqué un sándwich de mi mochila.

4. _____ jugamos fútbol en la playa.

   _____ tocó la guitarra y cantó.

2 Complete each sentence with the preterite form of the verb in parentheses.

1. Yo _____ la guitarra el sábado. (toqué / tocamos)

2. Yo _____ tarde al partido de fútbol. (llegó / llegué)

3. Tú _____ básquetbol y te duelen los brazos. (practiqué / practicaste)

4. Yo _____ a mi hermanita en su escuela. (busqué / buscaron)

5. Mi mamá _____ la ropa que compró mi hermano. (pagó / pagué)

3 Answer the following questions in complete sentences.

1. ¿Qué deporte practicaste ayer?

   _____

2. ¿A qué hora llegaste hoy a la escuela?

   _____

3. ¿Sacaste una buena nota en ciencias?

   _____

Gramática B *Stem-Changing Verbs: –car, –gar*

> **¡AVANZA!** **Goal:** Use **–car** and **–gar** verbs to talk about the past.

1 What did everyone do yesterday? Choose the correct form of the verb for each sentence below.

1. Yo _____ tarde a clases.

   a. llegaste **b.** llegamos **c.** llegué **d.** llegó

2. Juan _____ a sus amigos en la cafetería.

   a. busqué **b.** buscó **c.** buscaron **d.** buscamos

3. Yo _____ la guitarra en la fiesta de cumpleaños de Ana.

   a. tocaron **b.** tocaste **c.** toqué **d.** tocó

4. Los estudiantes _____ buenas notas en todas las clases.

   a. sacamos **b.** saqué **c.** sacaron **d.** sacaste

5. Yo _____ natación ayer.

   a. practicó **b.** practicaste **c.** practicaron **d.** practiqué

2 Complete the sentences with the preterite form of one of the verbs in the box.

1. Yo _____ el básquetbol y ahora me duele todo

   el cuerpo.

2. Yo _____ el piano en casa de un amigo.

3. Mi hermana _____ toda la ropa vieja del armario.

4. Nosotros _____ un buen lugar para cenar.

5. Yo _____ primero a la piscina.

> tocar
> sacar
> llegar
> practicar
> buscar

3 Create sentences about what you did yesterday. Use the preterite of the verbs provided.

1. pagar _____

2. buscar _____

3. llegar _____

Gramática C *Stem-Changing Verbs: –car, –gar*

> **¡AVANZA!** **Goal:** Use **–car** and **–gar** verbs to talk about the past.

1 Find out what everyone did yesterday by completing the sentences with the preterite form of the verb in parentheses.

1. Yo _____ a la escuela en autobús. (llegar)

2. Mis amigos _____ un lugar para comer. (buscar)

3. Yo _____ los libros que compraste. (pagar)

4. Luis _____ la basura para su padre. (sacar)

5. Yo _____ con el bate y el guante de béisbol. (practicar)

2 Write complete sentences to tell if you did or did not do the following activities.

1. comenzar la tarea tarde _____

_____

2. practicar un deporte _____

_____

3. llegar a casa temprano _____

_____

4. tocar la guitarra _____

_____

5. jugar videojuegos _____

_____

3 Write a paragraph about a recent trip to the mall. Be sure to tell when you arrived, what you looked for and how much you paid.

_____

_____

_____

_____

_____

_____

UNIDAD 6
Lección 2 • Gramática C

Integración: Hablar

Miriam's friend Rodrigo loves sports, but he has not been feeling well lately. Rodrigo calls
Miriam to ask if her father can help him. Miriam's father is a doctor who writes articles
about health issues for an online publication.

Fuente 1 Leer

Read Dr. Salinas's Web page article on health issues...

La salud es importante

¡Hola! Soy el doctor José Salinas. Hoy voy a hablar de la salud y de las
actividades para estar sano. También quiero hablar sobre las cosas que hacen
doler el cuerpo, como actividades y alimentos peligrosos para la salud. Si
juegas mucho al tenis, debes levantar pesas para tener los brazos siempre
fuertes. Tienes que comer muchas frutas porque son nutritivas. Debes comer
bien todos los días. Si haces actividades sanas como correr dos o más veces
por semana y tienes dolor en las piernas, debes correr más despacio o
caminar por quince minutos y después, correr.

Fuente 2 Escuchar *CD 03 track 32*

Listen to Rodrigo's voicemail for Miriam. Take notes.

_____

_____

_____

_____

Hablar

What advice will Miram's father, Dr. Salinas, give to Rodrigo?

modelo: A Rodrigo le duele(n)..., el doctor Salinas va a decir que debe...

Integración: Escribir

Level 1, pp. 339–340
WB CD 03 track 33

Gabriela and Beatriz went to Puerto Plata, Dominican Republic on vacation, but Gabriela is from Arkansas and did not know much about the beach, while Beatriz is from southern California and has spent a lot of time at the beach.

Fuente 1 Leer

Read Gabriela's e-mail to Beatriz...

> ¡Hola Beatriz!
>
> Me duelen la piel y la cabeza pero no es importante porque estoy muy contenta. Ayer, Norberto, mis amigas y yo pasamos el día en la playa. Tú sabes cuánto me gusta tomar el sol. Todos hablamos por horas y horas. Caminamos por la playa y nadamos en el mar. Tomamos el sol y escuchamos música. Tengo las piernas, los brazos y la nariz rojos como tomates, pero pasamos un día muy divertido en la playa. ¿Qué hicieron ustedes?
>
> Gabriela

Fuente 2 Escuchar *CD 03 track 34*

Listen to Beatriz's voice message to Gabriela. Take notes.

_____

_____

_____

_____

Escribir

Explain why Gabriela is in pain but Beatriz is not.

modelo: A Gabriela le duelen...Pero Beatriz está bien porque...

_____

_____

_____

_____

_____

_____

_____

Escuchar A

Level 1, pp. 346–347
WB CD 03 tracks 35-36

> **¡AVANZA!** **Goal:** Listen to discussions about the body and past activities.

1 Listen to Graciela. Then, read each sentence and answer **Cierto** (*True*) or **Falso** (*False*).

C   F   **1.** Graciela pasó el día en la playa.

C   F   **2.** Miriam tomó sol.

C   F   **3.** Miriam usó mucho bloqueador de sol.

C   F   **4.** A Miriam le duelen las piernas.

C   F   **5.** Graciela caminó con Miriam por la playa.

2 Listen to Miriam. Then, complete the sentences with the correct word.

1. Ayer, Miriam tomó mucho _____ . (sol / refrescos)

2. El sol en la playa es muy _____ . (sano / fuerte)

3. La amiga de Miriam la llamó para saber de su _____ . (salud / amigo)

4. Miriam hoy está _____ . (enferma / tranquila)

Escuchar B

> **¡AVANZA!** **Goal:** Listen to discussions about the body and past activities.

1 Listen to Lourdes and take notes. Then, match the people with what they did at the beach. People may have done more than one thing.

1. ____ Todos
2. ____ Las chicas
3. ____ Juan
4. ____ Norma
5. ____ Marcos
6. ____ Julia y Diego
7. ____ Lourdes

a. caminar por la playa
b. cantar en la noche
c. bailar
d. tocar la guitarra
e. celebrar el cumpleaños de Lourdes
f. llegar a casa tarde
g. preparar un pastel
h. practicar esquí acuático

2 Listen to Marcos. Take notes. Then, complete the sentences below:

1. Marcos y sus amigos pensaron en _____ .

2. Allí, ellos _____ de la amiga de Marcos.

3. Marcos tocó _____ y _____ música rock.

4. A Marcos le duelen _____ .

5. Todos _____ el día muy felices.

Escuchar C

¡AVANZA! **Goal:** Listen to discussions about the body and past activities.

1 Listen to the doctor and take notes. Then, complete the table with the causes of each person's pain.

Dolor de	Qué hicieron
Estómago	
Piel	
Cabeza u ojos	
Brazos	
Orejas	

2 Listen to Luis' conversation with the doctor. Take notes. Then, answer the following questions:

1. ¿Por qué va Luis a ver al doctor?

_____

_____

2. ¿Por qué está enfermo Luis?

_____

_____

3. ¿Por qué el doctor le preguntó cuándo celebraron el cumpleaños de la hermana de Luis?

_____

_____

4. ¿Qué tiene que hacer Luis?

_____

_____

Leer A

> ¡AVANZA! **Goal:** Read about past events.

Jaime wrote an e-mail message to his friends inviting them to spend the day at the beach.

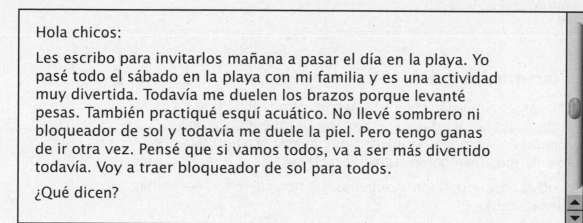

Hola chicos:

Les escribo para invitarlos mañana a pasar el día en la playa. Yo pasé todo el sábado en la playa con mi familia y es una actividad muy divertida. Todavía me duelen los brazos porque levanté pesas. También practiqué esquí acuático. No llevé sombrero ni bloqueador de sol y todavía me duele la piel. Pero tengo ganas de ir otra vez. Pensé que si vamos todos, va a ser más divertido todavía. Voy a traer bloqueador de sol para todos.

¿Qué dicen?

¿Comprendiste?

Read Jaime's e-mail message. Then, write **sí** next to the things that Jaime said he did at the beach and **no** next to the things he didn't mention.

1. _____ ir a la playa con su familia

2. _____ llevar bloqueador de sol

3. _____ levantar pesas

4. _____ nadar toda la tarde

5. _____ mirar el mar

6. _____ practicar esquí acuático

7. _____ cantar con sus amigos.

8. _____ no llevar sombrero

¿Qué piensas?

Read Jaime's e-mail message. Then write two sentences describing what you did the last time you went to the beach or pool with your friends.

_____

_____

_____

Leer B

> **¡AVANZA!** **Goal:** Read about past events.

The basketball team players are sick. Before they leave the gym, they are given the following informational leaflet:

➕ ¡Atención chicos!

Muchos jugadores están enfermos. Ayer, ganamos el partido y a muchos chicos hoy les duele el estómago. Después del partido celebraron en el parque. Cocinaron una comida poco nutritiva y hoy están enfermos. No jugaron el partido de la tarde.

La salud es muy importante y tenemos que hacer las cosas necesarias para estar sanos.

¡Tenemos que comer comida sana!

¿Comprendiste?

Read the leaflet. Then, complete the following sentences.

1. Los chicos no jugaron el partido de hoy porque _____

2. A los chicos les duele _____

3. Les duele porque _____

4. Una de las cosas más importantes es _____

5. Tenemos que hacer todo para _____

¿Qué piensas?

Read the leaflet. Answer the first question in a complete sentence then explain your answer.

1. ¿Piensas que es importante comer comida nutritiva? ¿Por qué?

_____

_____

2. ¿Qué cosas hiciste ayer para estar sano(a)?

_____

_____

Leer C

> **¡AVANZA!** **Goal:** Read about past events.

This morning, Claudia's mother found this note on the table.

> *Mamá:*
>
> *Hoy no voy a la escuela porque me duele mucho la cabeza. Ayer estudié toda la noche y hoy no puedo abrir los ojos. Ya hablé con Susana y ella me trae la tarea en la tarde.*
>
> *Ya preparé el desayuno; está en la mesa de la cocina. Mi papá me ayudó y cocinó unos huevos. También están en la mesa.*
>
> *Encontré el libro que tú buscaste ayer en el armario del primer piso. Está encima de la mesita de la sala.*
>
> *Hablamos después*
>
> *Claudia*

¿Comprendiste?

Read Claudia's note. Then answer the questions.

1. ¿Por qué Claudia no va a la escuela?

   _____

2. ¿Qué buscó Claudia?

   _____

3. ¿Quién ayudó a Claudia? ¿Cómo?

   _____

4. ¿Por qué Susana llevó la tarea a la casa de Claudia en la tarde?

   _____

¿Qué piensas?

Read Claudia's note. Write a short description about what you did the last time you stayed home from school because you were sick.

_____

_____

_____

_____

Escribir A

> **¡AVANZA!** **Goal:** Write about past events.

Step 1

In the first column, list the top parts of the body. In the second column, list the bottom parts of the body.

En la parte de arriba	En la parte de abajo

Step 2

Answer the following questions about your life in complete sentences:

1. ¿Qué celebraste el último mes?

_____

2. ¿Qué música escuchaste ayer?

_____

3. ¿Qué estudiaste esta semana?

_____

Step 3

Evaluate your writing using the information in the table below.

Writing Criteria	Excellent	Good	Needs Work
Content	You have responded to the questions completely.	You have responded to the questions partially.	You have not responded to the questions.
Communication	Most of your response is clear.	Some of your response is clear.	Your message is not very clear.
Accuracy	You make few mistakes in grammar and vocabulary.	You make some mistakes in grammar and vocabulary.	You make many mistakes in grammar and vocabulary.

Escribir B

> **¡AVANZA!** **Goal:** Write about past events.

Step 1

Read the definitions and write them in the spaces below. Then, write down each of the letters in the circles and you will discover the hidden word.

1. Parte del cuerpo con la que escribimos.
2. Partes del cuerpo con las que caminamos.
3. Parte del cuerpo que recibe la comida.

4. Parte del cuerpo con la que vemos.
5. Parte del cuerpo con la que hablamos y comemos.

1. ___ ___ ___ ◯
2. ___ ___ ___ ◯ ___ ___ ___
3. ◯ ___ ___ ___ ___ ___ ___
4. ___ ◯ ___
5. ___ ___ ___ ◯

Hidden word: _____

Step 2

Complete the following sentences using the words from the previous activity and the preterite:

1. mano /escribir _____
2. ojos / ver _____
3. oreja / escuchar _____

Step 3

Evaluate your responses to Actividad 2 using the information in the table below.

Writing Criteria	Excellent	Good	Needs Work
Content	You include all of the information.	You include some of the information.	You include little information.
Communication	Most of your message is organized and easy to follow.	Parts of your message are organized and easy to follow.	Your message is disorganized and hard to follow.
Accuracy	You make few mistakes in grammar and vocabulary.	You make some mistakes in grammar and vocabulary.	You make many mistakes in grammar and vocabulary.

Escribir C

> ¡AVANZA! **Goal:** Write about past events.

Step 1

Complete the table with the parts of the body and what we do with each of them.

Partes del cuerpo	¿Qué hacemos con ellas?

Step 2

You are in bed, sick. Write a four-sentence letter to a classmate telling him or her why you are sick and did not go to school. Use the preterite.

_____

_____

_____

_____

_____

_____

_____

Step 3

Evaluate your writing using the information in the table below.

Writing Criteria	Excellent	Good	Needs Work
Content	You include all of the information.	You include some of the information.	You include little information.
Communication	Most of your message is organized and easy to follow.	Parts of your message are organized and easy to follow	Your message is disorganized and hard to follow.
Accuracy	You make few mistakes in grammar and vocabulary.	You make some mistakes in grammar and vocabulary.	You make many mistakes in grammar and vocabulary.

Cultura A

¡AVANZA! **Goal:** Review cultural information about the Dominican Republic.

1 **Dominican Republic** Complete the following sentences with one of the multiple-choice answers.

1. The Dominican Republic shares the island of Hispaniola with ____.

   a. Puerto Rico   **b.** Haití   **c.** Cuba

2. The Festival del Merengue includes music and ____.

   a. baseball   **b.** surfing   **c.** cart races

3. The Dominican Republic is in the ____.

   a. Caribbean Sea   **b.** Pacific Ocean   **c.** Gulf of Mexico

2 **Dominican culture** Complete the following sentences by choosing the correct word.

1. The Festival del Merengue is celebrated every (winter / summer) in Santo Domingo.

2. The athlete Félix Sánchez won a (gold / silver) medal in the 2004 Olympic games.

3. The Dominican Republic has a (warm / cold) climate.

4. The **Altar de la (Nación / Patria)** is a monument to the Dominican heroes from the battle of 1844.

3 **Merengue** Merengue is considered to be a symbol of the Dominican Republic. Describe what instruments are used in playing merengue and what occurs at the Festival del Merengue. What would you enjoy most at the festival and why?

_____

_____

_____

_____

_____

_____

Cultura B

| ¡AVANZA! | **Goal:** Review cultural information about the Dominican Republic. |

1 **Dominican culture** Draw lines to match the phrases and names on the left with their explanation on the right.

baseball	famous Dominican singer
La Hispañola	typical Dominican food
cazabe	national sport of the Dominican Republic
merengue	island of the Dominican Republic
Juan Luis Guerra	music of the Dominican Republic

2 **The Dominican Republic** Answer the following questions about the Dominican Republic.

1. What is the capital of the Dominican Republic? _____

2. What are some events at the Festival del Merengue? _____

_____

3. What instruments are used to play merengue? _____

_____

3 **Atletas famosos** Compare the athletes Félix Sánchez and Daniela Larreal with an athlete you admire or are familiar with. Mention where each athlete is from, which sport they participate in, and any championships they have competed in or awards they have won.

_____

_____

_____

_____

_____

_____

UNIDAD 6 • Cultura B
Lección 2

290

Unidad 6, Lección 2
Cultura B

¡Avancemos! 1
Cuaderno: Práctica por niveles

Cultura C

> **¡AVANZA!** **Goal:** Review cultural information about the Dominican Republic.

1 **Dominican Republic** Read the following sentences and answer *true* or *false*.

T   F   **1.** The Festival del Merengue of Santo Domingo is held during the summer.

T   F   **2.** The athlete Félix Sánchez was born in the Dominican Republic.

T   F   **3.** One of the instruments used to play merengue is the accordion.

T   F   **4.** Paella is a typical food of the Dominican Republic.

T   F   **5.** The Dominican Republic is located in the Caribbean Sea.

2 **Dominican Culture** Answer the following questions with complete sentences.

1. What did the athlete Félix Sánchez promise he would do until he won a gold metal?

_____

_____

2. What is the currency of the Dominican Republic? _____

_____

3. What can people do at the Festival del Merengue?

_____

_____

3 Look at the painting on page 332 of your book. Describe the images and style of the painting. What feelings does it evoke? What does it tell you about the climate and landscape of the Dominican Republic?

_____

_____

_____

_____

_____

Comparación cultural: Deportes favoritos *Level 1, pp. 349–350*

Lectura y escritura

After reading the paragraphs about the favorite sports of Felipe, Gloria, and Agustín, write a paragraph about your favorite sport. Use the information on your sports chart to write sentences, and then write a paragraph that describes your favorite sport.

Step 1

Complete the sports chart describing as many details as possible about your favorite sport.

Categoría	Detalles
nombre del deporte	
lugar	
participantes	
equipo necesario	
ropa apropiada	

Step 2

Now take the details from your sports chart and write a sentence for each topic on the chart.

_____

_____

_____

_____

_____

_____

_____

_____

Comparación cultural: Deportes favoritos
Level 1, pp. 349–350

Lectura y escritura (continued)

Step 3

Now write your paragraph using the sentences you wrote as a guide. Include an introduction sentence and use the verbs **jugar** and **saber** to write about your favorite sport.

_____

_____

_____

_____

_____

_____

Checklist

Be sure that…

☐ all the details about your favorite sport from your sports chart are included in the paragraph;

☐ you use details to describe where the sport is played, as well as the participants and necessary equipment and clothing.

☐ you include new vocabulary words and the verbs **jugar** and **saber.**

Rubric

Evaluate your writing using the rubric below.

Writing criteria	Excellent	Good	Needs Work
Content	Your description includes many details about your favorite sport.	Your description includes some details about your favorite sport.	Your description includes little information about your favorite sport.
Communication	Most of your description is organized and easy to follow.	Parts of your description are organized and easy to follow.	Your description is disorganized and hard to follow.
Accuracy	Your description has few mistakes in grammar and vocabulary	Your description has some mistakes in grammar and vocabulary.	Your description has many mistakes in grammar and vocabulary.

Comparación cultural: Deportes favoritos
Level 1, pp. 349–350

Compara con tu mundo

Now write a comparison about your favorite sport and that of one of the three students from page 349. Organize your comparison by topics. First, write the name of the sport, then describe where is played and who participates, and lastly the clothing and equipment.

Step 1

Use the chart to organize your comparison by topics. Write details for each topic about your favorite sport and that of the student you chose.

Categoría	Mi deporte	El deporte de _____
nombre del deporte		
lugar		
participantes		
ropa apropiada		

Step 2

Now use the details from the mind map to write a comparison. Include an introduction sentence and write about each category. Use the verbs **jugar** and **saber** to describe your favorite sport, and that of the student you chose.

_____

_____

_____

_____

_____

_____

_____

_____

_____

Vocabulario A

> **¡AVANZA!** **Goal:** Talk about technology.

1 Place an "x" next to words related to computers and the Internet.

1. ____ la pantalla
2. ____ los jeans
3. ____ el mensajero instantáneo
4. ____ el teclado
5. ____ el sitio web

6. ____ la alfombra
7. ____ el icono
8. ____ el ratón
9. ____ las decoraciones
10. ____ la dirección electrónica

2 Early in the morning, Lucas connected to the Internet. Complete the following sentences with the correct word from the ones in parentheses:

1. Lucas conecta a Internet para _____ . (estar en línea / estar enfermo)

2. Para mandar un correo electrónico a su amiga, Lucas necesita

   _____ . (la cámara digital / la dirección electrónica)

3. Lucas usa _____ para hablar con amigos. (el mensajero instantáneo / quemar un disco compacto)

4. Lucas hace clic en _____ . (la pantalla / el icono)

5. Lucas escribe correos electrónicos con _____ . (el teclado / la cámara digital)

3 Complete the following sentences about using the computer:

1. Necesito buscar algo. ¿Tú sabes _____ ?

2. Me gusta la música salsa pero no la tengo. Mi amigo la tiene y va a

   _____ .

3. Yo tomo fotos con mi _____ .

Vocabulario B

> ¡AVANZA! **Goal:** Talk about technology.

1 Nicolás wants to send a few pictures to his friends. Put the steps below in logical order from a (for the first step) to e (for the last step).

1. Hacer clic en un icono para mandarlas _____ .

2. Conectar a Internet _____ .

3. Poner la dirección electrónica de su amigo _____ .

4. Escribir un correo electrónico con las fotos _____ .

5. Tomar las fotos con su cámara digital _____ .

2 Nicolás goes to the library to connect to the Internet. Complete the sentences using words from the box.

quemar un disco compacto	la pantalla teclado	en línea el sitio web

1. _____ está muy bien.

2. _____ es muy interesante, encuentro muchas cosas.

3. Quiero música nueva. Necesito _____ , pero en la casa no puedo.

4. Me gusta escribir pero no me gusta usar el lápiz. Es más fácil escribir en mi

   _____ . Me gusta más.

5. Mi computadora conecta a Internet. Estoy _____ en un minuto.

3 Answer the following questions about your life in complete sentences:

1. ¿Quemaste un disco compacto la semana pasada?

   _____

2. ¿Usaste el mensajero instantáneo anteayer?

   _____

3. ¿Tomaste fotos con la cámara digital el año pasado?

   _____

Vocabulario C

> ¡AVANZA! **Goal:** Talk about technology.

1 Mariela wants to send pictures in an e-mail to her mother. Underline the correct word of the ones in parentheses to complete each sentence.

1. Mariela toma fotos con (una pantalla / un icono / una cámara digital).

2. Para mandar las fotos por correo electrónico, primero tiene que (hacer clic / conectar a Internet / quemar un disco compacto).

3. Después, pone (la dirección electrónica / el Internet / el teclado) de su madre.

4. Mariela manda un correo electrónico con (las fotos / el ratón / la pantalla).

5. Mariela quiere tener siempre las fotos. Entonces ella piensa (un sitio web / quemar un disco compacto / la computadora).

2 Mariela connected to the Internet from a friend's house. Complete the following sentences:

1. Mariela navega _____

2. Mariela conecta _____

3. Mariela manda _____

4. Mariela toma _____

3 Write three sentences about your own computer use. Use the words from the box.

anteayer	por fin	la dirección electrónica
luego	el ratón	conectar a Internet

1. _____

2. _____

3. _____

Gramática A *Preterite of Regular –er and –ir Verbs*

> **¡AVANZA!** **Goal:** Talk about what you and others did in the past.

1 Circle the correct verb form in the sentences below:

1. Ayer, Lorena (perdí / perdió) el dinero en el centro comercial.

2. Anteayer, Lorena y Carmen (volvieron / volvió) muy tarde.

3. Ernesto y yo (salimos / salieron) a beber un refresco.

4. Yo (subió / subí) las escaleras.

5. Tú (viste / vimos) la camisa que quieres.

2 Inés and her friends went shopping. Answer the questions with the correct form of the verb and the element in parentheses.

1. ¿A qué hora salieron ustedes de tu casa? (3:00) _____

_____

2. ¿Qué vieron Inés y Cecilia? (zapatos) _____

_____

3. ¿Dónde perdió Inés el dinero? (en la tienda de deportes) _____

_____

4. ¿Volviste a la tienda para buscarlo? (Sí)_____

_____

3 Create sentences using the following elements. Conjugate the verbs in the preterite tense. Follow the model:

modelo: ayer / nosotros / comer / para celebrar el cumpleaños de mi tía:
Ayer nosotros comimos para celebrar el cumpleaños de mi tía.

1. mi tía y Norberto / compartir / el postre: _____

2. luego / ella / abrir / los regalos: _____

3. por fin /nosotros / volver / a casa: _____

Gramática B *Preterite of Regular –er and –ir Verbs*

> **¡AVANZA!** **Goal:** Talk about what you and others did in the past.

1 Several friends went to the park the day before yesterday. Choose the correct form of the verb to complete the sentences.

1. Inés ____ por una hora.

  a. corriste   **b.** corrió   **c.** corrí   **d.** corrimos

2. ¿Tú ____ temprano?

  a. volví   **b.** volvieron   **c.** volvió   **d.** volviste

3. Inés y yo ____ nuestras chaquetas.

  a. perdimos   **b.** perdió   **c.** perdí   **d.** perdieron

4. Ustedes ____ su almuerzo.

  a. compartieron   **b.** compartió   **c.** compartí   **d.** compartimos

5. Yo ____ a las diez.

  a. salimos   **b.** salió   **c.** saliste   **d.** salí

2 Lorena and her friends did a lot of things the day before yesterday. Complete the sentences with the correct form of the verb in parentheses.

1. Yo _____ un correo electrónico. (escribir)

2. Lorena y Armando _____ al cine. (salir)

3. ¿Señora Barros, usted _____ el suelo de su casa? (barrer)

4. Tú _____ en el parque. (correr)

5. ¿Lorena y tú _____ el mensaje instantáneo de la fiesta? (recibir)

3 Write three sentences to describe what this family did last year. Use the preterite of the verbs in parentheses.

  modelo: Nosotros (vivir): Nosotros vivimos en otra casa.

1. Mis padres (salir): _____

2. Yo (volver): _____

3. Mi madre (vender): _____

Gramática C *Preterite of Regular –er and –ir Verbs*

> **¡AVANZA!** **Goal:** Talk about what you and others did in the past.

❶ Ernesto and his friends played a baseball game the day before yesterday. Complete the following text with the correct form of the verbs in the box:

Mi equipo de béisbol **1.** _____ muchos regalos ayer.

Nosotros **2.** _____ a jugar un partido de béisbol.

Yo **3.** _____ como nunca. Juan y Ariel no

4. _____ ninguna pelota. Todos jugamos muy bien.

El otro equipo también jugó muy bien. Entonces, nosotros

5. _____ los regalos con los chicos del otro equipo.

correr
perder
compartir
recibir
salir

❷ Complete the following sentences about a sports event. Use the preterite of the verbs **correr, ver, perder, comprender las reglas,** and **recibir.**

1. Mis amigos y yo _____

2. Los chicos del equipo _____

3. Yo _____

4. ¿Tú _____

5. El equipo _____

❸ Write three complete sentences to describe what happened at a soccer game.
To begin, use one of these two expressions: **la semana pasada, el año pasado.**

_____

_____

_____

Gramática A *Affirmative and Negative Words*

> ¡AVANZA! **Goal:** Talk about indefinite or negative situations.

1 Sofía and her family went to a restaurant and did not enjoy the experience. Draw a line from the question on the left to its correct answer on the right.

1. ¿Quién sirve la comida?   **a.** Ni el uno ni el otro.

2. ¿Hay sopa o pescado?   **b.** No, nunca tengo.

3. ¿Tiene algo con brócoli?   **c.** No, no hay nada.

4. ¿Siempre tiene carnes?   **d.** Tampoco hay.

5. No hay carne. ¿Hay pollo?   **e.** No hay nadie.

2 Valeria is not having a good day. Underline the word that best completes each sentence.

1. No quiere (nada / algo) de comer.

2. No quiere hablar con (alguien / nadie).

3. Valeria no quiere ni salir (ni / o) escuchar música.

4. Valeria no quiere ir al cine y, (tampoco / también) al teatro.

5. No quiere comprar (algunos / ningunos) jeans.

3 Ramiro is looking for something to do with his friends. Below are a few things they have decided not to do. Complete the sentences.

1. Ramiro no quiere ver _____ película en el cine.

2. Sus amigos no tienen hambre. No tienen ganas de comer _____ .

3. Las entradas para el teatro cuestan mucho. _____ puede comprarlas.

Gramática B *Affirmative and Negative Words*

 Goal: Talk about indefinite or negative situations.

1 Complete the following dialog using **o...o, tampoco, algo, ni...ni...** or **alguien.**

1. **Alejo:** Hola. ¿ _____ sabe quemar un disco compacto?

2. **Sara:** No, yo no sé y Rita _____ sabe.

3. **Rita:** Yo sé hacerlo. Necesitas usar_ el ratón _ el teclado.

4. **Sara:** No. Pienso que no necesitas _ el ratón _ el teclado.

5. **Rita:** ¡Pero él tiene que usar ___!

2 Osvaldo and Carmen are always opposites in what they do and want. Write complete sentences stating what Carmen does or wants. Follow the model.

modelo: Osvaldo quiere comprar algunos pantalones. Carmen no quiere comprar ningún pantalón.

1. Osvaldo prefiere un jugo o un refresco. Carmen _____

2. Osvaldo siempre está contento. Carmen _____

3. Osvaldo siempre habla con alguien por Internet. Carmen nunca _____

_____

4. A Osvaldo también le gusta usar el mensajero instantáneo. A Carmen _____

_____

3 Use the information in the table below to create three complete sentences about what Osvaldo does or does not do. Use each element once:

Nunca	comprar	nada
Siempre	recibir	alguna cosa
De vez en cuando	compartir	alguien

1. _____

2. _____

3. _____

_____

Gramática C *Affirmative and Negative Words*

Level 1, pp. 366-368

¡AVANZA! **Goal:** Talk about indefinite or negative situations.

1 Elena is angry with Miriam. Rewrite the following sentences about what she is feeling, to make them negative.

1. Quiero saber algo de Miriam hoy.

_____

2. Hay alguna persona tan enojada como yo ahora.

_____

3. Ella siempre compartió sus libros y sus discos compactos.

_____

4. Ella sale con alguien.

_____

5. Ella quiere tener muchos amigos.

_____

2 Miriam is sad because one of her friends is angry with her. That's why she is not in the mood to do anything today. Complete the sentences. Use **ningún, nunca, nada, nadie** y **tampoco.**

1. Miriam no quiere _____

2. Miriam _____

3. Miriam no quiere _____

4. Miriam _____

5. Miriam no tiene _____

3 Write two complete sentences about what you do at the times in parentheses. Use affirmative or negative expressions. Follow the model.

modelo: (después de trabajar) Yo siempre como papas fritas después de trabajar.

1. (antes del desayuno) _____

2. (los domingos) _____

3. (después de las clases) _____

Integración: Hablar

Level 1, pp. 369-371
CD 04 track 01

Guillermo sends an e-mail to all his friends with pictures he took with his new digital camera.

Fuente 1 Leer

Read Guillermo's e-mail to all of his friends.

De: Guillermo   A: Todos mis amigos

Tema: Fotos nuevas

¡Hola a todos!

Estoy muy contento porque anteayer recibí regalos. ¡Qué fantástico! Mi papá me compró una cámara digital y también otra cosa. Cuando volví de la escuela, ¡mi papá abrió una computadora nueva! Ayer tomé algunas fotos con la cámara digital y las mando con este correo electrónico. Ustedes son los primeros que las ven, pero más tarde voy a ponerlas en un sitio web. Hoy mando más fotos a todos los chicos de la escuela.

Guillermo

Fuente 2 Escuchar   CD 04 track 02

Listen to the message Luis left on Guillermo's voicemail. Take notes.

_____

_____

_____

_____

Hablar

Tell what Luis is trying to do and what problem he encounters.

modelo: Luis quiere... Pero...

Integración: Escribir

Soledad has a digital camera and repeatedly tries to send pictures attached in her e-mails without success. She goes to a Web site to get instructions, Still, she doesn't seem to be able to do what she wants, so she calls and leaves a message with customer service.

Fuente 1 Leer

Read Soledad's digital camera Web site instructions...

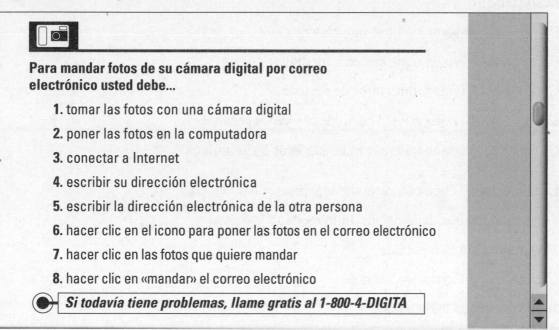

Para mandar fotos de su cámara digital por correo electrónico usted debe...

1. tomar las fotos con una cámara digital
2. poner las fotos en la computadora
3. conectar a Internet
4. escribir su dirección electrónica
5. escribir la dirección electrónica de la otra persona
6. hacer clic en el icono para poner las fotos en el correo electrónico
7. hacer clic en las fotos que quiere mandar
8. hacer clic en «mandar» el correo electrónico

Si todavía tiene problemas, llame gratis al 1-800-4-DIGITA

Fuente 2 Escuchar *CD 04 track 04*

Listen to Soledad's message to a customer service department. Take notes.

_____

_____

_____

_____

Escribir

Explain why Soledad's pictures are not being sent in her e-mails.

modelo: Soledad no... Ella tampoco...

_____

_____

_____

_____

_____

Escuchar A

> ¡AVANZA! **Goal:** Listen to discussions of various activities.

1 Listen to Viviana. Then, read each sentence below and answer **cierto** (true) or **falso** (false).

C F **1.** Viviana no tiene una casa nueva.

C F **2.** Viviana tiene una cámara digital.

C F **3.** Viviana tomó fotos de personas.

C F **4.** Viviana mandó las fotos el viernes pasado.

C F **5.** Viviana quiere mandar las fotos a sus amigos.

2 Listen to Julio. Then complete the sentences.

1. En su cumpleaños, la amiga de Julio recibió _____ .

2. Viviana recibió el regalo de _____ .

3. La amiga de Julio manda fotos de _____ .

4. Julio y su amiga hablan por _____ .

Escuchar B

> **¡AVANZA!** **Goal:** Listen to discussions of various activities.

1 Listen to Sebastián and take notes. Then, draw a line between the people and the photos they take.

1. Nicolás   **a.** de coches y autobuses

2. Miriam   **b.** del mar y la playa

3. Sebastián   **c.** de parques

4. Silvana   **d.** de personas

5. Pedro   **e.** de casas viejas

2 Listen to the conversation between Pedro and Silvana. Take notes. Then, complete the following sentences:

1. Pedro no mandó las fotos al _____

2. Pedro piensa que a nadie _____

3. Anteayer, Silvana mandó a Pedro fotos de_____

_____

4. Cuando Pedro vio las fotos, nunca pensó en _____

_____

Escuchar C

 Goal: Listen to discussions of various activities.

1 Listen to Armando and take notes. Then complete the following table with the information:

Persona que trae el regalo	Regalos	¿Para qué usa el regalo?
padre		
tío		
hermano		

2 Listen to the conversation between Javier and Sandra. Take notes. Then answer the following questions:

1. ¿Por qué tiene el hermano de Javier muchos regalos?

_____

2. ¿Dónde vivió el hermano de Javier el año pasado?

_____

3. ¿Quién vivió en la casa de la abuela: Javier o su hermano?

_____

4. ¿Por qué alguien tiene que estar con la abuela?

_____

5. ¿Cuándo es el cumpleaños de Javier?

_____

Leer A

> ¡AVANZA! **Goal:** Read about various activities.

Soledad is on vacation in Argentina. She sends this e-mail to her friend Agustín.

Hola, Agustín:

Estoy muy contenta. Ayer tomé muchas fotos y las mando con este correo electrónico. No sé la dirección electrónica de Jimena. ¿Puedes mandar tú las fotos? O mejor, ¿puedes mandar su dirección electrónica? Yo voy a mandar las fotos de ayer y las que mandé la semana pasada.

Ayer, comí una carne muy rica y salí a caminar por unos parques muy grandes.

¿Recibiste mi correo electrónico anteayer?

¿Vas a contestar algún día? Todavía no mandas ningún correo electrónico.

Adiós,

Soledad

¿Comprendiste?

Read Soledad's e-mail. Then place an "x" next to the things she did.

1. tomar fotos ____

2. ir al centro comercial ____

3. comer ____

4. caminar ____

5. escribir a Jimena ____

6. ir a la playa ____

7. almorzar en un restaurante muy grande ____

8. estar enferma una semana ____

¿Qué piensas?

Read Soledad's e-mail. Then answer the following questions:

¿Quieres ir a otros países y tomar fotos ¿Por qué?

_____

_____

Leer B

> **¡AVANZA!** **Goal:** Read about various activities.

Santiago uses the instant messaging every day with a group of friends from other countries.

Santiago dice:

> ¡Hola a todos! ¿Cómo están? Estoy triste. Ayer hablé
> con los chicos de Argentina pero no vi a ninguno en el
> mensajero instantáneo.

Sofía dice:

> ¡Hola, Santiago! Yo ayer no hablé por mensajero
> instantáneo porque salí con algunas amigas al cine.

Ernesto dice:

> ¡Hola, Santiago! ¿Cómo estás? Yo tampoco hablé por
> mensajero instantáneo porque estudié toda la tarde.

Viviana dice:

> ¡Hola, Santiago! Yo no hablé por mensajero instantáneo
> porque salí a almorzar con mis padres y después salimos
> a comprar algunas cosas para mi cuarto. Nadie habló
> ayer por mensajero instantáneo.

¿Comprendiste?

Read the instant messenger conversation. Then, choose the correct answer about what each person did.

1. Ernesto: ____
2. Viviana: ____
3. Santiago: ____
4. Sofía: ____

a. comió en un restaurante

b. pasó un rato con amigas

c. conectó a Internet

d. estudió mucho

¿Qué piensas?

¿Te gusta hablar con amigos por mensajero instantáneo? ¿Por qué?

_____

_____

Leer C

> ¡AVANZA! **Goal:** Read about various activities.

Víctor is on a trip. He writes a diary to remember everything he did in each place.

15 de marzo: Hoy paseé por parques muy grandes. Salí a caminar con unos amigos nuevos. Comí una carne muy rica y bebí jugos de frutas de aquí.

16 de marzo: Hoy no salí con amigos. Volví a los parques porque ayer perdí mi cámara digital en el parque. Por fin, la encontré.

Después comí pescado y ensalada.

17 de marzo: Hoy abrí la puerta de mi cuarto y encontré a todos mis amigos. Algunos prepararon una fiesta porque mañana voy a volver a mi país.

¿Comprendiste?

Read Victor's diary and imagine that today is March 17th. Then, list the things he did in the appropriate column.

Hoy	Ayer	Anteayer
1.	1.	1.
2.	2.	2.
3.	3.	3.
		4.

¿Qué piensas?

Read Victor's diary. Answer the first question in a complete sentence. Then, explain your answer.

1. ¿Piensas que puedes viajar solo?

_____

2. ¿Por qué?

_____

Escribir A

> **¡AVANZA!** **Goal:** Write about various activities.

Step 1

List three places where you have taken photos with a digital camera.

1.	
2.	
3.	

Step2

Write three sentences about the places where you have taken photos and what you did there. Include the words **hoy**, **ayer**, and **anteayer**:

_____

_____

_____

_____

_____

Step 3

Evaluate your writing using the information in the table below.

Writing Criteria	Excellent	Good	Needs Work
Content	You have included three sentences about the places you have been and what you did there.	You have included two sentences about the places you have been and what you did there.	You have included one sentence or less about the places you have been and what you did there.
Communication	Most of your response is clear.	Some of your response is clear	Your message is not very clear.
Accuracy	You make few mistakes in grammar and vocabulary.	You make some mistakes in grammar and vocabulary.	You make many mistakes in grammar and vocabulary.

Escribir B

> **¡AVANZA!** **Goal:** Write about various activities.

Step 1

Write a list of four activities you do during the summer.

1.	
2.	
3.	
4.	

Step 2

Write four complete sentences that describe what you did last summer. Use the preterite of three different **–er** and **–ir** verbs.

_____

_____

_____

Step 3

Evaluate your writing using the information in the table.

Writing Criteria	Excellent	Good	Needs Work
Content	You included four sentences that describe what you did last summer.	You included three sentences that describe what you did last summer.	You included two or fewer sentences that describe what you did last summer.
Communication	Most of your message is organized and easy to follow.	Parts of your message are organized and easy to follow.	Your message is disorganized and hard to follow.
Accuracy	You make few mistakes in grammar and vocabulary.	You make some mistakes in grammar and vocabulary.	You make many mistakes in grammar and vocabulary.

Escribir C

> ¡AVANZA! **Goal:** Write about various activities.

Step 1

Write a list of four things you and your friends buy at the mall.

1.
2.
3.
4.

Step2

The day before yesterday you went to the mall with your friends. Use the list above to write five complete sentences that describe what all or some of you did. Include the words **alguna** and **ninguna**.

_____

_____

_____

_____

_____

Step3

Evaluate your writing using the information in the table below.

Writing Criteria	Excellent	Good	Needs Work
Content	You include five sentences that describe what you and your friends did at the mall.	You include three to four sentences that describe what you and your friend did at the mall.	You include two sentences or less that describe what you and your friend did at the mall.
Communication	Most of your message is organized and easy to follow.	Parts of your message are organized and easy to follow.	Your message is disorganized and hard to follow.
Accuracy	You make few mistakes in grammar and vocabulary.	You make some mistakes in grammar and vocabulary.	You make many mistakes in grammar and vocabulary.

Cultura A

| ¡AVANZA! | **Goal:** Review cultural information about Argentina. |

1 **Argentina** Read the following sentences about Argentina and answer *true* or *false*.

T   F   **1.** The capital of Argentina is Buenos Aires.

T   F   **2.** Argentina is located in South America.

T   F   **3.** Jorge Luis Borges was a famous Argentine painter.

T   F   **4.** The **bandoneón** is an Argentine musical instrument similar to the accordion.

T   F   **5.** Many Argentines use **vos** instead of **tú**.

2 **Argentine culture** Draw lines to match the names or phrases on the left with their explanation on the right.

asado	a variety of slang from Buenos Aires
Carlos Gardel	the widest street in the world
gaucho	typical Argentine food
Avenida 9 de Julio	Argentine cattleman
lunfardo	famous tango singer

3 **Visiting Argentina** In Argentina there are many places to visit and many interesting things to see. Write down the interesting things to see in the following places in Argentina.

Places to visit	**Interesting things to see**
el Barrio de San Telmo	_____
las **pampas**	_____
Plaza de la República	_____
the city of Mar del Plata	_____
	_____

Cultura B

> ¡AVANZA! **Goal:** Review cultural information about Argentina.

1 **Argentina** Choose the correct word to complete the sentences.

1. The city of Mar del Plata is famous for its _____ .

2. The _____ is a popular Argentine dance.

3. Many Argentines don't use **tú,** but instead use _____ .

4. The capital of Argentina is _____ .

5. The _____ raise cattle and are cultural icons in Argentina.

2 **About Argentina** Answer the following questions about Argentina in complete sentences.

1. What was the profession of Carlos Gardel? _____

2. What do the **lunfardo** terms **gomias** and **zapi** mean? _____

3. What is the name of the musical instrument that is similar to an accordion and used in

   tango music? _____

3 Write a description of how you would spend a day at the beach in Mar del Plata, Argentina. What time of year would you travel there and why? What activities would you participate in? What might you see there?

_____

_____

_____

_____

_____

_____

_____

_____

UNIDAD 7
Lección 1

Cultura B

Unidad 7, Lección 1
Cultura B

316

¡Avancemos! 1
Cuaderno: Práctica por niveles

Cultura C

> **¡AVANZA!** **Goal:** Review cultural information about Argentina.

1 **Sites in Argentina** In Argentina, there are many interesting things to see. Write down what can be seen at the following famous sites of Argentina.

Famous sites of Argentina	What to see
Barrio de San Telmo	_____
Las pampas	_____
Plaza de la República	_____
Mar del Plata	_____

2 **Argentina** Answer these questions about Argentina using complete sentences.

1. What do some people call the city of Buenos Aires because of its European architecture?

_____

2. Which avenue in Argentina is considered to be the widest in the world?

_____

3. What people of Argentina are considered to be cultural icons? _____

_____

3 **Lunfardo** Describe what **lunfardo** is. How and where did it develop? What are some examples of **lunfardo?**

_____

_____

_____

_____

_____

_____

_____

Vocabulario A

Level 1, pp. 380-384

¡AVANZA! **Goal:** Discuss where you like to go with your friends.

1 Griselda and Raúl go to fun places. Place an X next to the logical sentences.

1. Griselda prepara la comida en el acuario. _____

2. Raúl y Griselda aprenden mucho en el museo. _____

3. Griselda y sus amigos leen mucho en el parque de diversiones. _____

4. A Griselda le gustan los animales y va mucho al zoológico. _____

5. Raúl compra el boleto de los autitos chocadores. _____

6. Griselda aprende de animales del mar en la vuelta al mundo. _____

2 It was fun! Look at the drawings and complete the following sentences.

| 1. | 2. | 3. | 4. | 5. |

1. A Griselda le gustan _____.

2. Raúl mira el arte en _____.

3. Raúl y Griselda tienen miedo de subir a _____.

4. A Griselda le gusta ir _____.

5. Raúl siempre va _____.

3 Answer the following questions about your life in complete sentences.

1. ¿Te gustaría conocer museos de otros países?

_____

2. ¿Tus amigos dejan el mensaje cuando llaman y tú no estás?

_____

3. ¿Adónde invitas a tus amigos para pasar un rato divertido?

_____

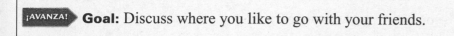

Nombre _____ Clase _____ Fecha _____

Vocabulario B

┌───┐
│ ¡AVANZA! **Goal:** Discuss where you like to go with your friends.   │
└───┘

1 Laura and her friends want to have fun. List related words from the box in the appropriate columns of the table.

parque de diversiones	biblioteca	acuario
museo	autitos chocadores	zoológico

Para pasar un rato divertido	Para aprender de animales	Para aprender otras cosas

2 Laura wants to ask Tomás to go to the amusement park. She calls him on the phone. Complete their conversation with an appropriate expression.

Laura: **1.** ¿_____ ? **2.** ¿_____ hablar con Tomás?

Madre de Tomás: ¿Laura? ¿Cómo estás? Un momento, a ver... no, él no

3. _____. Quieres dejar un mensaje?

Laura: ¿No está? **4.** ¡ _____ ! Sí. Quiero dejar un mensaje.

Quiero saber si **5.** _____ ir al parque de diversiones.

Madre de Tomás: ¡Claro que sí! Él invitó a su hermano Diego, pero Diego no puede ir.

Yo pienso que **6.** _____ .

3 **¿Qué prefiere?** Complete the first part of the following sentences with something each person does not want to do and the second part with what each person prefers instead.

1. A Lucas no le gustaría ir a _____ , prefiere

_____ .

2. Carina tiene miedo de _____ , le gustaría más

_____ .

3. Norma no quiere subir a _____ , pero le encantaría

_____ .

Vocabulario C

Level 1, pp. 380-384

> **¡AVANZA!** **Goal:** Discuss where you like to go with your friends.

1 My friends do many fun things. Draw a line between the activity they want and the place for it.

1. Los chicos quieren ver animales.

a. Van al parque de diversiones.

2. Los chicos quieren ver animales del mar.

b. Van al zoológico.

3. Los chicos quieren subir a la vuelta al mundo.

c. Van al museo.

4. Los chicos quieren ver el arte.

d. Van al acuario.

2 I went to the amusement park and other fun places with Gastón. Complete the following sentences with what you think happened.

1. Gastón subió a los autitos chocadores pero primero _____

_____

2. Gastón y yo vimos todo el parque de diversiones cuando _____

_____

3. A Gastón no le gustan los lugares peligrosos, entonces _____

_____

4. También, en el zoológico _____

_____

5. «¡Qué aburrido!» dice Gastón cuando _____

_____

3 Write three complete sentences describing fun activities that you would like to do with your friends this weekend.

_____

_____

_____

Gramática A *Preterite of **ir, ser, hacer***

Level 1, pp. 385-389

> ¡AVANZA! **Goal:** Say where you went, what you did, and how it was.

1 Fabiana and her friends did many things. Underline the correct form of each verb below.

1. Fabiana (fueron / fue) al museo.

2. Fabiana y yo (hicimos / hizo) algunas llamadas a nuestros amigos.

3. Adrián y Fabiana (hizo / hicieron) esquí acuático.

4. Subir a la vuelta al mundo (fue / fuimos) divertido.

5. ¿Tú (fue / fuiste) al acuario?

2 What did Fabiana's friends do? Complete the sentences with the preterite of the verbs in parentheses.

1. Fabiana _____ muy simpática con Jorge. (ser)

2. Fabiana y Josefina _____ a comer a un restaurante bueno. (ir)

3. ¿Tú _____ el campeón de tenis el año pasado? (ser)

4. ¿Qué _____ ustedes anteayer? (hacer)

5. Pablo _____ esquí acuático. (hacer)

6. Fabiana, Pablo y yo _____ al parque de diversiones. (ir)

7. Roberto y Patricio no fueron al parque de diversiones, ellos _____

   las tareas. (hacer)

8. _____ muy divertida la actividad. (ser)

3 Write three sentences about what happened last Saturday. Use the following elements.

1. Yo / ir / casa de mis amigos _____

   _____

2. Yo / ser / estudioso _____

   _____

3. Yo / hacer / la tarea _____

   _____

Gramática B *Preterite of ir, ser, hacer*

 ¡AVANZA! **Goal:** Say where you went, what you did, and how it was.

1 Fabio and his friends went out last week. Read the information in the table and write complete sentences with it.

Fabio	fui a la casa de Fabio.
Fabio y yo	hiciste una comida muy rica.
Yo	hicimos algunas compras.
Fabio y Soledad	fue al acuario.
Tú	fueron buenos amigos y compraron los boletos para nosotros.

1. _____

2. _____

3. _____

4. _____

5. _____

2 Federico and Agustina invited a friend to dinner. Complete the friend's sentences using the preterite of **ir, ser,** or **hacer**.

1. Federico _____ una sopa nutritiva. ¡Qué rica!

2. Federico y Agustina _____ a comprar las cosas para preparar la cena.

3. Federico y Agustina _____ muy simpáticos en la cena.

4. Yo _____ el postre.

5. Agustina y yo _____ a comprar el jugo de naranja.

3 What did you do for fun last week? Write three complete sentences using the preterite of **ir, ser,** and **hacer**. Follow the model:

modelo: Yo hice esquí acuático.

1. _____

2. _____

3. _____

UNIDAD 7 • Gramática B
Lección 2

322

Unidad 7, Lección 2
Gramática B

¡Avancemos! 1
Cuaderno: Práctica por niveles

Gramática C *Preterite of ir, ser, hacer*

> **¡AVANZA!** **Goal:** Say where you went, what you did, and how it was.

1 Emiliano spent a fun day with his friends. Complete the text with the correct form of **ir, ser,** or **hacer.**

Anteayer, mis amigos y yo **1.** _____ a pasar un día en

la playa. ¡Qué divertido! Fernando y Lupe **2.** _____

esquí acuático y también bucearon. Después, ellos y yo tocamos la guitarra

y cantamos. Por la tarde, **3.** _____ mucho sol y calor,

entonces algunos chicos **4.** _____ a buscar más refrescos

y los otros nadaron en el mar. **5.** ¡ _____ un día perfecto!

2 Create five sentences about the activities and relationships of Emiliano and his friends, using the preterite of **ir, ser,** and **hacer.**

| Emiliano |
| Fernando |
| yo |
| Marcos |

1. _____

2. _____

3. _____

4. _____

5. _____

3 ¿Qué hiciste la semana pasada? Write an e-mail to a friend about last week's activities. Write four complete sentences using the preterite of **ir, ser,** and **hacer.**

_____

_____

_____

_____

Gramática A *Pronouns after Prepositions*

¡AVANZA! **Goal:** Talk about activities you did with friends.

1 Patricia invited her friends to the movies. Circle the correct pronoun for each sentence below.

1. Patricia buscó a Pablo y él fue con (ella / nosotros).

2. Nosotros fuimos al cine a las dos. Los chicos hablaron con (ellos / nosotros) a las dos y media.

3. Mi semana fue muy triste. Ir al cine fue muy bueno para (ti / mí).

4. Fui (contigo / conmigo) al cine porque tú eres una buena amiga.

5. ¡Qué divertido fue el día que tú fuiste (contigo / con nosotros) al cine!

2 Patricia and her friends had a good time at the movies. Complete each sentence with the correct pronoun.

1. A Patricia le gustó la película. Fue muy interesante para _____ .

2. Yo invité a Matías porque me gusta estar con _____ .

3. Tú invitaste a Juana porque te gusta hablar con _____ .

4. A _____ también me gustó la película.

5. No sabemos qué le gusta a Patricia. Nunca habla de _____ .

3 Answer the following questions about your life in complete sentences. Use the same prepositions in your answer as in the question and the correct pronouns after them.

1. ¿A ti te gusta ir de compras?

_____

2. ¿Vas al cine con tus amigos el fin de semana?

_____

3. ¿Tus padres van contigo al centro comercial?

_____

UNIDAD 7 • **Gramática A**
Lección 2

Unidad 7, Lección 2
Gramática A

324

¡Avancemos! 1
Cuaderno: Práctica por niveles

Gramática B *Pronouns after Prepositions*

> ¡AVANZA! **Goal:** Talk about activities you did with friends.

1 Sarita and her friends went shopping last weekend. Choose the correct pronoun to complete the sentences.

1. Al padre de Ana le gustan las camisas y Ana compró algunas para _____ .

 a. él **b.** nosotros **c.** mí

2. Sandra compró un libro para _____ , porque sabe que me gusta leer.

 a. ella **b.** yo **c.** mí

3. Sarita fue _____ a la tienda de deportes porque yo sé de deportes.

 a. contigo **b.** conmigo **c.** con ella

2 Use the information given to create complete sentences. Exchange the correct pronoun for the information in parentheses.

 modelo: Yo / hablar con (Julia). Yo hablé con ella.

1. Yo / comprar un regalo para (mi hermano). _____

2. Mis amigos / compartir con (tú) su almuerzo. _____

_____

3. Tú / no encontrar el disco compacto para (Soledad) y para (yo). _____

_____

4. ¡Qué divertido! Nosotros / cantar "feliz cumpleaños" para (tú). _____

_____

3 Answer the following questions about your life in complete sentences. Use the correct pronoun after the prepositions given.

1. Para ti, ¿cuál es el deporte más peligroso?

_____

2. ¿Quién va al cine contigo?

_____

3. En tu familia, ¿quién compra los regalos de cumpleaños para ustedes?

_____

_____

Gramática C *Pronouns after Prepositions*

¡AVANZA! **Goal:** Talk about activities you did with friends.

1 Yesterday, Silvia and some friends went to the museum. Read the sentences below and complete the second part with the correct pronoun after each preposition.

1. Yo invité a mis amigos al museo. A _____ les gusta el arte.

2. Mis amigos dicen que buscan a Norma y vienen con _____ .

3. Joaquín, el autobús llega cerca de tu casa. Está cerca de _____ .

4. El museo está al lado de la escuela. Está al lado de _____ .

5. Silvia compra los boletos para Joaquín, para José, para Norma y para mí. Ella los compra

para _____ .

2 Our friends got to the museum late. Write complete sentences using the pronouns in parentheses after a preposition.

1. (mí) _____

2. (ti) _____

3. (nosotros) _____

4. (ella) _____

5. (conmigo) _____

3 Write three complete sentences about what you did last week. Use pronouns after prepositions.

1. _____

2. _____

3. _____

UNIDAD 7 • Gramática C
Lección 2

326

Unidad 7, Lección 2
Gramática C

¡Avancemos! 1
Cuaderno: Práctica por niveles

Integración: Hablar

Alejandra and Cecilia want to meet on Saturday. But they have different plans and are available at different times.

Fuente 1 Leer

Read Alejandra's e-mail to Cecilia...

> De: Alejandra   A: Cecilia
>
> Tema: Invitación para el sábado
>
> ¡Hola Cecilia!
>
> El fin de semana pasado fui al parque de diversiones y, ¡qué divertido! ¿Te gustaría venir conmigo el sábado? Hay una vuelta al mundo muy grande. Yo sé que te gustan mucho la vuelta al mundo y los autitos chocadores. ¿Puedes venir o por la mañana o por la tarde? Si vamos por la tarde, podemos almorzar en un café en el parque. Manda un correo electrónico o llama por teléfono. Si me llamas a casa y no estoy, me puedes dejar un mensaje en mi teléfono celular.
>
> Alejandra

Fuente 2 Escuchar   *CD 04 track 12*

Listen to Cecilia's message on Alejandra's cell phone. Take notes.

_____

_____

_____

Hablar

According to their schedules, when can Alejandro and Cecilia meet on Saturday? What activities can they do together? What can't they do?

modelo: Alejandra y Cecilia pueden ir... Luego, ellas... No pueden...

Integración: Escribir

Level 1, pp. 393-395
CD 04 track 13

There is a new baseball museum in the city. It is advertised in newspapers and people are interested in going there.

Fuente 1 Leer

Read the Museum's newspaper ad...

MUSEO DEL BÉISBOL

¿Te gusta el béisbol?

¿Quieres saber más sobre los jugadores y la historia del deporte?

De vez en cuando algunos jugadores famosos vienen al museo para hablar. El fin de semana pasado, abrimos para ti un museo en el centro comercial de la calle Santa Fe, cerca del parque. Es un museo donde puedes aprender muchas cosas de tu deporte favorito.

En el museo hay premios de campeonatos. También tenemos muchas cosas de los jugadores.

Fuente 2 Escuchar   *CD 04 track 14*

Listen to the explanations given through loudspeakers in the museum. Take notes.

_____

_____

_____

Escribir

Describe what people can see in the museum.

modelo: En el museo... También las personas pueden...

_____

_____

_____

_____

Escuchar A

Level 1, pp. 400-401
CD 04 tracks 15-16

> ¡AVANZA! **Goal:** Listen to discussions about fun activities with friends.

---

1 Listen to Federico. Then, place an "x" next to the sentences that describe what happened.

1. Federico y sus amigos fueron al parque de diversiones. ____

2. Federico y sus amigos fueron al zoológico. ____

3. Todos subieron a la vuelta al mundo pero Susana no subió. ____

4. Raúl habló con sus amigos para subir a los autitos chocadores. ____

5. Raúl subió a los autitos chocadores pero nadie más subió. ____

6. Todos subieron a los autitos chocadores. ____

2 Listen to Susana. Then, complete the sentences.

1. Susana tiene _____ de los lugares peligrosos.

2. Susana cree que _____ es peligrosa.

3. Todos hablaron _____ pero no subió.

4. Después del _____ , fueron a la casa de Noemí.

Escuchar B

> **¡AVANZA!** **Goal:** Listen to discussions about fun activities with friends.

1 Listen to Teresa and take notes. Then, underline the word that completes each sentence.

1. Teresa invitó a Jaime al (acuario / zoológico).

2. A Teresa le gusta ir con (él /ella).

3. Jaime sacó buenas notas en ciencias el (mes pasado /año pasado).

4 Teresa aprendió cosas de (animales / buenas notas).

5. Teresa piensa que el zoológico es un lugar muy (aburrido / interesante).

2 Listen to Jaime and take notes. Then, complete the table below with the information requested.

¿Qué recibió Jaime?	¿De quién?	¿Cuándo?
el boleto	de Teresa	
un libro de los zoológicos de todos los países	de su papá	
un libro con fotos de todos los animales	de su mamá	

Escuchar C

> ¡AVANZA! **Goal:** Listen to discussions about fun activities with friends.

1 Listen to Luis. Then, write four things that happened in Catalina's house and four things that happened in the movie.

En la casa de Catalina	**En la película**
1. _____	1. _____
2. _____	2. _____
3. _____	3. _____
4. _____	4. _____

2 Listen to Catalina's conversation and take notes. Then, answer the following questions:

1. ¿Quiénes fueron a la casa de Catalina?

_____

2. ¿Cuándo fueron los chicos a comprar refrescos?

_____

3. ¿Qué tiene Manuel?

_____

4. ¿Por qué tocó Luis la guitarra para María?

_____

5. ¿Qué piensa Catalina de recibir amigos en su casa?

_____

Leer A

¡AVANZA! **Goal:** Read about a few activities.

Vanesa has a diary. Yesterday, she went out with friends and she wrote about it in her diary.

Martes, 23 de septiembre.

Hoy salí con Gastón y Julieta. Fuimos al parque de diversiones. ¡Qué divertido! A Julieta le gusta ir conmigo cuando sale. Dice que le encanta salir conmigo. Vamos a todos los lugares. También es muy divertido salir con Gastón. Gastón y yo subimos a la vuelta al mundo. Julieta fue a comprar algo de beber y no subió. Ella tiene miedo de subir tan alto. Gastón y Julieta subieron a los autitos chocadores y yo saqué mi teléfono celular y hablé con otro amigo. No me gustan los autitos chocadores. Les tengo miedo.

Volvimos muy tarde pero contentos.

¿Comprendiste?

Read Vanessa's diary. Draw a line from the people's names below to what each person did.

1. Julieta   **a.** Hizo una llamada.

2. Julieta, Vanesa y Gastón   **b.** Sale siempre con Vanesa.

3. Vanesa   **c.** Fue a comprar refrescos.

4. Vanesa y Gastón   **d.** No tiene miedo de subir alto.

5. Vanesa y Julieta   **e.** Salieron para divertirse.

¿Qué piensas?

Read Vanessa's diary. Answer the following question in a complete sentence.

1. ¿Qué te gustaría hacer: subir a la vuelta al mundo, a la montaña rusa o a los autitos chocadores?

_____

_____

2. ¿Con quién o quiénes te gustaría ir al parque de diversiones? ¿Por qué?

_____

_____

Leer B

> **¡AVANZA!** **Goal:** Read about a few activities.

Ramiro writes an e-mail to his best friend to tell him what he did over the weekend.

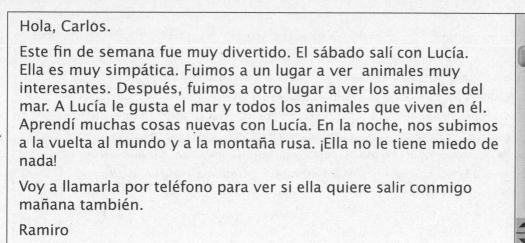

Hola, Carlos.

Este fin de semana fue muy divertido. El sábado salí con Lucía. Ella es muy simpática. Fuimos a un lugar a ver animales muy interesantes. Después, fuimos a otro lugar a ver los animales del mar. A Lucía le gusta el mar y todos los animales que viven en él. Aprendí muchas cosas nuevas con Lucía. En la noche, nos subimos a la vuelta al mundo y a la montaña rusa. ¡Ella no le tiene miedo de nada!

Voy a llamarla por teléfono para ver si ella quiere salir conmigo mañana también.

Ramiro

¿Comprendiste?

Read Ramiro's e-mail. Then, circle the words that best complete each sentence, based on the text.

1. El primer lugar al que fueron Ramiro y Lucía es (el acuario / el zoológico).

2. A Lucía le gusta ir al (acuario / parque de diversiones).

3. A Ramiro le gusta salir con Lucía porque aprende mucho con (él / ella).

4. El tercer lugar donde fueron Ramiro y Lucía fue (el parque de diversiones / el museo)

5. Ramiro va a (dejar un mensaje / hacer una llamada) a Lucía para invitarla a salir el domingo.

¿Qué piensas?

Read Ramiro's e-mail. Answer the first question in a complete sentence. Then, give an example of your answer.

1. ¿Alguna vez saliste e hiciste muchas cosas en un solo día?

_____

_____

2. Ejemplo:

_____

_____

Leer C

> **Goal:** Read about a few activities.

Ester didn't go to school today and wrote this note to her friend Carina. She sends it with her brother.

> *Carina:*
>
> *Hoy no fui a la escuela porque me duelen las piernas. Ayer corrí en la mañana, jugué al tenis a las doce y levanté pesas a las cuatro. Gustavo y yo salimos a las siete y volví a mi casa después de ocho horas. También fui con él al parque y encontramos una feria del libro. Tú sabes que a Gustavo le encanta leer de todo y compró libros de muchos temas. Él fue muy buen amigo y me regaló uno de salud y ejercicios muy interesante. Son los que más me gustan. Después del almuerzo también subimos a la montaña rusa. ¡Él no le tiene miedo! Y Gustavo compró los boletos para nosotros. Me encantó el día.*
>
> *Besos,*
> *Ester*

¿Comprendiste?

Read Ester's note. Then, draw a line from the beginning of each sentence in the left column to the correct ending in the right, based on the text.

1. A Ester le duelen las piernas porque   **a.** al parque de diversiones con ella.

2. Al parque Ester y Gustavo encontraron   **b.** una feria del libro.

3. Gustavo también fue   **c.** hizo muchos deportes ayer.

4. Gustavo pagó   **d.** fue divertido.

5. Para Ester, el día   **e.** los boletos para los dos.

¿Qué piensas?

Read Ester's note. Answer the following question in two complete sentences:

¿Piensas que es divertido ir a una feria del libro? ¿Por qué?

_____

_____

_____

_____

Escribir A

> **¡AVANZA!** **Goal:** Write about various activities.

Step 1

List three places where you had fun on your summer vacation last year.

1. _____
2. _____
3. _____

Step 2

Use the list above to write three sentences about what you did at those places.

_____

_____

_____

Step 3

Evaluate your writing using the information in the table.

Writing Criteria	Excellent	Good	Needs Work
Content	You have included three sentences about what you did on your vacation last year.	You have included two sentences about what you did on your vacation last year.	You have included only one sentence about what you did on your vacation last year.
Communication	Most of your response is clear.	Some of your response is clear.	Your message is not very clear.
Accuracy	You make few mistakes in grammar and vocabulary.	You make some mistakes in grammar and vocabulary.	You make many mistakes in grammar and vocabulary.

¡Avancemos! 1
Cuaderno: Práctica por niveles

UNIDAD 7
Lección 2 • Escribir A

Unidad 7, Lección 2
Escribir A **335**

Escribir B

> ¡AVANZA! **Goal:** Write about various activities.

Step 1

Complete the following table with places where you can go in the left column. In the other column, write what you do there.

Lugares	¿Qué haces allí?

Step 2

Using the information you listed above, write an e-mail to your friends telling them where you went and what you did.

_____

_____

_____

_____

_____

Step 3

Evaluate your writing using the information in the table.

Writing Criteria	Excellent	Good	Needs Work
Content	You include several sentences that tell where you went and what you did.	You include some sentences that tell where you went and what you did.	You include few sentences that tell where you went and what you did.
Communication	Most of your message is organized and easy to follow.	Parts of your message are organized and easy to follow.	Your message is disorganized and hard to follow.
Accuracy	You make few mistakes in grammar and vocabulary.	You make some mistakes in grammar and vocabulary.	You make many mistakes in grammar and vocabulary.

Escribir C

> ¡AVANZA! **Goal:** Write about various activities.

Step 1

List four fun things you did last summer.

1.

2.

3.

4.

Step 2

Write a paragraph about your activities last summer using the list, with an introductory sentence.

_____

_____

_____

_____

Step 3

Evaluate your writing using the information in the table.

Writing Criteria	Excellent	Good	Needs Work
Content	You include six sentences about your activities.	You include four to five sentences about your activities.	You include three or fewer sentences about your activities.
Communication	Most of your message is organized and easy to follow.	Parts of your message are organized and easy to follow.	Your message is disorganized and hard to follow.
Accuracy	You make few mistakes in grammar and vocabulary.	You make some mistakes in grammar and vocabulary.	You make many mistakes in grammar and vocabulary.

Cultura A

> **¡AVANZA!** **Goal:** Review cultural information about Argentina.

1 **Argentina** Complete the following questions with one of the multiple-choice answers.

1. The **Museo al Aire Libre** of Argentina is on which street? ____

   a. El Pueblito   **b.** El Vallecito   **c.** El Caminito

2. In Argentina, the people who are from Buenos Aires are called ____

   a. porteños   **b.** norteños   **c.** costeños

3. The Obelisk of Buenos Aires is in the Plaza de ____

   a. la Patria   **b.** la República   **c.** la Independencia

2 **Argentine culture** Read the following sentences about Argentina and answer *true* or *false*.

T   F   **1.** The currency of Argentina is the Argentine peso.

T   F   **2.** The Argentine painter Benito Quinquela Martín grew up in the neighborhood of San Telmo.

T   F   **3.** **Matambre** is a typical Argentine dish.

T   F   **4.** In the neighborhood La Boca there are many multicolored houses.

T   F   **5.** Argentina is located in Central America.

3 **Argentine cuisine** Argentina's landscape includes the **pampas,** or sprawling grasslands. Many immigrants also came to Argentina from Italy. Explain how each of these factors have influenced the type of cuisine popular in Argentina today.

_____

_____

_____

_____

_____

_____

Cultura B

¡AVANZA! **Goal:** Review cultural information about Argentina.

---

1 **Argentina** Choose the correct word to complete the following sentences.

1. **El Parque de la Costa** is the largest (national / amusement) park in South America.

2. Argentina is located in (South / North) America.

3. La Boca was the first (port / skyscraper) of Buenos Aires.

4. Benito Quinquela Martín is a famous Argentine (writer / painter).

5. In Argentina, (French / Italian) food is very popular in addition to meat.

2 **In Argentina** Answer the following questions about Argentina in complete sentences.

1. What are **estancias?** _____

2. What is the capital of Argentina? _____

3. On which famous Argentine street can you find the **Museo al Aire Libre?**
_____

4. What is the Argentine curency? _____

3 **Museums** Write a comparison of **El Museo al Aire Libre** and **El Museo de Instrumentos Musicales.** Where is each museum located and what can you find there? Which museum would you prefer to visit and why?

_____

_____

_____

_____

_____

_____

_____

_____

_____

_____

_____

Cultura C

> ¡AVANZA! **Goal:** Review cultural information about Argentina.

1 **In Argentina** Draw lines to match the words on the left with their explanation on the right.

parrillas	ranches
asados	people from Buenos Aires
bife	restaurants where they sell meat
estancias	open-air barbecues
porteños	meat or steak

2 **Argentina** Answer the following questions with complete sentences.

1. Aside from meat or steak, what other foods are popular in Argentina? _____ . _____

2. Why is beef a common food in Argentina? _____ _____

3. The painter Benito Quinquela Martín lived in which neighborhood, or **barrio,** of Argentina? _____

3 **Argentine life** The **gauchos** live in **las pampas** and earn a living raising cattle, while many Argentine artists live in the neighborhood La Boca where they sell and create their art. Which of these two lifestyles would you like to lead? Write a paragraph about how your life would be. Where would you live? What would you do every day?

_____

_____

_____

_____

_____

_____

Comparación cultural: ¿Conoces un lugar divertido?

Level 3, pp. 402-403

Lectura y escritura

After reading the paragraphs about the places that Luis, Liliana and Eva visited, write a paragraph about a place that you recently visited. Use the information on your activity timeline to write sentences and then write a paragraph that describes your visit.

Step 1

Complete the activity timeline, showing what you did first, second, third, and so on. Describe as many details as you can about the place you went and what you did.

Primero   Segundo   Tercero

_____   _____   _____

_____   _____   _____

_____   _____   _____

_____   _____   _____

_____   _____   _____

_____   _____   _____

Step 2

Now take the details from the activity timeline and write a sentence for each topic on the timeline.

_____

_____

_____

_____

_____

_____

_____

_____

_____

Comparación cultural: ¿Conoces un lugar divertido?

Lectura y escritura (continued)

Step 3

Now write your paragraph using the sentences you wrote as a guide. Include an introduction sentence and use **primero, más tarde, luego, después,** and **por fin** to write about the place you visited and what you did.

_____

_____

_____

_____

_____

_____

_____

_____

Checklist

Be sure that…

☐ all the details about your visit from your timeline are included in the paragraph;

☐ you use details to describe, as clearly as possible, sequence of your activities;

☐ you include expressions of time and new vocabulary words.

Rubric

Evaluate your writing using the rubric below.

Writing criteria	Excellent	Good	Needs Work
Content	Your description includes many details about where you went.	Your description includes some details about where you went.	Your description includes little information about where you went.
Communication	Most of your description is organized and easy to follow.	Parts of your description are organized and easy to follow.	Your description is disorganized and hard to follow.
Accuracy	Your description has few mistakes in grammar and vocabulary.	Your description has some mistakes in grammar and vocabulary.	Your description has many mistakes in grammar and vocabulary.

Comparación cultural: ¿Conoces un lugar divertido?

Compara con tu mundo

Now write a comparison about your visit and that of one of the three students from page 403. Organize your comparison in chronological order. Describe what you did first, then second, and finally the last activities you did or places you visited.

Step 1

Use the table to organize your comparison in chronological order. Write details for each activity of your visit and that of the student you chose.

Categoría	Mis actividades	Las actividades de _____
Primero		
Después		
Luego		
Por fin		

Step 2

Now use the details from the table to write a comparison. Include an introduction sentence and write about each activity. Use the words **primero, más tarde, luego, después,** and **por fin** to describe your visit and that of the student you chose.

_____

_____

_____

_____

_____

_____

_____

UNIDAD 7 • Comparación cultural
Lección 2

Vocabulario A

> **¡AVANZA!** **Goal:** Talk about daily routines.

1 Lucía and Lucas get up early to go to school. Place an "x" next to the activities they might do in the morning before going to school.

1. _____ acostarse

5. _____ maquillarse

2. _____ ducharse

6. _____ peinarse

3. _____ afeitarse

7. _____ dormirse

4. _____ cepillarse los dientes

8. _____ quedarse en un hotel

2 Look at the drawings below to see what people use to get ready for work. Then complete the sentences.

1.   **2.**   **3.**   **4.**   **5.**

1. Jaime usa _____ para cepillarse los dientes.

2. Nora se baña con agua y _____ .

3. Roberto usa _____ para lavarse el pelo.

4. María usa una _____ para secarse.

5. Ángel se peina con un _____ .

3 Complete the sentences with what you might do on a trip.

1. Puedo ir de vacaciones a la ciudad o _____

2. Puedo hacer un viaje en tren, en barco o _____

3. Llego y busco un buen _____ para dormir.

Vocabulario B

¡AVANZA! **Goal:** Talk about daily routines.

---

1 Irma's routine is the same every day. Draw a line from what she does to what she uses to do it.

1. peinarse   **a.** la pasta y el cepillo de dientes

2. bañarse   **b.** el espejo

3. cepillarse los dientes   **c.** el peine

4. maquillarse   **d.** la ropa

5. vestirse   **e.** el jabón y el champú

2 Andrea is going on a trip. Complete her conversation with her friend Gustavo.

Gustavo: ¡Hola, Andrea! ¿Ya vas **1.**_____ ?

Andrea: ¡Hola, Gustavo! Sí, voy al **2.**_____ , lejos de la

ciudad. Tengo muchas cosas que hacer todavía.

Gustavo: ¿Vas en **3.**_____ ?

Andrea: No, voy en **4.**_____ . No es tan rápido

pero puedo mirar lugares muy bonitos.

Gustavo: ¿Y sabes a qué **5.**_____ vas?

Andrea: No, no voy a un hotel. Voy a casa de unos tíos.

3 Answer the following questions about your routine.

1. ¿A qué hora te acuestas generalmente?

_____

_____

2. ¿A qué hora te despiertas generalmente?

_____

_____

3. ¿Cuántas veces por día te cepillas los dientes?

_____

_____

Vocabulario C

¡AVANZA! **Goal:** Talk about daily routines.

1 Santiago has to wake up early; he's taking a trip. In one column, place words related to his daily routine and, in the other column, place words related to taking trips.

el hotel	el peine	el secador de pelo	el tren
la toalla	el campo	el viaje	el jabón
el avión	el cepillo de dientes	el champú	el barco

La rutina

1. _____
2. _____
3. _____
4. _____
5. _____
6. _____

Las vacaciones

7. _____
8. _____
9. _____
10. _____
11. _____
12. _____

2 Marcos woke up late and might miss his train. Complete the following sentences with what he needs to do.

1. Marcos va a llegar tarde. Tiene que _____

2. Marcos está sucio. Tiene que _____

3. Marcos acaba de lavarse el pelo. Necesita _____

4. Marcos tiene diez años. No tiene que _____

3 Write three complete sentences to describe your own daily routine.

1. _____
2. _____
3. _____

Unidad 8, Lección 1
Vocabulario C

346

¡Avancemos! 1
Cuaderno: Práctica por niveles

UNIDAD 8 • Vocabulario C
Lección 1

Gramática A *Reflexive Verbs*

> **¡AVANZA!** **Goal:** Use reflexive verbs to talk about daily routines.

1 Laura and her friends all have the same routine. Circle the correct form of each verb.

1. Laura (se acuesta / me acuesto) temprano.

2. Laura y Verónica (se maquilla / se maquillan) después de secarse el pelo.

3. Laura y yo (te lavas / nos lavamos) el pelo con un champú muy bueno.

4. Yo (se viste / me visto) .

5. Y tú, ¿ (se cepillan / te cepillas) los dientes antes o después de ducharte?

2 The following people start their day early. Complete the sentences with the correct form of the verbs in parentheses.

1. Mario _____ a las seis de la mañana. (despertarse)

2. Laura y yo _____ antes de ir a la escuela. (ducharse)

3. Laura y Patricia _____ el pelo antes de bañarse. (bañarse)

4. ¿Cuándo _____ usted? (peinarse)

5. Yo_____ el pelo antes de vestirme. (secarse)

3 Answer the following questions about daily routines.

1. ¿Qué haces después de despertarte?

   _____

   _____

2. ¿Qué haces después de bañarte?

   _____

   _____

3. ¿Qué hacen tus hermanos o los hermanos de tus amigos antes de vestirse?

   _____

   _____

UNIDAD 8
Lección 1 • Gramática A

Gramática B *Reflexive Verbs*

> ¡AVANZA! **Goal:** Use reflexive verbs to talk about daily routines.

1 Francisco and his friends have a set daily routine from Monday to Friday. Choose the correct form of each verb below.

1. Francisco y yo _____ a las siete de la mañana.

   a. te despiertas   **b.** nos despertamos   **c.** se despiertan   **d.** me despierto

2. Los amigos de Francisco _____ antes de afeitarse.

   a. se duchan   **b.** te duchas   **c.** se ducha   **d.** nos duchamos

3. Yo nunca_____ después de ducharme.

   a. te afeitas   **b.** se afeita   **c.** nos afeitamos   **d.** me afeito

4. ¿Tú _____ el pelo con un secador de pelo?

   a. se secan   **b.** te secas   **c.** se seca   **d.** me seco

5. Todos los días, Francisco _____ a las diez.

   a. se acuesta   **b.** nos acostamos   **c.** te acuestas   **d.** se acuestan

2 On Saturdays, their routines are a little different. Complete the following sentences with the verb in parentheses.

1. Francisco _____ a las diez de la mañana. (despertarse)

2. Francisco y Norberto _____ antes de ducharse. (afeitarse)

3. Norberto y yo _____ antes de vestirnos. (secarse el pelo)

4. ¿Ustedes _____ antes de desayunar? (vestirse)

5. Yo_____ a medianoche. (dormirse)

3 Write three sentences to state at what time the following people wake up and go to bed.

1. Tus amigos: _____

   _____

2. Una persona en tu familia: _____

   _____

3. Tú: _____

   _____

Gramática C *Reflexive Verbs*

> ¡AVANZA! **Goal:** Use reflexive verbs to talk about daily routines.

1 Javier's friends play soccer on the weekends. Complete the text with the correct form of the verbs in parentheses.

Hoy es sábado y nosotros (despertarse) **1.** _____

muy temprano. Estoy cansado porque los viernes yo (dormirme)

2. _____ tarde. Antes de ir al partido, mi hermano

(ducharse) **3.** _____ y (lavarse)

4. _____ el pelo. Todos los chicos del equipo

(ponerse) **5.** _____ pantalones cortos negros y

camisetas anaranjadas para el partido.

2 What is your routine? Use reflexive verbs to complete the following sentences.

1. Normalmente, yo _____

2. Todos los días, yo _____

3. Los fines de semana, yo _____

4. Yo nunca _____

5. De vez en cuando, yo _____

3 Use reflexive verbs to write an e-mail to your penpal about your Monday routine. Write three sentences.

_____

_____

_____

_____

_____

_____

_____

_____

Gramática A *Present Progressive*

> **¡AVANZA!** **Goal:** Use the present progressive to talk about what people are doing right now.

1 Lorenzo's family is going on a trip. Draw a line from the people to what each of them are doing right now to get ready.

1. Los hermanos de Lorenzo   **a.** está afeitándose.

2. Lorenzo   **b.** estamos hablando del hotel.

3. La madre de Lorenzo y yo   **c.** están sacando las maletas.

4. Tú   **d.** estás pidiendo la comida.

2 The following people are busy doing many things. Complete each sentence with the present progressive of the verb in parentheses.

1. Javier _____ por teléfono. (hablar)

2. Nora y Carla _____ en el bosque. (caminar)

3. Yo _____ las maletas. (hacer)

4. ¿Usted _____ ? (vestirse)

5. ¿Chicos, ustedes _____ ? (dormir)

3 Look at the drawings below and write what each person is doing right now.

1.   2.   3.

1. **Mauro está limpiando su cuarto.**

2. _____

3. _____

UNIDAD 8
Lección 1

Gramática A

Unidad 8, Lección 1
Gramática A

350

¡Avancemos! 1
Cuaderno: Práctica por niveles

Gramática B *Present Progressive*

> **¡AVANZA!** **Goal:** Use the present progressive to talk about what people are doing right now.

1 These friends are doing a few things to get ready for their trip. Complete these sentences with the present progressive form of the verbs in parentheses.

1. Camila les _____ a todos los chicos qué tienen que hacer. (decir)

2. Ariadna y Fernanda _____ . (bañarse)

3. Abel y yo _____ los boletos del tren. (comprar)

4. Tú _____ información sobre los hoteles. (leer)

5. Yo_____ para ir de vacaciones. (vestirse).

2 The people below are on vacation. Write sentences using the present progressive.

1. Los chicos / viajar en tren.

   _____

2. Armando y yo / hablar del viaje.

   _____

3. Tú / tomar fotos.

   _____

2. Yo / no dormir.

   _____

3 Using the information in the table below, write three sentences about what each of the students are doing right now.

Camila	mirar	el parque
Camila y yo	caminar	el campo
Camila y Armando	correr	la playa

1. _____

2. _____

3. _____

Gramática C *Present Progressive*

> **¡AVANZA!** **Goal:** Use the present progressive to talk about what people are doing right now.

1 We have just returned from vacation and are now doing several things. Complete the following sentences with the present progressive of the verb in parentheses.

1. Marcos y yo _____ a nuestras casas. (llegar)

2. Marcos _____ su ropa con jabón. (lavar)

3. Yo _____ un disco compacto con las fotos de las vacaciones. (quemar)

4. Marcos y Mariela _____ sus correos electrónicos. (leer)

5. Tú _____ antes de dormir. (bañarse)

2 The following students just got back from a trip to the country. Complete these sentences with what you think they might be doing right now. Use the present progressive.

1. Marcos y Natalia _____

_____

2. Natalia _____

_____

3. Natalia y yo _____

_____

4. Yo _____

_____

5. Ustedes _____

_____

3 Write three sentences about what your family members are doing right now. Use the present progressive.

_____

_____

_____

_____

UNIDAD 8 • Gramática C
Lección 1

Unidad 8, Lección 1
Gramática C

352

¡Avancemos! 1
Cuaderno: Práctica por niveles

Integración: Hablar

Level 1, pp. 45-47
CD 04 track 21

Agustín decided to go on vacation to the countryside after reading an ad in the newspaper. He is having a really good experience and calls his roomates to let them know about it.

Fuente 1 Leer
Read the newspaper ad that Agustín read...

¿Vacaciones en el campo?

¿Estás pensando en pasar tus vacaciones en el campo?
Con nosotros, vas a pasar las mejores vacaciones.
Organizamos tu viaje completo.

Primero, te buscamos en coche en tu casa y te llevamos a tomar el tren. Después, te llevamos al hotel.

Organizamos todo para tu familia.

Puedes llamarnos al 555-4567

¡Tus vacaciones en nuestras manos son vacaciones de película!

Fuente 2 Escuchar *CD 04 track 22*
Listen to Agustín's message for his roomates. Take notes.

_____

_____

_____

_____

Hablar
What did Agustín do in the first day of his vacation?

modelo: Antes de llegar al hotel, Agustín... Después de llegar al hotel, Agustín...

Integración: Escribir

Level 1, pp. 45-47
WB CD 04 track 23

Vilma is on vacation and forgets some things at home. She e-mails her brother and he calls her back and teases her a bit in his message.

Fuente 1 Leer

Read the email that Vilma writes to her brother.

De: Vilma   A: Roberto

Tema: Mis vacaciones

Hola Roberto:

Estoy aburrida, no estoy haciendo nada divertido. Me desperté temprano. Me bañé pero no me maquillé. No hay champú en el hotel. No tengo un peine y tú me tienes que ayudar. Todas las cosas para maquillarme están en casa. ¡Mándame mis cosas ya! Las necesito para estar bonita, porque quiero salir a bailar. No quiero estar aburrida.

Adiós,

Vilma

Fuente 2 Escuchar   *CD 04 track 24*

Listen to Roberto's voicemail to Vilma. Take notes.

_____

_____

_____

_____

Escribir

What does Vilma need and why? What solutions does Roberto offer?

modelo: Vilma necesita... porque... Roberto es cómico y dice que Vilma puede...
Por fin Roberto dice que va a...

_____

_____

_____

_____

_____

Escuchar A

Level 1, pp. 52-53
CD 04 tracks 25-26

> **¡AVANZA!** **Goal:** Listen to discussions about daily routines.

1 Listen to Fernando. Then, place an "x" next to the things that happen to him.

1. Casi siempre llega tarde a la escuela. ____

2. No puede despertarse temprano. ____

3. Todos los días, se acuesta temprano. ____

4. A Fernando no le gusta mirar la televisión. ____

5. La madre de Fernando está enojada. ____

6. De vez en cuando, Fernando se levanta a las siete. ____

2 Listen to Marta. Then, complete the sentences with the words from the box.

se viste	se acuesta	la rutina	despertarse

1. El hijo de Marta _____ tarde.

2. El hijo de Marta no puede _____ .

3. El hijo de Marta _____ después de afeitarse.

4. Mirar la televisión o escuchar música por la noche es _____ del hijo de Marta.

¡Avancemos! 1
Cuaderno: Práctica por niveles

UNIDAD 8
Lección 1 • Escuchar A

Unidad 8, Lección 1
Escuchar A **355**

Escuchar B

> ¡AVANZA! **Goal:** Listen to discussions of daily routines.

1 Listen to Jorge. Then, complete the table with each person's routine.

Jorge	La hermana de Jorge

2 Listen to Daniela. Then, complete the following sentences:

1. Daniela comparte el baño con _____

_____

2. Todas las mañanas, Daniela necesita _____

_____

3. Daniela le dice a su hermano que _____

_____

4. El hermano de Daniela dice que _____

_____

5. Daniela no tiene un espejo en _____

_____

UNIDAD 8
Lección 1

Escuchar B

Unidad 8, Lección 1
Escuchar B

356

¡Avancemos! 1
Cuaderno: Práctica por niveles

Escuchar C

> **Goal:** Listen to discussions of daily routines.

1 Listen to Gabriela and take notes. Then, put her routine below in order, numbering the sentences 1 through 8.

a. ____ Se baña.

b. ____ Se seca con la toalla y con el secador de pelo.

c. ____ Se lava el pelo.

d. ____ Se despierta temprano.

e. ____ Se maquilla.

f. ____ Se cepilla los dientes.

g. ____ Se viste.

h. ____ Se peina.

2 Listen to Gabriela's conversation with her mother. Take notes. Then, answer the following questions.

1. ¿Por qué llama la mamá a su hija?

_____

2. ¿Qué está haciendo Gabriela?

_____

3. ¿Cuántos minutos necesita ella para maquillarse?

_____

4. ¿Qué están haciendo la mamá y el papá de Gabriela?

_____

5. ¿Qué cosa importante necesita hacer Gabriela antes de salir?

_____

¡Avancemos! 1
Cuaderno: Práctica por niveles

Unidad 8, Lección 1
Escuchar C **357**

UNIDAD 8
Lección 1 • Escuchar C

Leer A

> ¡AVANZA! **Goal:** Read about people's routines and trips.

This hotel organizes trips to the country and placed this ad in the newspaper.

¡Vamos al campo!

¿Tienes vacaciones?
¿Estás pensando en viajar
y no sabes adónde?

El hotel "Cinco estrellitas" organiza viajes para toda la familia,
para grupos de amigos y también viajes individuales.

¿Te gusta el campo? ¿Quieres despertarte y ver
bellos lugares por tu ventana?

Puedes venir en tren o en avión.

**Nosotros organizamos las otras cosas
para unas vacaciones fantásticas.**

¿Comprendiste?

Read the hotel's ad. Then, read each sentence and answer **cierto** (true) or **falso** (false).

C F **1.** No pueden ir grupos de amigos.

C F **2.** Pueden ir familias.

C F **3.** El hotel está en el campo.

C F **4.** Puedes ver una escuela por la ventana del hotel.

C F **5.** Puedes llegar en barco.

¿Qué piensas?

¿A qué lugar prefieres ir de vacaciones, al campo o a la ciudad? ¿Por qué?

_____

_____

_____

_____

Leer B

> ¡AVANZA! **Goal:** Read about people's routines and trips.

Emiliano wrote this letter to his friend. In it, he describes what he is doing on his trip.

Hola Hugo.

No sabes qué vacaciones fantásticas estoy pasando en el campo. Me despierto todos los días a las nueve de la mañana. Miro por la ventana y veo unos lugares muy bonitos. Este lugar es muy bueno para la salud. Mi familia y yo llegamos en tren. Cuando vi el campo, pensé que quiero vivir aquí para siempre. ¡El lugar es fantástico!

Ahora me estoy durmiendo, mañana te escribo más.

Emiliano

¿Comprendiste?

Read Emiliano's letter. Then, place an "x" next to what he describes.

1. Las vacaciones de Emiliano son aburridas. _____

2. Las vacaciones de Emiliano son en la playa. _____

3. A Emiliano le gusta el campo. _____

4. El campo es bueno para la salud. _____

5. La rutina de Emiliano empieza temprano. _____

6. Emiliano fue con sus padres. _____

7. Emiliano fue con sus amigos. _____

¿Qué piensas?

1. ¿Qué haces cuando estás de vacaciones?

_____

_____

2. ¿Tienes una rutina cuando vas de vacaciones? ¿Cuál?

_____

_____

_____

Leer C

> **¡AVANZA!** **Goal:** Read about people's routines and trips.

Jimena went on a trip to another city. She writes an e-mail about it to her friend.

Hola, Viviana.

Mi familia y yo llegamos a la ciudad muy bien. El viaje en avión fue tranquilo. El hotel está muy bien. Yo prefiero las vacaciones en el campo pero mi papá fue a comprar los boletos de avión y compró boletos para la ciudad. Él prefiere la ciudad.

En la ciudad hay muchas cosas para ver: teatros, cines y parques. En el campo podemos hacer actividades que son buenas para la salud y los lugares son más bonitos.

Todos los días estamos almorzando en un restaurante del centro. El lugar es bonito. ¿Puedes conectarte a Internet a las tres? Hablamos por mensajero instantáneo.

Besos,

Jimena

¿Comprendiste?

Read Jimena's e-mail. Then, answer the questions below:

1. ¿Cómo llegó Jimena a la ciudad? _____

2. ¿Dónde se quedó Jimena? _____

3. ¿Dónde prefiere ir de vacaciones Jimena? _____

4. ¿Por qué prefiere ir de vacaciones al campo? _____

   _____

5. ¿Dónde comen? _____

¿Qué piensas?

1. ¿Qué te gusta hacer cuando vas de vacaciones a una ciudad?

   _____

   _____

2. ¿A qué ciudades fuiste de vacaciones? ¿Cuál te gustó más?

   _____

   _____

Escribir A

> ¡AVANZA! **Goal:** Write about daily routines and trips.

Step 1

List the methods of transportation you know.

1. _____   4. _____

2. _____   5. _____

3. _____

Step 2

Complete the following sentences with your daily routine.

1. Yo, cuando me despierto, _____

2. Después, yo _____

3. Después, yo _____

4. Cuando estoy viajando, yo _____

Step 3

Write three complete sentences about your daily routine when you are traveling by boat, airplane, or train.

modelo: Cuando hago un viaje en avión ...

_____

_____

Step 4

Evaluate your writing using the information in the table.

Writing Criteria	Excellent	Good	Needs Work
Content	Your sentences include many details about your routine.	Your sentences include some details about your routine.	Your sentences include little information about your routine.
Communication	Most of your sentences are clear.	Some of your sentences are clear.	Your sentences are not very clear.
Accuracy	Your sentences have few mistakes in grammar and vocabulary.	Your sentences have some mistakes in grammar and vocabulary.	Your sentences have many mistakes in grammar and vocabulary.

Escribir B

> **¡AVANZA!** **Goal:** Write about daily routines and trips.

Step 1

Complete the table with your daily routine.

Por la mañana	¿A qué hora?	Por la noche	¿A qué hora?

Step 2

Using the information in the table above, describe your daily routines. Write four complete sentences. Also describe how your routine changes when you are taking a trip. Follow the model.

modelo: Generalmente me despierto a las seis y media de la mañana ...

_____

_____

_____

Step 3

Evaluate your writing using the information in the table.

Writing Criteria	Excellent	Good	Needs Work
Content	You include all of the information.	You include some of the information.	You include little information.
Communication	Most of your sentences are clear.	Some of your sentences are clear.	Your sentences are not very clear.
Accuracy	Your sentences have few mistakes in grammar and vocabulary.	Your sentences have some mistakes in grammar and vocabulary.	Your sentence have many mistakes in grammar and vocabulary.

Escribir C

> **¡AVANZA!** **Goal:** Write about daily routines and trips.

Step 1

Complete the following sentences about your morning routine.

1. Antes de bañarme, yo _____
2. Después, yo _____
3. Después de bañarme, yo _____
4. Después, yo _____
5. Después, yo _____
6. Después, yo _____

Step 2

You are on a trip. Write a five-sentence e-mail to your friend describing your routine there. Use the present progressive at least once.

_____

_____

_____

_____

_____

_____

Step 3

Evaluate your writing using the information in the table.

Writing Criteria	Excellent	Good	Needs Work
Content	Your email includes all of the information.	Your email includes some of the information.	Your email includes little information.
Communication	Most of your email is organized and easy to follow.	Parts of your email are organized and easy to follow.	Your email is disorganized and hard to follow.
Accuracy	Your email has few mistakes in grammar and vocabulary.	Your email has some mistakes in grammar and vocabulary.	Your email has many mistakes in grammar and vocabulary.

UNIDAD 8
Lección 1   •   Escribir C

Cultura A

┌──┐
│ **¡AVANZA!** **Goal:** Review cultural information about Costa Rica. │
└──┘

1 **Costa Rica** Complete the following questions with one of the multiple-choice answers.

1. The capital of Costa Rica is _____

   a. San Juan   **b.** San José   **c.** San Luis

2. The _____ of Tabacón are popular with tourists.

   a. carretas   **b.** beaches   **c.** hot springs.

3. The **carretas,** or oxcarts, which are a symbol of Costa Rica, were used to _____

   a. transport coffee   **b.** transport sugarcane   **c.** transport bananas

2 **Costa Rican culture** Read the following sentences about Costa Rica and answer *true* or *false*.

T   F   **1.** Costa Rica was the headquarters of the Kayak Surf World Championship in 2005.

T   F   **2.** **Gallo pinto** is a typical dish from Costa Rica.

T   F   **3.** Costa Rica is located in South America.

T   F   **4.** Arenal is an active volcano in Costa Rica.

T   F   **5.** Costa Ricans use **tú** instead of **vos.**

3 **Costa Rican geography** Costa Rica has many varied landscapes. Write a description of some of the landscapes found in Costa Rica. Which land feature do you like most and why?

_____

_____

_____

_____

_____

_____

_____

UNIDAD 8
Lección 1

Cultura A

Unidad 8, Lección 1
Cultura A

364

¡Avancemos! 1
Cuaderno: Práctica por niveles

Cultura B

> **¡AVANZA!** **Goal:** Review cultural information about Costa Rica.

❶ Costa Rica Draw lines to match the names or phrases on the left with their explanation on the right.

Arenal	were used to transport coffee
Sarchí	typical Costa Rican food
colón	active volcano
gallo pinto	Costa Rican currency
carretas	where the **carreta** festival is held

❷ Costa Rican culture Answer the following questions about Costa Rica.

1. What is the name of the active volcano in Costa Rica? _____

2. Which aquatic sport can you do on Costa Rica's beaches? _____

3. What is the capital of Costa Rica? _____

4. In general, Costa Ricans do not use **tú,** but instead use _____.

5. In Costa Rica, family members often use _____ when speaking with each other.

❸ Costa Rican travel You work at a travel agency and must create an advertisement to get tourists interested in traveling to Costa Rica. Write an ad describing the types of activities and scenery that the tourists could enjoy in Costa Rica.

_____

_____

_____

_____

_____

_____

_____

_____

Cultura C

> **¡AVANZA!** **Goal:** Review cultural information about Costa Rica.

1 **Costa Rica** Complete the sentences about Costa Rica.

1. Costa Rica is located in _____ America.

2. _____ is an active volcano in Costa Rica.

3. Costa Ricans use _____ rather than **tú,** but many family members use
_____ with each other.

4. Casado is a typical Costa Rican _____.

5. _____ is the capital of Costa Rica.

2 **In Costa Rica** Answer the following questions using complete sentences.

1. What is the name of the Costa Rican town where the **carreta** festival is held every year?

_____

2. What is Costa Rica's landscape like? _____

_____

3. What is the name of Costa Rica's currency? _____

3 **Souvenirs** You work at a souvenir shop in Costa Rica. Write about a typical souvenir
from Costa Rica that you would recommend for a tourist. What would you tell the tourist
to convince them to buy the item? Describe what the souvenir looks like, as well as any
interesting facts.

_____

_____

_____

_____

_____

_____

UNIDAD 8 • Cultura C
Lección 1

366

Unidad 8, Lección 1
Cultura C

¡Avancemos! 1
Cuaderno: Práctica por niveles

Vocabulario A

> **¡AVANZA!** Read about what people do on vacation.

1 We like to go away on vacation and do lots of activities. Match the words in the left column with related words in the right column.

a. estar al aire libre   comprar cerámica

b. hacer una parrillada   surf de vela

c. buscar artesanía   preparar carne

d. hacer surfing   acampar

e. buscar joyas   comprar un collar

2 We do a lot of things on our vacation. Complete the following sentences with words from the box.

1. En el mercado de artesanías, compramos _____

   para nuestras familias.

2. Me encantan los anillos de _____ que compré ayer.

3. Este artículo de madera es muy _____ .

4. Nos divertimos mucho cuando vamos a _____ .

5. Berta compró unos _____ de plata muy bonitos.

aretes
oro
montar a caballo
recuerdos
barato

3 Complete the sentences with what these people like to do on vacation.

modelo: (a mí) / acampar / vacaciones.

Me gusta acampar en vacaciones.

1. (a ti) / comprar / de madera

   _____

   _____

2. (a / María) / regatear mercado

   _____

   _____

3. (hermano) / comprar artículos / calidad

   _____

   _____

Vocabulario B

Level 1, pp. 434-438

> ¡AVANZA! **Goal:** Read about what people do on vacation.

1 Martín and his friends go on vacation. Choose the correct word in parentheses to complete each sentence.

1. Martín da _____ al aire libre. (caminatas / mercados / aretes)

2. Martín compra artesanías en el _____ . (surf / mercado / collar)

3. Los chicos tienen mucho _____ . (barato / recuerdo / tiempo libre)

4. Martín compra algunas _____ para su mamá. (joyas / parrilladas / caminatas)

2 Martín goes to the handicrafts market. Complete the dialogue with words from the box.

lo dejo	le puedo ofrecer	me deja ver	Qué caro

Martín: ¡Buenos días! ¿ _____ el anillo de plata?

Artesano: Claro. También _____ algunos de oro. El precio está debajo de cada artículo.

Martín: ¡ _____ !

Artesano: Bueno, _____ más barato si compra dos.

3 Look at the pictures and complete the sentences.

1.
2.
3.

1. Claudia _____ en la playa.

2. Alejandro _____ en su casa.

3. Los chicos van a _____ al aire libre.

Vocabulario C

| ¡AVANZA! | **Goal:** Read about what people do on vacation. |

1 Natalia and her friends went on a summer vacation. Write the related words in the correct column.

dar una caminata	hacer una parrillada	acampar
artesanías	anillos	artículos de madera
hacer surfing	aretes	comer al aire libre
recuerdos	artículos de cerámica	montar a caballo

Actividades   **Mercado**

_____   _____
_____   _____
_____   _____
_____   _____
_____   _____
_____   _____

2 Do you like to go on vacation? Complete the sentences with things that you like to do when you go on vacation.

1. A mí me gusta _____
2. Normalmente yo _____
3. Yo prefiero _____
4. Cuando voy de vacaciones, yo _____
5. En mis vacaciones, yo siempre _____

3 Write a three-sentence text to describe what you did on your vacation.

_____
_____
_____

¡Avancemos! 1
Cuaderno: Práctica por niveles

Unidad 8, Lección 2
Vocabulario C 369

UNIDAD 8 • Vocabulario C
Lección 2

Gramática A Indirect Object Pronouns

¡AVANZA!	**Goal:** Use indirect object pronouns to talk about vacations.

1 Pablo's friends went on vacation together. Underline the correct pronoun for each sentence.

1. ¿Quieres ir de vacaciones? Yo (te / me) mando el nombre del hotel.

2. Susana no encuentra su peine. Yo (le / nos) doy mi peine.

3. Patricia y yo compramos artesanías. (Nos / Te) gustan las artesanías.

4. ¿Sabes hacer surfing? ¿(Me / Te) gusta hacerlo?

5. ¿(Me / Le) puedes comprar el bloqueador de sol?

2 These friends help each other. Complete the sentences with the correct pronoun.

1. Necesito el jabón. ¿ _____ lo das?

2. Claudia quiere unos aretes. ¿ _____ puedes comprar unos aretes de plata?

3. Mis padres no saben cómo estoy. ¿Puedes mandar_____ un correo electrónico?

4. ¿Estás enfermo? ¿Puedo dar_____ algo?

5. Álvaro y yo vamos a hacer una parrillada. ¿ _____ puedes decir cómo hacerlo?

3 Complete the sentences with things you can buy at a handicrafts market.

modelo: Comprar un anillo (mamá).

Puedo comprarle un anillo a mamá.

1. Comprar recuerdos (amigos)

_____

_____

2. Comprar aretes (hermana)

_____

_____

3. Comprar artículos de madera (tú)

_____

_____

UNIDAD 8 • Gramática A
Lección 2

370

Unidad 8, Lección 2
Gramática A

¡Avancemos! 1
Cuaderno: Práctica por niveles

Gramática B Indirect Object Pronouns

> **¡AVANZA!** **Goal:** Use indirect object pronouns to talk about vacations.

1 Everyone went to the handicrafts market. The following sentences are out of order; rewrite each one in the correct order.

1. madre algunas mi joyas compré a le

   _____

2. los cerámica gustaron me de artículos

   _____

3. algunos amigos llevo madera artículos de a les mis

   _____

4. muy recuerdos compré bonitos te unos

   _____

5. unos chicos los compraron bonitos nos anillos muy

   _____

2 After the handicrafts market, everyone did other activities. Rewrite the sentences, replacing the person with the correct indirect object pronoun.

1. Traemos un caballo para Lucas. _____

2. Hacemos una parrillada para todos los chicos. _____

3. Los chicos traen frutas para nosotros. _____

4. Yo compro algo de comer para ustedes. _____

3 Answer the questions with a complete sentence.

1. ¿A quién le dices tus secretos?

   _____

   _____

2. ¿A quiénes les pides regalos de cumpleaños?

   _____

   _____

¡Avancemos! 1
Cuaderno: Práctica por niveles

Unidad 8, Lección 2
Gramática B **371**

UNIDAD 8 • Gramática B
Lección 2

Gramática C *Indirect Object Pronouns*

Level 1, pp. 439-443

> **¡AVANZA!** **Goal:** Use indirect object pronouns to talk about vacations.

1 Read the following sentences about a day at the handicrafts market. Complete each sentence using an indirect object pronoun.

1. Necesito saber cuánto cuesta el anillo. ¿Puedes decir_____ cuánto cuesta?

2. Quieres un collar y _____ compré un collar de plata.

3. A nosotros _____ gustan las artesanías de madera.

4. Los chicos no vienen con nosotros, pero podemos comprar_____

algunos recuerdos.

5. ¿Quieres comprar_____ algo a tu madre?

2 Write complete sentences about what happens at the handicrafts market. Use indirect object pronouns.

modelo   (nosotros) buscar un regalo / para Armando:

Le buscamos un regalo muy bonito.

1. (ellos) / llevar recuerdos / para mis padres:

_____

2. (yo) comprar un anillo / para mí:

_____

3. (él) traer frutas / para nosotros:

_____

3 Write a four-sentence e-mail to a friend. Tell your friend what things you buy at the handicrafts market. Use indirect object pronouns.

_____

_____

_____

_____

UNIDAD 8 • Gramática C
Lección 2

372

Unidad 8, Lección 2
Gramática C

¡Avancemos! 1
Cuaderno: Práctica por niveles

Gramática A *Demonstrative Adjectives*

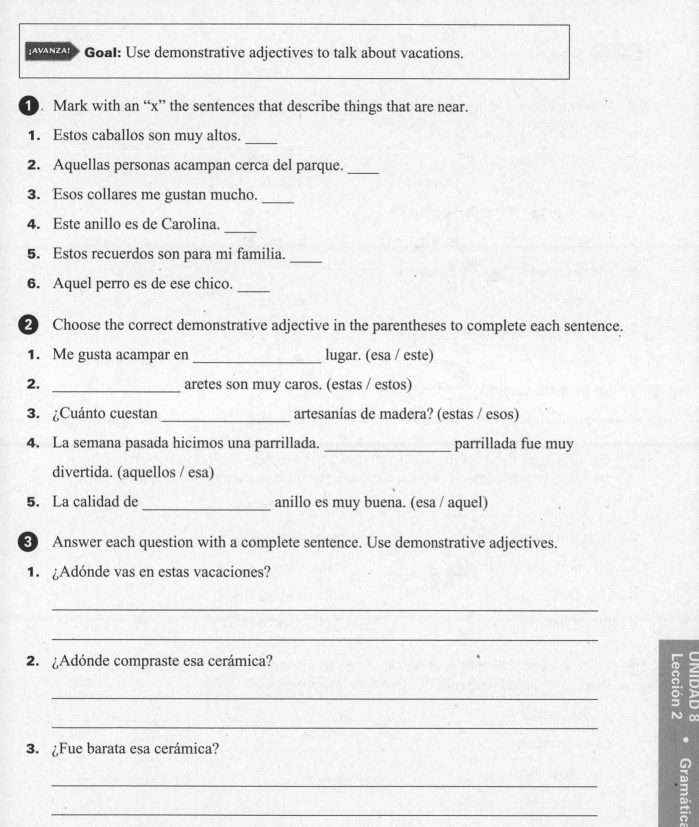

> **¡AVANZA!** **Goal:** Use demonstrative adjectives to talk about vacations.

1. Mark with an "x" the sentences that describe things that are near.

1. Estos caballos son muy altos. _____

2. Aquellas personas acampan cerca del parque. _____

3. Esos collares me gustan mucho. _____

4. Este anillo es de Carolina. _____

5. Estos recuerdos son para mi familia. _____

6. Aquel perro es de ese chico. _____

2. Choose the correct demonstrative adjective in the parentheses to complete each sentence.

1. Me gusta acampar en _____ lugar. (esa / este)

2. _____ aretes son muy caros. (estas / estos)

3. ¿Cuánto cuestan _____ artesanías de madera? (estas / esos)

4. La semana pasada hicimos una parrillada. _____ parrillada fue muy

divertida. (aquellos / esa)

5. La calidad de _____ anillo es muy buena. (esa / aquel)

3. Answer each question with a complete sentence. Use demonstrative adjectives.

1. ¿Adónde vas en estas vacaciones?

_____

_____

2. ¿Adónde compraste esa cerámica?

_____

_____

3. ¿Fue barata esa cerámica?

_____

_____

UNIDAD 8 • Gramática A
Lección 2

Gramática B *Demonstrative Adjectives*

> ¡AVANZA! **Goal:** Use demonstrative adjectives to talk about vacations.

1 We bought some things at the handicrafts market. Complete the sentences with the correct adjective.

1. Yo compré_____ aretes.

   a. este   **b.** estos   **c.** esta   **d.** aquel

2. Luis compró _____ collar de oro.

   a. esos   **b.** esta   **c.** aquel   **d.** aquella

3. Marta compró _____ artesanías.

   a. estos   **b.** esta   **c.** estas   **d.** aquel

4. Mis amigos compraron _____ joya.

   a. ese   **b.** esa   **c.** este   **d.** aquel

5. Mi hermana compró _____ recuerdos para ustedes.

   a. esas   **b.** estas   **c.** aquel   **d.** aquellos

2 We all bought things at the handicrafts market. Complete the following sentences with **ese** (that) or **este** (this) in singular or plural, feminine or masculine, as appropriate.

1. Yo vi_____ recuerdos. (cerca)

2. Nosotros compramos _____ artesanías. (cerca)

3. Mi hermana compró _____ joyas. (lejos)

4. Ustedes compraron _____ anillo de plata. (lejos)

5. Iván compró _____ artículo de madera. (cerca)

3 Write sentences about things we buy at the handicrafts market. Change the adjective to singular or plural, feminine or masculine, as appropriate.

1. Aquel / aretes: _____

2. Este / recuerdos: _____

3. Ese / artesanías: _____

Unidad 8, Lección 2
Gramática B

374

¡Avancemos! 1
Cuaderno: Práctica por niveles

UNIDAD 8 • Gramática B
Lección 2

Gramática C *Demonstrative Adjectives*

> **¡AVANZA!** **Goal:** Use demonstrative adjectives to talk about vacations.

1 Yesterday, you went to the handicrafts market. Complete the following sentences with the correct demonstrative adjectives. Use the words in parentheses as clues.

1. Yo compré _____ aretes de plata. (cerca)

2. Mis amigos vieron _____ collares que tú quieres. (muy lejos)

3. Tú compraste _____ recuerdos muy baratos. (lejos)

4. Yo vi_____ artesanías muy bonitas. (lejos)

5. Ustedes compraron _____ joya de oro. (cerca)

2 What did you buy at the handicrafts market? Write sentences using the demonstrative adjectives in parentheses.

1. (este) _____

_____

2. (aquellas) _____

_____

3. (esos) _____

_____

4. (esa) _____

_____

5. (estos) _____

_____

3 Write three sentences about things that are near to you and things that are far from you at this moment. Use demonstrative adjectives.

1. _____

2. _____

3. _____

Integración: Hablar

Level 1, pp. 447-449
CD 04 track 31

Iván and his friends go on vacation, and decide to go to an arts and crafts fair. Ivan's friends are interested in shopping but he wants to do other activities in the area.

Fuente 1 Leer

Read the newspaper article on the **Feria de Artesanías**...

Feria de Artesanías

Todos los que pasan sus vacaciones en nuestra playa pueden ir a la Feria de Artesanías. Es un lugar fantástico. En la feria venden todas las cosas que las personas buscan. Después de un día de actividades al aire libre, pueden dar una caminata por la playa y llegar al Parque Victorino. En este parque pueden montar a caballo y comer al aire libre. Es un buen lugar para hacer una parrillada.

Fuente 2 Escuchar   *CD 04 track 32*

Listen to what the announcer says through the loudspeakers at the Feria de Artesanías. Take notes.

_____

_____

_____

_____

Hablar

What can Ivan's friends buy at the **Feria de Artesanías**? What other activities can Ivan and his friends do nearby? Tell when they should do each activity.

modelo: Primero, Iván y sus amigos pueden... Luego, también pueden...

Unidad 8, Lección 2
Integración: Hablar

376

¡Avancemos! 1
Cuaderno: Práctica por niveles

UNIDAD 8 • Integración:
Lección 2   Hablar

Integración: Escribir

Lucía went on vacation with her classmates. Olga couldn't join them for the trip.

Fuente 1 Leer

Read the email Olga sent to Lucía.

Queridos amigos:

Ya es de noche y les escribo porque no estoy triste. No ir de vacaciones fue mejor porque estoy enferma. Me duelen la cabeza y el estómago. Es cierto, no tengo ganas salir. Ahora quiero dormir. Pero voy a estar bien. Quisiera pedir una cosa pequeña. Si tienen tiempo y pueden, quiero que compren un recuerdo del lugar donde ustedes están. Si me traen un recuerdo de ese lugar, cuando lleguen voy a estar contenta.

Adiós,

Olga

Fuente 2 Escuchar   *CD 04track 34*

Listen to Federico's voice message to Olga. Take notes.

_____

_____

_____

_____

Escribir

Now answer this question: Olga had to stay home, but what's going to happen for her to feel better? Explain why.

Modelo: Olga quiere...Entonces sus amigos

_____

_____

_____

_____

_____

_____

Escuchar A

> **¡AVANZA!** **Goal:** Listen to people talking about vacation activities.

1 Listen to Cecilia talking about her vacation. Then, read each sentence and answer **cierto** (true) or **falso** (false).

C F **1.** A Cecilia le gustan las actividades al aire libre.

C F **2.** A Cecilia no le gusta montar a caballo.

C F **3.** A los amigos de Cecilia les gusta montar a caballo.

C F **4.** Estas vacaciones, Cecilia va al campo.

C F **5.** Cecilia siempre va a la playa con su familia.

2 Listen to Inés. Then, complete the sentences using the correct word in parentheses.

1. Inés va de _____ (vacaciones / caballo) con sus amigos.

2. Los amigos de Inés son _____ . (divertidos / baratos)

3. Inés tiene _____ . (la calidad / una pelota)

4. Inés va a comprarle a su madre _____ como recuerdo. (unos aretes / artesanías)

UNIDAD 8 • Escuchar A
Lección 2

Unidad 8, Lección 2
Escuchar A

378

¡Avancemos! 1
Cuaderno: Práctica por niveles

Escuchar B

Level 1, pp. 454-455
CD 04 tracks 37-38

| ¡AVANZA! | **Goal:** Listen to people talking about vacation activities. |

1 Listen to Victoria. Then, draw lines to match each person with what he or she bought at the handicrafts market.

a. Verónica   Anillo

b. Hugo   Artículo de madera

c. Mauro   Recuerdos

d. Sandra   Aretes de plata

e. Victoria   Collar

2 Listen to Ernesto. Then, complete the following sentences.

1. Victoria le compró _____

   a Ernesto.

2. Este regalo es _____

3. No fue cara porque _____

4. La persona de la tienda las vendió baratas porque _____

5. Victoria les compró estos artículos a _____

Escuchar C

¡AVANZA! **Goal:** Listen to people talking about vacation activities.

1 Listen to the handicrafts seller and take notes. Then, complete the chart.

¿Quién compró?	¿Qué compró?	¿De qué es?

2 Listen to Miriam and take notes. Then, answer the questions with complete sentences.

1. ¿Qué compró Miriam y para quién lo compró?

_____

2. ¿Qué le gusta a la mamá de Miriam?

_____

3. ¿Cómo son las joyas que más le gustan a la mamá de Miriam?

_____

4. ¿Por qué Miriam no le compró nada a su padre?

_____

Leer A

> **¡AVANZA!** **Goal:** Read about vacation activities.

A campground places an ad in the local newspaper.

¿Te gusta acampar?

Si te gusta acampar, conocemos el lugar ideal para hacerlo.

• Puedes hacer muchas actividades al aire libre: puedes montar a caballo, hacer surfing o dar una caminata.

¿Quieres venir a un lugar fantástico?

• Este lugar es un lugar como los de las películas.

• Si vienen en grupo les podemos ofrecer precios muy baratos.

¿Comprendiste?

Read the ad from a campground. Mark with an "x" those sentences that name things you can do.

1. acampar _____

2. hacer actividades en el agua _____

3. montar a caballo _____

4. caminar al aire libre _____

5. comprar recuerdos _____

6. ver animales _____

7. hacer deportes en el agua _____

8. llevar a tus amigos _____

¿Qué piensas?

¿Te gustaría ir a un lugar como el que describe la publicidad? ¿Por qué?

_____

_____

_____

¡Avancemos! 1
Cuaderno: Práctica por niveles

UNIDAD 8
Lección 2

•

Leer A

Unidad 8, Lección 2
Leer A **381**

Leer B

Level 1, pp. 454-455

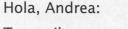 **Goal:** Read about vacation activities.

Before going away on vacation with some friends, Andrea receives an e-mail.

Hola, Andrea:

Te escribo este correo electrónico porque sé que sales de viaje a las 2:45 pm y yo salgo de mi clase de ciencias a las 3:00 pm.

Las vacaciones son muy divertidas cuando vas con cuatro personas. ¿Puedes tomar fotos de todo el grupo? ¿Me mandas las fotos por correo electrónico?

Conozco un lugar bonito, donde pueden acampar y hacer parrilladas. ¡Es buenísimo! Está al lado del mercado de artesanías.

Adios,

Javier

¿Comprendiste?

Read Javier's e-mail. Then complete the sentences.

1. Javier le escribe un correo electrónico a Andrea porque _____

2. Andrea va de vacaciones con un _____

3. Javier le pide _____

4 . Javier le habla de un lugar muy bueno para _____

5. Ese lugar está cerca _____

¿Qué piensas?

¿Te gusta ir de vacaciones en grupo o con pocas personas? ¿Por qué?

_____

_____

_____

_____

_____

_____

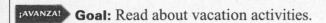

Nombre _____ Clase _____ Fecha _____

Leer C

> ¡AVANZA! **Goal:** Read about vacation activities.

Verónica received a letter from her friend Raúl.

> Hola, Verónica.
>
> Todavía estoy en la playa. No encuentro una computadora para mandarte un correo electrónico, entonces te escribo esta carta.
>
> Ayer fui al mercado de artesanías y te compré un recuerdo. Vi un collar de plata que me gustó mucho pero no sé si te gustaría. Todo fue muy barato porque regateé y el señor me vendió todo a un buen precio.
>
> También hice surf de vela. Fue divertido. Como al aire libre todas las mañanas y leo un libro en mi tiempo libre por las tardes. Estoy muy contento, y tú, ¿cómo estás?
>
> Raúl

¿Comprendiste?

Read the letter from Raúl. Then answer the following questions using complete sentences.

1. ¿Por qué Raúl escribe una carta?

_____

2. ¿Qué hizo en el mercado?

_____

3. ¿Por qué pagó poco dinero por las cosas que compró?

_____

4. ¿Qué más hace Raúl?

_____

¿Qué piensas?

1. ¿Tú les escribes a tus amigos cuando estás de vacaciones?

_____

2. Da un ejemplo:

_____

_____

Escribir A

> ¡AVANZA! **Goal:** Write about vacation activities.

Step 1

Write a list of things you can buy in a handicrafts market.

1. _____
2. _____
3. _____
4. _____
5. _____
6. _____

Step 2

Using the information from the list, write three sentences about which of these items you can buy for your friends and family, and why. Use indirect object pronouns.

_____

_____

_____

_____

_____

Step 3

Evaluate your writing using the information in the table.

Writing Criteria	Excellent	Good	Needs Work
Content	Your sentences include many details and new vocabulary.	Your sentences include some details and new vocabulary.	Your sentences include little information or new vocabulary.
Communication	Most of your sentences are clear.	Some of your sentences are clear.	Your sentences are not very clear.
Accuracy	Your sentences have few mistakes in grammar and vocabulary.	Your sentences have some mistakes in grammar and vocabulary.	Your sentences have many mistakes in grammar and vocabulary.

UNIDAD 8 • **Escribir A** • **Lección 2**

Unidad 8, Lección 2
Escribir A

384

¡Avancemos! 1
Cuaderno: Práctica por niveles

Escribir B

> ¡AVANZA! **Goal:** Write about vacation activities.

Step 1

Make a list about activities you can do on vacation.

1. _____

2. _____

3. _____

4. _____

Step 2

Using the information from the list, write four sentences about vacation activities.
Use indirect object pronouns and demonstrative adjectives.

_____

_____

_____

_____

_____

Step 3

Evaluate your writing using the information in the table.

Writing Criteria	Excellent	Good	Needs Work
Content	Your sentences include many details and new vocabulary.	Your sentences include some details and new vocabulary.	Your sentences include little information or new vocabulary.
Communication	Most of your sentences are organized and easy to follow.	Some of your sentences are organized and easy to follow.	Your sentences are disorganized and hard to follow.
Accuracy	Your sentences have few mistakes in grammar and vocabulary.	Your sentences have some mistakes in grammar and vocabulary.	Your sentences have many mistakes in grammar and vocabulary.

UNIDAD 8
Lección 2

•

Escribir B

Escribir C

> **¡AVANZA!** **Goal:** Write about vacation activities.

Step 1

You are going to go shopping at a handicrafts market. Complete this chart with what you buy, what is made of, and who you buy it for.

¿Qué?	¿De qué?	¿Para quién?

Step 2

Using the information from the chart, write a paragraph about a visit to a handicrafts market. Use demonstrative adjectives and indirect object pronouns.

_____

_____

_____

_____

_____

Step 3

Evaluate your writing using the information in the table.

Writing Criteria	Excellent	Good	Needs Work
Content	Your text includes many details and vocabulary.	Your text includes some details and vocabulary.	Your text includes little information or vocabulary.
Communication	Most of your text is organized and easy to follow.	Parts of your text are organized and easy to follow.	Your text is disorganized and hard to follow.
Accuracy	Your text has few mistakes in grammar and vocabulary.	Your text has some mistakes in grammar and vocabulary.	Your text has many mistakes in grammar and vocabulary.

Cultura A

> **¡AVANZA!** **Goal:** Review cultural information about Costa Rica.

1 **Costa Rica** Complete the following sentences with one of the multiple-choice answers.

1. The taxis in Costa Rica are _____

   a. blue   **b.** yellow   **c.** red

2. Costa Rica is located in _____

   a. Central America   **b.** North America   **c.** South America

3. The **quetzal** and the **tucán** are examples of _____ found in Costa Rica.

   a. typical dishes   **b.** tropical birds   **c.** tropical plants

2 **Costa Rican culture.** Choose the correct word to complete the following sentences.

1. (Gold / Coffee) is one of Costa Rica's most exported products.

2. In Costa Rica coffee is harvested between the months of (November and January / April and June).

3. Arenal is a well-known (volcano/ river) in Costa Rica.

3 **Markets** At San José's **Mercado Central** there are many stalls that sell a variety of things. Do you remember what is sold in this market? Write about the types of items that you can buy at the **Mercado Central.** Which items would you buy if you visited this market?

_____

_____

_____

_____

Cultura B

> ¡AVANZA! **Goal:** Review cultural information about Costa Rica.

1 **Costa Rica** Read the following sentences about Costa Rica and answer *true* or *false*.

T   F   **1.** The product that Costa Rica exports the most is coffee.

T   F   **2.** At the **Mercado Central** in San José, you can buy fruit and flowers.

T   F   **3.** Costa Rica is larger than México.

T   F   **4.** Costa Rica has a very cold climate.

T   F   **5.** **Casado** is a typical Costa Rican food.

2 **Costa Rican culture** Answer the following questions about Costa Rica.

1. What color are the airport taxis in Costa Rica? _____

2. In which region of the Americas Costa Rica located? _____

3. When is the coffee harvest in Costa Rica? _____

4. What are three common transportation methods in Costa Rica? _____

3 **Transportation** Compare the modes of transportation that are popular in Costa Rica with those that are popular in your city or state. How do people travel short and long distances, typically? What are the pros and cons of each type of transportation?

_____

_____

_____

_____

Cultura C

> **¡AVANZA!** **Goal:** Review cultural information about Costa Rica.

1 **Life in Costa Rica** In Costa Rica, there are many places to visit and many things to do. Where do you go in Costa Rica to do the following things?

Things to do	Places to go
Buy fruit, coffee, or flowers	_____
Surfing	_____
go to the *carreta* festival	_____

2 **Costa Rica** Answer the following questions about Costa Rica using full sentences.

1. When is coffee harvested in Costa Rica? _____

_____

2. What is the currency of Costa Rica? _____

3. What are three common transportation methods in Costa Rica? _____

_____

3 **Markets** Write a comparison of Costa Rica's **Mercado Central** and Uruguay's **Mercado del Puerto**. In which cities are the markets located? What can you buy and where can you eat at each market?

_____

_____

_____

_____

_____

_____

_____

¡Avancemos! 1
Cuaderno: Práctica por niveles

Unidad 8, Lección 2
Cultura C   **389**

UNIDAD 8
Lección 2   •   Cultura C

Comparación cultural: ¡De vacaciones!

Level 1, pp. 456-457

Lectura y escritura

After reading the paragraphs about how Ernesto, Isabel, and Osvaldo describe their vacations, write a short paragraph about a real or imaginary vacation. Complete the information in the three boxes and then write a paragraph that describes your vacation.

Step 1

Complete the boxes describing as many details as you can about your place, activities, and your opinion about the location.

Lugar	Actividades	Opinión

Step 2

Now take the details from the boxes and write a sentence for each one according to their category.

_____

_____

_____

_____

_____

_____

_____

_____

_____

_____

UNIDAD 8 • Comparación
Lección 2   cultural

Comparación cultural: ¡De vacaciones!

Level 1, pp. 456-457

Lectura y escritura (continued)

Step 3

Now write your paragraph using the sentences you wrote as a guide. Include an introductory sentence and use **hacer un viaje, quedarse** and **gustar** to write about your own vacation.

_____

_____

_____

_____

_____

_____

Checklist

Be sure that…

☐ all the details about your vacation from your boxes are included in the paragraph;

☐ you use details to describe, as clearly as possible, all of your activities;

☐ you include new vocabulary words and the verbs **hacer un viaje, quedarse,** and **gustar.**

Rubric

Evaluate your writing using the rubric below.

Writing criteria	Excellent	Good	Needs Work
Content	Your paragraph includes many details about your vacation.	Your paragraph includes some details about your vacation.	Your paragraph includes little information about your vacation.
Communication	Most of your paragraph is organized and easy to follow.	Parts of your paragraph are organized and easy to follow.	Your paragraph is disorganized and hard to follow.
Accuracy	Your paragraph has few mistakes in grammar and vocabulary.	Your paragraph has some mistakes in grammar and vocabulary.	Your paragraph has many mistakes in grammar and vocabulary.

UNIDAD 8 • Comparación cultural
Lección 2

Comparación cultural: ¡De vacaciones!

Level 1, pp. 456-457

Compara con tu mundo

Now write a comparison about your vacation and that of one of the three students from page 457. Organize your comparison by topics. First, compare the place where you go, then the activities, and lastly your opinions about the locations.

Step 1

Use the table to organize your comparison by topics. Write details for each topic about yourself and the student you chose.

Categoría	Mis vacaciones	Las vacaciones de _____
lugar(es)		
actividades		
opinión		

Step 2

Now use the details from your chart to write the comparison. Include an introductory sentence and write about each topic. Use **hacer un viaje, quedarse,** and **gustar** to describe your vacation and that of the student you chose.

_____

_____

_____

_____

_____

_____

_____

_____

_____

Unidad 8
Comparación cultural: ¡De vacaciones!

¡Avancemos! 1
Cuaderno: Práctica por niveles

392

UNIDAD 8 • Comparación
Lección 2   cultural

Greet People and Say Goodbye

GREETINGS

Buenos días.	Good morning.
Buenas tardes.	Good afternoon.
Buenas noches.	Good evening.
Hola.	Hello./Hi.

SAY GOODBYE

Adiós.	Goodbye.
Buenas noches.	Good night.
Hasta luego.	See you later.
Hasta mañana.	See you tomorrow.

SAY HOW YOU ARE

¿Cómo estás?	How are you? (familiar)
¿Cómo está usted?	How are you? (formal)
¿Qué tal?	How is it going?
Bien.	Fine.
Mal.	Bad.
Más o menos.	So-so.
Muy bien.	Very well.
Regular.	Okay.
¿Y tú?	And you? (familiar)
¿Y usted?	And you? (formal)
¿Qué pasa?	What's up?

Say Which Day It Is

¿Qué día es hoy?	What day is today?
Hoy es...	Today is...
Mañana es...	Tomorrow is...
el día	day
hoy	today
mañana	tomorrow
la semana	week

Describe the Weather

¿Qué tiempo hace?	What is the weather like?
Hace calor.	It is hot.
Hace frío.	It is cold.
Hace sol.	It is sunny.
Hace viento.	It is windy.
Llueve.	It is raining.
Nieva.	It is snowing.

Say Where You Are From

¿De dónde eres?	Where are you (familiar) from?
¿De dónde es?	Where is he/she from?
¿De dónde es usted?	Where are you (formal) from?
Soy de...	I am from...
Es de...	He/She is from...

Make Introductions

¿Cómo se llama?	What's his/her/your (formal) name?
Se llama...	His/Her name is...
¿Cómo te llamas?	What's your (familiar) name?
Me llamo...	My name is...
Te/Le presento a...	Let me introduce you (familiar/formal) to...
El gusto es mío.	The pleasure is mine.
Encantado(a).	Delighted./Pleased to meet you.
Igualmente.	Same here./Likewise.
Mucho gusto.	Nice to meet you.
¿Quién es?	Who is he/she/it?\\
Es...	He/She/It is...

Exchange Phone Numbers

¿Cuál es tu/su número de teléfono?	What's your (familiar/formal) phone number?
Mi número de teléfono es...	My phone number is...

Other Words and Phrases

la clase	class
el (la) maestro(a) de español	Spanish teacher (male/female)
Perdón.	Excuse me.
el país	country
(Muchas) Gracias.	Thank you (very much).
el señor (Sr.)	Mr.
la señora (Sra.)	Mrs.
la señorita (Srta.)	Miss
sí	yes
no	no

Talk About Activities

alquilar un DVD	to rent a DVD
andar en patineta	to skateboard
aprender el español	to learn Spanish
beber	to drink
comer	to eat
comprar	to buy
correr	to run
descansar	to rest
dibujar	to draw
escribir correos electrónicos	to write e-mails
escuchar música	to listen to music
estudiar	to study
hablar por teléfono	to talk on the phone
hacer la tarea	to do homework
jugar al fútbol	to play soccer
leer un libro	to read a book
mirar la televisión	to watch television
montar en bicicleta	to ride a bike
pasar un rato con los amigos	to spend time with friends
pasear	to go for a walk
practicar deportes	to practice / play sports
preparar la comida	to prepare food / a meal
tocar la guitarra	to play the guitar
trabajar	to work

Say What You Like and Don't Like to Do

¿Qué te gusta hacer?	What do you like to do?
¿Te gusta...?	Do you like...?
Me gusta...	I like...
No me gusta...	I don't like...

Snack Foods and Beverages

el agua (fem.)	water
la fruta	fruit
la galleta	cookie
el helado	ice cream
el jugo	juice
las papas fritas	French fries
la pizza	pizza
el refresco	soft drink

Other Words and Phrases

la actividad	activity
antes de	before
después (de)	afterward, after
la escuela	school
más	more
o	or
pero	but
también	also

Describe Yourself and Others

¿Cómo eres?	What are you like?
PERSONALITY	
artístico(a)	artistic
atlético(a)	athletic
bueno(a)	good
cómico(a)	funny
desorganizado(a)	disorganized
estudioso(a)	studious
inteligente	intelligent
malo(a)	bad
organizado(a)	organized
perezoso(a)	lazy
serio(a)	serious
simpático(a)	nice
trabajador(a)	hard-working
APPEARANCE	
alto(a)	tall
bajo(a)	short (height)
bonito(a)	pretty
grande	big, large; great
guapo(a)	good-looking
joven (pl. jóvenes)	young
pelirrojo(a)	red-haired
pequeño(a)	small
viejo(a)	old
Tengo...	I have...
Tiene...	He / She has
pelo rubio	blond hair
pelo castaño	brown hair

People

el (la) amigo (a)	friend
la chica	girl
el chico	boy
el (la) estudiante	student
el hombre	man
la mujer	woman
la persona	person

Other Words and Phrases

muy	very
un poco	a little
porque	because
todos(as)	all

Subject Pronouns and ser

Ser means *to be*. Use **ser** to identify a person or say where he or she is from.

Singular		Plural	
yo	**soy**	nosotros(as)	**somos**
tú	**eres**	vosotros(as)	**sois**
usted	**es**	ustedes	**son**
él, ella	**es**	ellos(as)	**son**

Gustar with an Infinitive

Use **gustar** to talk about what people like to do.

A mí **me gusta** dibujar.

A ti **te gusta** dibujar.

A usted **le gusta** dibujar.

A él, ella **le gusta** dibujar.

A nosotros(as) **nos gusta** dibujar.

A vosotros(as) **os gusta** dibujar.

A ustedes **les gusta** dibujar.

A ellos(as) **les gusta** dibujar.

Nota gramatical: Use **de** with the verb **ser** to talk about where someone is from.
*Yo **soy** de Miami. Ellos **son** de California.*

Definite and Indefinite Articles

In Spanish, articles match nouns in gender and number.

		Definite Article	Noun	Indefinite Article	Noun
Masculine	Singular	**el**	chico	**un**	chico
	Plural	**los**	chicos	**unos**	chicos
Feminine	Singular	**la**	chica	**una**	chica
	Plural	**las**	chicas	**unas**	chicas

Noun-Adjective Agreement

In Spanish, adjectives match the gender and number of the nouns they describe.

	Singular	Plural
Masculine	el chico alto	los chicos altos
Feminine	la chica alta	las chicas altas

Nota gramatical: Use **ser** to describe what people are like.
*Ella **es** alta. Mis amigos **son** simpáticos.*

Tell Time and Discuss Daily Schedules

¿A qué hora es...?	At what time is . . . ?
¿Qué hora es?	What time is it?
A la(s)...	At . . . o'clock.
Es la... / Son las...	It is . . . o'clock.
de la mañana	in the morning (with a time)
de la tarde	in the afternoon (with a time)
de la noche	at night (with a time)
la hora	hour; time
el horario	schedule
menos	to, before (telling time)
el minuto	minute
...y cuarto	quarter past
...y (diez)	(ten) past
...y media	half past

Describe Classes

casi	almost
¿Cuántos(as)...?	How many . . . ?
difícil	difficult
en	in
el examen (pl. los exámenes)	exam
fácil	easy
hay...	there is, there are . . .
muchos(as)	many
tarde	late
temprano	early
tener que	to have to

NUMBERS FROM 11 TO 100 p. 87

Describe Frequency

de vez en cuando	once in a while
muchas veces	often, many times
mucho	a lot
nunca	never
siempre	always
todos los días	every day

Other Words and Phrases

Describe Classroom Objects

el borrador	eraser
la calculadora	calculator
el cuaderno	notebook
el escritorio	desk
el lápiz (pl. los lápices)	pencil
el mapa	map
la mochila	backpack
el papel	paper
el pizarrón (pl. los pizarrones)	board
la pluma	pen
la puerta	door
el reloj	clock; watch
la silla	chair
la tiza	chalk
la ventana	window

School Subjects

SCHOOL SUBJECTS	
el arte	art
las ciencias	science
el español	Spanish
la historia	history
el inglés	English
las matemáticas	math

Classroom Activities

CLASSROOM ACTIVITIES	
contestar	to answer
enseñar	to teach
llegar	to arrive
necesitar	to need
sacar una buena / mala nota	to get a good / bad grade
tomar apuntes	to take notes
usar la computadora	to use the computer

Describe Classes

aburrido(a)	boring
divertido(a)	fun
interesante	interesting

Places in School

el baño	bathroom
la biblioteca	library
la cafetería	cafeteria
el gimnasio	gymnasium
la oficina del (de la) director(a)	principal's office
el pasillo	hall

Say Where Things Are Located

al lado (de)	next to
cerca (de)	near (to)
debajo (de)	underneath, under
delante (de)	in front (of)
dentro (de)	inside (of)
detrás (de)	behind
encima (de)	on top (of)
lejos (de)	far (from)

Talk about How You Feel

cansado(a)	tired
contento(a)	content, happy
deprimido(a)	depressed
emocionado(a)	excited
enojado(a)	angry
nervioso(a)	nervous
ocupado(a)	busy
tranquilo(a)	calm
triste	sad

Other Words and Phrases

¿(A)dónde?	(To) Where?
¿Cuándo?	When?
cuando	when
el problema	problem

The Verb **tener**

Use the verb **tener** to talk about what you have.

tener *to have*		
yo	**tengo**	nosotros(as)	**tenemos**
tú	**tienes**	vosotros(as)	**tenéis**
usted	**tiene**	ustedes	**tienen**
él, ella		ellos(as)	

Tener + **que** + **infinitive** is used to talk about what someone has to do.

Present Tense of **–ar** Verbs

To form the present tense of a regular verb that ends in **–ar**, drop the **–ar** and add the appropriate ending.

hablar *to talk, to speak*		
yo	**habl**o	nosotros(as)	**habl**amos
tú	**habl**as	vosotros(as)	**habl**áis
usted	**habl**a	ustedes	**habl**an
él, ella		ellos(as)	

Nota gramatical: For the numbers 21, 31, and so on, use **veintiún, treinta y un,** and so on before a masculine noun. Use **veintiuna, treinta y una,** and so on before a feminine noun.

The Verb **estar**

Use **estar** to indicate location and say how people feel.

estar *to be*		
yo	**estoy**	nosotros(as)	**estamos**
tú	**estás**	vosotros(as)	**estáis**
usted	**está**	ustedes	**están**
él, ella		ellos(as)	

The Verb **ir**

Use **ir** to talk about where someone is going.

ir *to go*		
yo	**voy**	nosotros(as)	**vamos**
tú	**vas**	vosotros(as)	**vais**
usted	**va**	ustedes	**van**
él, ella		ellos(as)	

Nota gramatical: To form a question, you can switch the position of the verb and the subject.

Talk About Foods and Beverages

MEALS

el almuerzo	lunch
la bebida	beverage, drink
la cena	dinner
compartir	to share
la comida	food; meal
el desayuno	breakfast
vender	to sell

FOR BREAKFAST

el café	coffee
el cereal	cereal
el huevo	egg
el jugo de naranja	orange juice
la leche	milk
el pan	bread
el yogur	yogurt

FOR LUNCH

la hamburguesa	hamburger
el sándwich de jamón y queso	ham and cheese sandwich
la sopa	soup

FRUIT

la banana	banana
la manzana	apple
las uvas	grapes

Describe Feelings

tener ganas de...	to feel like . . .
tener hambre	to be hungry
tener sed	to be thirsty

Ask Questions

¿Cómo?	How?
¿Cuál?	Which?; What?
¿Por qué?	Why?
¿Qué?	What?
¿Quién?	Who?

Other Words and Phrases

ahora	now
Es importante.	It's important.
horrible	horrible
nutritivo(a)	nutritious
otro(a)	other
para	for; in order to
rico(a)	tasty, delicious

Talk About Family

la abuela	grandmother
el abuelo	grandfather
los abuelos	grandparents
la familia	family
la hermana	sister
el hermano	brother
los hermanos	brothers, brother(s) and sister(s)
la hija	daughter
el hijo	son
los hijos	son(s) and daughter(s), children
la madrastra	stepmother
la madre	mother
el padrastro	stepfather
el padre	father
los padres	parents
el (la) primo(a)	cousin
los primos	cousins
la tía	aunt
el tío	uncle
los tíos	uncles, uncle(s) and aunt(s)

Ask, Tell, and Compare Ages

¿Cuántos años tienes?	How old are you?
Tengo... años.	I am . . . years old.
mayor	older
menor	younger

Give Dates

¿Cuál es la fecha?	What is the date?
Es el... de...	It's the . . . of . . .
el primero de...	the first of . . .
el cumpleaños	birthday

Pets

¡Feliz cumpleaños!	Happy birthday!
la fecha de nacimiento	birth date
el (la) gato(a)	cat
el (la) perro(a)	dog

Other Words and Phrases

vivir	to live
ya	already

NUMBERS FROM 200 TO 1,000,000

doscientos (as)	200
trescientos (as)	300
cuatrocientos (as)	400
mil	1000
un millón (de)	1,000,000

MONTHS

enero	January
febrero	February
marzo	March
abril	April
mayo	May
junio	June
julio	July
agosto	August
septiembre	September
octubre	October
noviembre	November
diciembre	December

Gustar with Nouns

To talk about the things that people like, use **gustar** + **noun**.

Singular	Plural
me gusta la sopa	**me gustan** los jugos
te gusta la sopa	**te gustan** los jugos
le gusta la sopa	**le gustan** los jugos
nos gusta la sopa	**nos gustan** los jugos
os gusta la sopa	**os gustan** los jugos
les gusta la sopa	**les gustan** los jugos

Present Tense of –er and –ir Verbs

vender *to sell*	
vendo	vendemos
vendes	vendéis
vende	venden

compartir *to share*	
comparto	compartimos
compartes	compartís
comparte	comparten

Nota gramatical: To ask a question, use an interrogative word followed by a conjugated verb. *¿Cómo está usted? How are you?*

Nota gramatical: The verb **hacer** is irregular in the present tense only in the **yo** form (**hago**). In other forms, it follows the pattern for –er verbs.

Possessive Adjectives

In Spanish, **possessive adjectives** agree in number with the nouns they describe. **Nuestro(a)** and **vuestro(a)** must also agree in gender with the nouns they describe.

Singular Possessive Adjectives		Plural Possessive Adjectives	
mi	**nuestro(a)**	**mis**	**nuestros(as)**
my	*our*	*my*	*our*
tu	**vuestro(a)**	**tus**	**vuestros(as)**
your (familiar)	*your (familiar)*	*your (familiar)*	*your (familiar)*
su	**su**	**sus**	**sus**
your (formal)	*your (formal)*	*your*	*your*
su	**su**	**sus**	**sus**
his, her, its	*his, her, its*	*his, her, its*	*thier*

Comparatives

Use with an adjective to compare two things:

más... que...

menos... que...

tan... como...

If no adjective, use these phrases.

más que...

menos que...

tanto como...

Irregular comparative words.

mayor	**menor**	**mejor**	**peor**
older	*younger*	*better*	*worse*

Nota gramatical: Use **de** and a **noun** to show possesion. el gato de **Marisa** *Marisa's cat*

Nota gramatical: Use **tener** to talk about how old a person is. *¿Cuantos años* **tiene** *tu amiga? How old is your friend?*

Nota gramatical: To give the date, use the phrase: Es el + **number** + de + **month.** Hoy es el **diez** de **diciembre.**
Today is the tenth of December.
Es el **primeiro** de **diciembre.** *It is December first.*

Talk About Shopping

el centro comercial	shopping center, mall
¿Cuánto cuesta(n)?	How much does it (do they) cost?
Cuesta(n)...	It (They) cost . . .
el dinero	money
el dólar (pl. los dólares)	dollar
el euro	euro
ir de compras	to go shopping
pagar	to pay
el precio	price
la tienda	store

Describe Clothing

la blusa	blouse
los calcetines	socks
la camisa	shirt
la camiseta	T-shirt
la chaqueta	jacket
feo(a)	ugly
el gorro	winter hat
los jeans	jeans
llevar	to wear
nuevo(a)	new
los pantalones	pants
los pantalones cortos	shorts
la ropa	clothing
el sombrero	hat
el vestido	dress
los zapatos	shoes

COLORS

amarillo(a)	yellow
anaranjado(a)	orange
azul	blue
blanco(a)	white
marrón (pl. marrones)	brown
negro(a)	black
rojo(a)	red
verde	green

Expressions with tener

tener calor	to be hot
tener frío	to be cold
tener razón	to be right
tener suerte	to be lucky

Discuss Seasons

la estación (pl. las estaciones)	season
el invierno	winter
el otoño	autumn, fall
la primavera	spring
el verano	summer

Other Words and Phrases

durante	during
cerrar (ie)	to close
empezar (ie)	to begin
entender (ie)	to understand
pensar (ie)	to think, to plan
preferir (ie)	to prefer
querer (ie)	to want

Describe Places in Town

el café	café
el centro	center, downtown
el cine	movie theater; the movies
el parque	park
el restaurante	restaurant
el teatro	theater

In a Restaurant

el (la) camarero(a)	(food) server
costar (ue)	to cost
la cuenta	bill
de postre	for dessert
el menú	menu
la mesa	table
el plato principal	main course
la propina	tip

ORDERING FROM A MENU

pedir (i)	to order, to ask for
servir (i)	to serve

FOR DINNER

el arroz	rice
el bistec	beef
el brócoli	broccoli
la carne	meat
la ensalada	salad
los frijoles	beans
el pastel	cake
la patata	potato
el pescado	fish
el pollo	chicken
el tomate	tomato
las verduras	vegetables

Describe Events in Town

el concierto	concert
las entradas	tickets
la música rock	rock music
la película	movie
la ventanilla	ticket window

Getting Around Town

a pie	by foot
la calle	street
en autobús	by bus
en coche	by car
encontrar (ue)	to find
tomar	to take

Other Words and Phrases

allí	there
almorzar (ue)	to eat lunch
aquí	here
dormir (ue)	to sleep
el lugar	place
poder (ue)	to be able, can
tal vez	perhaps, maybe
ver	to see
volver (ue)	to return, to come back

Stem-Changing Verbs: e → ie

For **e → ie** stem-changing verbs, the **e** of the stem changes to ie in all forms except **nosotros(as)** and **vosotros(as).**

querer *to want*	
quiero	queremos
quieres	queréis
quiere	quieren

Direct Object Pronouns

Direct object pronouns can be used to replace **direct object nouns.**

Singular		Plural	
me	*me*	**nos**	*us*
te	*you (familiar)*	**os**	*you (familiar)*
lo	*you (formal), him, it*	**los**	*you, them*
la	*you (formal), her, it*	**las**	*you, them*

Nota gramatical: Use **tener** to form many expressions that in English would use *to be.*
Tengo frío. *I am cold*

Stem-Changing Verbs: o → ue

For **o → ue** stem-changing verbs, the last **o** of the stem changes to **ue** in all forms except **nosotros(as)** and **vosotros(as).**

poder *to be able, can*	
puedo	podemos
puedes	podéis
puede	pueden

Stem-Changing Verbs: e → i

For **e → i** stem-changing verbs, the last **e** of the stem changes to **i** in all forms except **nosotros(as)** and **vosotros(as).**

servir *to serve*	
sirvo	servimos
sirves	servís
sirve	sirven

Nota gramatical: **Ver** has an irregular **yo** form in the present tense.
Veo un autobús.

Nota gramatical: Use a form of **ir a** + **infinitive** to talk about what you are going to do.

Describe a House

el apartamento	apartment
el armario	closet; armoire
bajar	to descend
la casa	house
la cocina	kitchen
el comedor	dining room
el cuarto	room; bedroom
la escalera	stairs
ideal	ideal
el jardín (pl. los jardines)	garden
el patio	patio
el piso	floor (of a building)
la planta baja	ground floor
la sala	living room
subir	to go up
el suelo	floor (of a room)

Describe Household Items

la cosa	thing
el disco compacto	compact disc
el lector DVD	DVD player
el radio	radio
el televisor	television set

Furniture

la alfombra	rug
la cama	bed
la cómoda	dresser
las cortinas	curtains
el espejo	mirror
la lámpara	lamp
los muebles	furniture
el sillón (pl. los sillones)	armchair
el sofá	sofa, couch

el tocadiscos compactos	CD player
los videojuegos	video games

Ordinal Numbers

primero(a)	first
segundo(a)	second
tercero(a)	third
cuarto(a)	fourth
quinto(a)	fifth
sexto(a)	sixth
séptimo(a)	seventh
octavo(a)	eighth
noveno(a)	ninth
décimo(a)	tenth

Plan a Party

bailar	to dance
cantar	to sing
celebrar	to celebrate
dar una fiesta	to give a party
decorar	to decorate
las decoraciones	decorations
la fiesta de sorpresa	surprise party
el globo	balloon
los invitados	guests
invitar a	to invite (someone)
salir	to leave, to go out
el secreto	secret
venir	to come

Talk About Chores and Responsibilities

acabar de...	to have just . . .
ayudar	to help
barrer el suelo	to sweep the floor
cocinar	to cook
cortar el césped	to cut the grass
darle de comer al perro	to feed the dog
deber	should, ought to
hacer la cama	to make the bed
lavar los platos	to wash the dishes
limpiar (la cocina)	to clean the kitchen
limpio(a)	clean
pasar la aspiradora	to vacuum
planchar la ropa	to iron
poner la mesa	to set the table
los quehaceres	chores
sacar la basura	to take out the trash
sucio(a)	dirty

Talk About Gifts

abrir	to open
buscar	to look for

envolver (ue)	to wrap
el papel de regalo	wrapping paper
recibir	to receive
el regalo	gift
traer	to bring

Other Words and Phrases

decir	to say, to tell
hay que	one has to, one must
poner	to put, to place
si	if
todavía	still; yet

Ser or estar

Ser and **estar** both mean *to be*.

Use **ser** to indicate origin.

Use **ser** to describe personal traits and physical characteristics.

Ser is also used to indicate professions.

You also use **ser** to express possession and to give the time and the date.

Use **estar** to indicate location.

Estar is also used to describe conditions, both physical and emotional.

Ordinal Numbers

When used with a noun, an **ordinal number** must agree in number and gender with that noun.

Ordinals are placed before nouns.
Primero and **tercero** drop the **o** before a masculine singular noun.

More Irregular Verbs

Dar, decir, poner, salir, traer, and **venir** are all irregular.

decir *to say, to tell*		venir *to come*	
di**go**	decimos	ven**go**	venimos
dices	decís	vienes	venís
dice	dicen	viene	vienen

Some verbs are irregular only in the **yo** form of the present tense.

dar	poner	salir	traer
doy	pon**go**	sal**go**	trai**go**

Affirmative tú Commands

Regular **affirmative tú commands** are the same as the **él/ella** forms in the present tense.

Infinitive	Present Tense	Affirmative tú Command
lavar	(él, ella) **lava**	¡**Lava** los platos!
barrer	(él, ella) **barre**	¡**Barre** el suelo!
abrir	(él, ella) **abre**	¡**Abre** la puerta!

There are irregular **affirmative tú commands.**

decir	hacer	ir	poner	salir	ser	tener	venir
di	haz	ve	pon	sal	sé	ten	ven

Nota gramatical: When you want to say that something has just happened, use the verb **acabar de** + infinitive.

Acabamos de comprar el pastel para la fiesta.
We just bought the cake for the party.

Sports

el básquetbol	basketball
el béisbol	baseball
el fútbol americano	football
nadar	to swim
la natación	swimming
patinar	to skate
patinar en línea	to in-line skate
el tenis	tennis
el voleibol	volleyball

Locations and People

los aficionados	fans
el (la) atleta	athlete
el campeón (pl. los campeones), la campeona	champion
el campo	field
la cancha	court
el equipo	team
el estadio	stadium
el (la) ganador(a)	winner
el (la) jugador(a)	player
la piscina	pool

Sports Equipment

el bate	bat
el casco	helmet
el guante	glove
los patines en línea	in-line skates
la pelota	ball
la raqueta	racket

Talk About Sports

comprender las reglas	to understand the rules
favorito(a)	favorite
ganar	to win

el partido	game
peligroso(a)	dangerous
perder (ie)	to lose

Talk About Staying Healthy

enfermo(a)	sick
fuerte	strong
herido(a)	hurt
levantar pesas	to lift weights
la salud	health
sano(a)	healthy

PARTS OF THE BODY

la boca	mouth
el brazo	arm
la cabeza	head
el corazón (pl. los corazones)	heart
el cuerpo	body
el estómago	stomach
la mano	hand
la nariz (pl. las narices)	nose
el ojo	eye
la oreja	ear
el pie	foot
la piel	skin
la pierna	leg
la rodilla	knee
el tobillo	ankle

Make Excuses

doler (ue)	to hurt, to ache
Lo siento.	I'm sorry.

Other Words and Phrases

anoche	last night
ayer	yesterday
comenzar (ie)	to begin
terminar	to end
¿Qué hiciste (tú)?	What did you do?
¿Qué hicieron ustedes?	What did you do?

Outdoor Activities

el bloqueador de sol	sunscreen
bucear	to scuba-dive
caminar	to walk
hacer esquí acuático	to water-ski
el mar	sea
la playa	beach
tomar el sol	to sunbathe

The Verb jugar

Jugar is a stem-changing verb in which the **u** changes to ue in all forms except **nosotros(as)** and **vosotros(as).**

jugar *to play*	
juego	jugamos
juegas	jugáis
juega	juegan

When you use **jugar** with the name of a sport, use **jugar a** + **sport.**

The Verbs saber and conocer

Both **saber** and **conocer** mean *to know* and have irregular **yo** forms in the present tense.

saber *to know*		conocer *to know*	
sé	sabemos	conozco	conocemos
sabes	sabéis	conoces	conocéis
sabe	saben	conoce	conocen

· Use **saber** to talk about factual information you know. You can also use **saber + infinitive** to say that you know how to do something.

· Use **conocer** when you want to say that you are familiar with a person or place. You also use **conocer** to talk about meeting someone for the first time.

Nota gramatical: When a specific person is the direct object of a sentence, use the personal **a** after the verb and before the person.
No conozco **a** Raúl. *I don't know Raúl.*

Preterite of Regular –ar Verbs

To form the **preterite** of a regular **–ar** verb, add the appropriate preterite ending to the verb's stem.

nadar *to swim*	
nadé	nadamos
nadaste	nadasteis
nadó	nadaron

Preterite of –car, –gar, –zar Verbs

Regular verbs that end in **–car, –gar, or –zar** have a spelling change in the **yo** form of the preterite.

buscar	c	becomes → qu	(yo) busqué
jugar	g	becomes – › gu	(yo) jugué
almorzar	z	becomes – › c	(yo) almorcé

Nota gramatical: To express what hurts, use **doler (ue)** followed by a definite article and a part of the body.
Me **duele la cabeza.** *My head hurts.*

Talk About Technology

la cámara digital	digital camera
conectar a Internet	to connect to the Internet
la dirección electrónica (pl. las direcciones)	e-mail address
estar en línea	to be online
hacer clic en	to click on
el icono	icon
mandar	to send
el mensajero instantáneo	instant messaging
navegar por Internet	to surf the Internet
la pantalla	screen
quemar un disco compacto	to burn a CD
el ratón (pl. los ratones)	mouse
el sitio Web	Web site
el teclado	keyboard
tomar fotos	to take photos

Talk About Negative or Indefinite Situations

algo	something
alguien	someone
algún / alguno(a)	some, any
nada	nothing
nadie	no one, nobody
ni... ni	neither . . . nor
ningún / ninguno(a)	none, not any
o... o	either . . . or
tampoco	neither, not either

Talk About Events

anteayer	the day before yesterday
el año pasado	last year
entonces	then, so
luego	later on, then
más tarde	later on
por fin	finally
la semana pasada	last week

At the Amusement Park

los autitos chocadores	bumper cars
el boleto	ticket
la montaña rusa	roller coaster
subir a	to ride
¡Qué divertido!	How fun!
¡Qué miedo!	How scary!
tener miedo	to be afraid
la vuelta al mundo	Ferris wheel

Make a Phone Call

dejar un mensaje	to leave a message
la llamada	phone call
llamar	to call (by phone)
el teléfono celular	cellular phone

Talk on the Phone

¿Aló?	Hello?
¿Está...?	Is . . . there?
No, no está.	No, he's / she's not.
¿Puedo hablar con...?	May I speak with . . . ?
Un momento.	One moment.

Extended Invitations

¿Quieres acompañarme a...?	Would you like to come with me to . . . ?
¿Te gustaría...?	Would you like . . . ?
Te invito.	I'll treat you. / I invite you.
ACCEPT	
¡Claro que sí!	Of course!
Me gustaría...	I would like . . .
Sí, me encantaría.	Yes, I would love to.
DECLINE	
¡Qué lástima!	What a shame!

Places of Interest

el acuario	aquarium
la feria	fair
el museo	museum
el parque de diversiones	amusement park
el zoológico	zoo

Other Words and Phrases

con	with
el fin de semana	weekend

Preterite of Regular –er and –ir Verbs

In the preterite, –er and –ir verb endings are identical.

vender to sell	
vendí	vendimos
vendiste	vendisteis
vendió	vendieron

escribir to write	
escribí	escribimos
escribiste	escribisteis
escribió	escribieron

Affirmative and Negative Words

Affirmative Words	
algo	*something*
alguien	*someone*
algún / alguno(a)	*some, any*
o... o	*either... or*
siempre	*always*
también	*also*

Negative Words	
nada	*nothing*
nadie	*no one, nobody*
ningún / ninguno(a)	*none, not any*
ni... ni	*neither... nor*
nunca	*never*
tampoco	*neither, not either*

Alguno(a) and **ninguno(a)** must match the gender of the noun they replace or modify. They have different forms when used before masculine singular nouns.

Nota gramatical: Ningunos(as) is used only with nouns that are not typically singular.
No compro **ningunos** jeans. I'm ***not*** buying any **jeans.**

Preterite of ir, ser, and hacer

Ir, ser, and **hacer** are irregular in the preterite tense. The preterite forms of **ir** and **ser** are exactly the same.

ir to go / ser to be	
fui	fuimos
fuiste	fuisteis
fue	fueron

hacer to do, to make	
hice	hicimos
hiciste	hicisteis
hizo	hicieron

Pronouns After Prepositions

Pronouns that follow prepositions are the same as the subject pronouns except **mí (yo)** and **ti (tú).**

Pronouns After Prepositions	
mí	nosotros(as)
ti	vosotros(as)
usted, él, ella	ustedes, ellos(as)

The preposition **con** combines with **mí** and **ti** to form the words **conmigo** and **contigo.**

Nota gramatical: To express *How* + **adjective,** use Qué + **adjective** in the masculine singular form. Use the feminine form only when a feminine noun is being described.
¡Qué **divertido!** *How fun!*

Talk About a Daily Routine

acostarse (ue)	to go to bed
afeitarse	to shave oneself
bañarse	to take a bath
cepillarse los dientes	to brush one's teeth
despertarse (ie)	to wake up
dormirse (ue)	to fall asleep
ducharse	to take a shower
lavarse	to wash oneself
lavarse la cara	to wash one's face
levantarse	to get up
maquillarse	to put on makeup
peinarse	to comb one's hair
ponerse (la ropa)	to put on (clothes)
secarse	to dry oneself
secarse el pelo	to dry one's hair
vestirse (i)	to get dressed

TALK ABOUT GROOMING

el cepillo (de dientes)	brush (toothbrush)
el champú	shampoo
el jabón	soap
la pasta de dientes	toothpaste
el peine	comb
el secador de pelo	hair dryer
la toalla	towel

Talk About a Typical Day

generalmente	generally
normalmente	normally
la rutina	routine

Other Words and Phrases

el campo	the country
la ciudad	city
esperar	to wait (for)
hacer un viaje	to take a trip
en avión	by plane
en barco	by boat
en tren	by train
el hotel	hotel
quedarse en	to stay in
las vacaciones	vacation
de vacaciones	on vacation

Talk About Vacation Activities

acampar	to camp
comer al aire libre	to picnic, to eat outside
dar una caminata	to hike
hacer una parrillada	to barbecue
hacer surf de vela	to windsurf
hacer surfing	to surf
montar a caballo	to ride a horse
el tiempo libre	free time

Talk About Buying Souvenirs

barato(a)	inexpensive
la calidad	quality
caro(a)	expensive
demasiado	too much
el mercado	market
el recuerdo	souvenir

JEWELRY AND HANDICRAFTS

el anillo	ring
el arete	earring
las artesanías	handicrafts
los artículos	goods
de madera	wood
de oro	gold
de plata	silver
la cerámica	ceramics
el collar	necklace
las joyas	jewelry

BARGAINING

Le dejo... en...	I'll give . . . to you for . . .
Le puedo ofrecer...	I can offer you . . .
¿Me deja ver...?	May I see . . . ?
¡Qué caro(a)!	How expensive!
Quisiera...	I would like . . .
regatear	to bargain

Indicate Position

aquel (aquella)	that (over there)
aquellos(as)	those (over there)
ese(a)	that
esos(as)	those
este(a)	this
estos(as)	these
¿Qué es esto?	What is this?

Reflexive Verbs

Use reflexive pronouns with **reflexive verbs** when the subject in a sentence is the same as its object.

lavarse *to wash oneself*	
me lavo	nos lavamos
te lavas	os laváis
se lava	se lavan

Present Progressive

To form the present progressive in Spanish, use the present tense of **estar** + **present participle.**

-ar verbs	**-er** verbs	**-ir** verbs
caminar ← ando	poner ← iendo	abrir ← iendo
caminando	poniendo	abriendo

Some verbs have a spelling change or a stem change in the present participle.

Indirect Object Pronouns

Indirect Object pronouns use the same words as direct object pronouns except for le and les.

Singular		Plural	
me	*me*	nos	*us*
te	*you (familiar)*	os	*you (familiar)*
le	*you (formal), him, her*	les	*you, them*

Demonstrative Adjective

In Spanish, **demonstrative adjectives** must match the nouns they modify in gender and number.

	Singular	Plural
Masculine	este anillo	estos anillos
	ese anillo	esos anillos
	aquel anillo	aquellos anillos
Feminine	esta camiseta	estas camisetas
	esa camiseta	esas camisetas
	aquella camiseta	aquellas camisetas